PRICELESS

PRICELESS

How I Went Undercover to Rescue the World's Stolen Treasures

ROBERT K. WITTMAN

with John Shiffman

CROWN PUBLISHERS

NEW YORK

Robert K. Wittman is available for select
readings and lectures. To inquire about a possible appearance,
please visit www.rhspeakers.com or call 212–572–2013.

Published in the United States by Crown Publishers, an imprint of the
Crown Publishing Group, a division of Random House, Inc., New York.
www.crownpublishing.com

CROWN and the Crown colophon are registered trademarks of
Random House, Inc.

Library of Congress Cataloging-in-Publication Data

Wittman, Robert K.
  Priceless : how I went undercover to rescue the world's stolen treasures /
Robert K. Wittman.—1st ed.
      p. cm.
  1. Wittman, Robert K.   2. Art thefts—Investigation.   I. Title.   II. Title:
How I went undercover to rescue the world's stolen treasures.
  N8795.5.W58W58 2009
  364.16'287—dc22   2009049083

ISBN 978-0-307-46147-6

Printed in the United States of America

Design by Lauren Dong

5 7 9 10 8 6 4

To Donna, my wife, and our three children,
Kevin, Jeffrey, and Kristin

CONTENTS

ALLA PRIMA

Chapter 1: SOUTH BEACH   3

Chapter 2: CRIMES AGAINST HISTORY   13

PROVENANCE

Chapter 3: THE MAKING OF AN AGENT   25

Chapter 4: *MASK OF THE MAN WITH THE BROKEN NOSE*   33

Chapter 5: THE ACCIDENT   45

Chapter 6: LEARNING TO SEE   53

Chapter 7: A NEW LIFE   67

BODY OF WORK

Chapter 8: THE GOLD MAN   73

Chapter 9: HISTORY OUT THE BACK DOOR   93

Chapter 10: A BLOOD CLOTH   107

Chapter 11: BEFRIEND AND BETRAY   119

Chapter 12: THE CON ARTIST   143

Chapter 13: A HOT HAND   161

Chapter 14: THE PROPERTY OF A LADY   181

Chapter 15: NATIONAL TREASURE   199

Chapter 16: ART CRIME TEAM   217

Chapter 17: THE OLD MASTER   223

OPERATION MASTERPIECE

Chapter 18: MRS. GARDNER   *245*

Chapter 19: COLD CASE   *249*

Chapter 20: A FRENCH CONNECTION   *257*

Chapter 21: LAURENZ AND SUNNY   *263*

Chapter 22: ALLIES AND ENEMIES   *273*

Chapter 23: A COWARD HAS NO SCAR   *283*

Chapter 24: SUSPICIOUS MINDS   *287*

Chapter 25: ENDGAME   *309*

Author's Note   319

Acknowledgments   321

ALLA PRIMA

CHAPTER 1

SOUTH BEACH

Miami, 2007.

THE PLATINUM ROLLS-ROYCE WITH BULLETPROOF
windows glided east onto the Palmetto Expressway toward
Miami Beach, six stolen paintings stashed in its armor-plated trunk.

Great works by Degas, Dalí, Klimt, O'Keeffe, Soutine, and
Chagall were piled rudely in the rear, wrapped individually in thin
brown paper and clear packing tape. In the driver's seat, a Parisian millionaire named Laurenz Cogniat pushed the three-ton beast
hard. He entered the left lane approaching eighty, then ninety
miles an hour, the vehicle's menacing stainless-steel grille leading
the way.

At Interstate 95, the glimmering Rolls turned south, hurtling
down the raised concrete ribbon, the Miami skyline rising ahead.
Laurenz took the Martin Luther King Boulevard exit, made a sharp
U-turn, and jumped back on to the interstate, still southbound. His
cold green eyes flicked from the road to the rearview mirror and
back again. He craned his neck and searched a cobalt Florida sky.
Every few minutes, Laurenz stabbed the brakes, dropping down to
forty or fifty miles an hour and slipping into the right lane, then
abruptly punched the gas again. In the passenger seat, a plump
shaggy-haired fellow with a warm round face, a Frenchman who

called himself Sunny, sat stoically, an unlit Marlboro between his lips. He, too, searched for suspicious vehicles.

In the backseat, I glanced at my borrowed Rolex and watched with amusement as Laurenz's domed head bobbed and weaved with the traffic. At this rate, we were going to arrive early, assuming Laurenz didn't attract a traffic cop or get us killed first. He shifted lanes again, and I gripped the handle above the door. Laurenz was an amateur. A bored real-estate magnate in a V-neck T-shirt, faded blue jeans, and sandals, he longed for adventure and assumed that this was how criminals ought to act on the way to a big deal—drive erratically to make sure no one is tailing them. Just like in the movies.

Behind black-mirrored shades, I rolled my eyes. "Relax," I said. "Slow down."

Laurenz pursed his lips and pressed a sandal on the accelerator.

I tried again. "Um, it's kind of hard to be inconspicuous to the police when you're driving ninety miles an hour down I-95 in a platinum Rolls-Royce Phantom."

Laurenz pushed on. A self-made man, he didn't take orders from anyone. Sunny, still pouting because I wouldn't let him carry a gun, ignored me as well. He ran a stubby hand through his thick mane and quietly stared out the window. I knew he was nervous. He fretted that Laurenz was too temperamental—a whiner and ultimately a coward, a guy who might appear bold and buff, but couldn't be counted on if things turned violent. Sunny didn't speak much English and I didn't speak much French, but whenever we talked about Laurenz, we agreed on one thing: We needed his connections. I tugged my seat belt tighter and kept my mouth shut.

The two Frenchmen in the front seat knew me as Bob Clay. In using my true first name, I was following a cardinal rule of working undercover: Keep the lies to a minimum. The more lies you tell, the more you have to remember.

Sunny and Laurenz believed I was some sort of shady American art dealer, a guy who worked both sides of the legal and illicit art markets, an international broker comfortable with multimillion-dollar deals. They didn't know my true identity: Special Agent of the Federal Bureau of Investigation and senior investigator of the FBI's Art Crime Team. They didn't know that the European criminal who'd vouched for me in Paris was in fact a police informant.

Most important, Sunny and Laurenz viewed today's sale of six paintings as a mere prelude to the Big One.

Together, with their French underworld connections and my money, we were negotiating to buy a long-lost Vermeer, a couple of Rembrandts, and five sketches by Degas. This collection of art was worth $500 million, and far more significant, it was infamous. These were the very masterpieces stolen seventeen years ago during the greatest unsolved art crime in history, the 1990 theft from the Isabella Stewart Gardner Museum in Boston.

The Gardner heist had long haunted the art world and the many investigators who failed to run the thieves to ground and recover the stolen paintings. The Boston police and local FBI office had chased hundreds of dead-end leads, checking every lousy tip, wild rumor, and spurious sighting. They'd debunked theories floated by con men and gadflies angling for the $5 million reward. As years passed, new suspects surfaced and old ones died, some under mysterious circumstances. This spawned countless conspiracy theories: It was the mob; it was the IRA; it was a made-to-order heist by a foreign tycoon. The thieves didn't know what they were doing; they knew exactly what they were doing. The burglars were long dead; they were alive, living in Polynesia. It was an inside job; the police were involved. The paintings were buried in Ireland; they were hidden in a Maine farmhouse; they hung on the walls of a Saudi prince's palace; they were burned shortly after the crime. Journalists and authors investigated and wrote speculative and scandalous takeouts. Filmmakers produced documentaries. Each year, the legend of the Gardner heist grew. It became the holy grail of art crime.

Now I believed I was weeks away from solving it.

I'd spent nine painstaking months undercover luring Sunny and Laurenz, ingratiating myself with them to win their trust, and today's entire ruse on a leased yacht was a near-final step in that process, designed to prove to them beyond a doubt that I was a serious player. The six paintings in the trunk were rank forgeries, copies I'd picked out at a government warehouse, yet good enough to fool Laurenz and Sunny. The FBI script called for the three of us to go for a short cruise aboard the rented boat, *The Pelican*. There, we would meet a Colombian drug dealer and his entourage, and sell him the paintings for $1.2 million—to be paid with a mix of bank wire transfers, gold coins, and diamonds. Of course, the drug dealer and everyone else on the yacht—his henchmen, the hot women, the captain and stewards—were fellow FBI undercover agents.

As we rolled toward our exit, the script reeled through my head and I visualized last-minute preparations aboard *The Pelican:* the Colombian dealer opening a shipboard safe, withdrawing a handful of Krugerrands and a sack of diamonds; the four brunette babes, hard bodies in their late twenties, stashing their Glocks and slipping into bikinis; the stewards in white linen uniforms laying out tortilla chips, salsa, rare roast beef, shoving two magnums of champagne into ice buckets; a sullen Irishman alone on a curved cream sofa, hunching over text messages on a silver BlackBerry; the captain flipping on hidden surveillance cameras and hitting "record."

The Rolls sped east onto the MacArthur Causeway, the majestic link between downtown and Miami Beach. We were five minutes out.

I thought about the phone call I'd made to my wife earlier that morning. I always called Donna in the last moments before an undercover deal. I'd say I love you, and she'd say the same. I'd ask about her day and she'd talk about the kids. We always kept it short, a minute or two. I never said where I was or what I was about to do, and she knew better than to ask. The call not only calmed me, it reminded me not to play hero.

We pulled off the causeway and Laurenz eased into the marina parking lot. He stopped the Rolls in front of the blue-and-white-canopied dock house. He pushed a five-dollar bill into the valet's hand, took the ticket, and turned toward the yacht. Of the three of us, Laurenz was the youngest and in the best shape, but he marched straight to the great white boat, leaving Sunny and me to unload the paintings. Sunny didn't care. He was a connected guy in France, close to one of five Marseilles mob families known as La Brise de Mer, an organization whose signature hit is carried out by motorcycle assassins. But Sunny was no leader; he was a soldier, and one with mixed success. He didn't like to talk about his background, but I knew his history of theft and violence in southern France stretched back to the late 1960s. He'd spent the 1990s in harsh French prisons, then had been busted twice for aggravated assault before slipping off to South Florida.

Laurenz's story was a quintessential Florida immigrant tale: A former accountant and money changer for wiseguys in Paris, he had fled France a wanted man. Laurenz arrived in Miami with $350,000 in the mid-1990s, at the dawn of the last real estate boom. He smartly parlayed a combination of no-interest loans and a keen eye for distressed properties—plus a few well-timed bribes to the right lenders—into the American dream. Most of what Laurenz told me checked out, and on paper, he was probably worth $100 million. He lived in a gated $2 million house with a pool and Jet Skis docked on a private canal that fed into Miami Bay. He wore monogrammed shirts and rarely went a week without a manicure. Laurenz drove the Rolls everywhere, unless he needed to ferry his dogs. For that, he used the Porsche.

Sunny and Laurenz had not known each other in France. They'd met in Miami. But they knew some of the same people back home, wiseguys with access to the people holding the stolen Vermeer and Rembrandts in Europe. The French police wiretaps confirmed that Sunny and Laurenz spoke regularly with known European art thieves, and on the calls, they talked about selling a Vermeer. There was only one missing Vermeer in the world, the one from the Gardner.

As I approached the yacht, I took in the scene—the hearty welcome, the bikini babes, the thundering calypso music, and it struck me as slightly off key. I wondered if we weren't trying too hard. Sunny and Laurenz weren't stupid. They were good crooks.

We shoved off and cruised Miami Harbor for a good hour. We ate, we sipped bubbly, we soaked up the vista. It was a party. Two of the women cooed over Sunny while Laurenz and I chatted with the lead Colombian dealer. Once we were well under way, a third woman took it up a notch. She grabbed a champagne glass and a bowl of fruit and yelled "Strawberry-eating contest!" She raced out to the deck, laid a blanket down and got on her knees. Dangling a strawberry over her face, she covered it in whipped cream and lowered it lasciviously between her well-glossed lips. She sucked it slowly, and the other undercover female FBI agents took their turns. I guess it was all good drug-dealer bimbo fun until the undercover women made a dumb mistake. They crowned Sunny as judge of their contest, making him the center of attention. It didn't play right—the chubby, lowest-ranking guy in our gang getting the royal treatment. Sunny fidgeted uncomfortably. I shoved my hands in my pockets and glared at the women.

Once again, our investigation was veering dangerously off course—yet another instance of too many people too eager to play a role. And there wasn't much I could do about it.

I hated this helpless feeling. As the FBI's only undercover agent who worked art crime cases, I was used to calling the shots. True, I carried a reputation for taking risks, but I also got results. In eighteen years with the bureau, I'd already recovered $225 million worth of stolen artworks and antiquities—icons of American history, European classics, and artifacts from ancient civilizations. I'd built a career catching art thieves, scammers, and black-market traders in nearly every art venue, going undercover in places as distant as Philadelphia, Warsaw, Santa Fe, and Madrid. I'd rescued works of art by Rodin, Rembrandt, and Rockwell, and pieces of history as varied as Geronimo's headdress and a long-lost copy of the Bill of Rights. I was months away from recovering the original manuscript for Pearl Buck's *The Good Earth*.

I understood that art crime cases couldn't be handled like your garden-variety Miami cocaine deal or strong-arm Boston robbery. We weren't chasing common criminal commodities like cocaine, heroin, and laundered cash. We were in pursuit of the priceless—irreplaceable art, snapshots of human history. And this was the biggest unsolved case of them all.

No one else on the boat had ever worked an art crime investigation. Few FBI agents ever have. Most American law-enforcement agencies, the FBI included, don't give much thought to saving stolen art. They're much more comfortable doing what they do best, busting criminals for robbing banks, dealing drugs, or fleecing investors. Today's FBI is so focused on preventing another terrorist attack that nearly a third of the bureau's thirteen thousand agents now spend their time chasing the ghost of Bin Laden. There has long been no interest in art crime. For many years after 9/11, this worked to my advantage. I got to call the shots on my cases and remain in the shadows. Generally, my FBI supervisors were competent, or at least tolerable. They trusted me to do my job, and let me operate autonomously from Philadelphia.

Operation Masterpiece, the name another agent gave the Gardner case, was different. Agents on both sides of the Atlantic were hungry to share a chunk of this grand prize. Supervisors in almost every office involved—Miami, Boston, Washington, Paris, Madrid—demanded a major role. For when the case was solved, they all wanted a stake in the glory, their picture in the paper, their name in the press release.

The FBI is a giant bureaucracy. By protocol, the bureau generally assigns cases to the appropriate squad in the city where the crime occurred, regardless of expertise. Most art crime investigations are run by the same local FBI unit that handles routine property theft—the bank robbery/violent crime squad. Once assigned, the cases are rarely transferred afterward. For most middle managers, the priority isn't cases, it's careers. No supervisor wants to make a controversial decision, such as transferring a big case to headquarters or to an elite unit like the Art Crime Team, because it might insult or embarrass another supervisor, potentially crippling someone's career. So the Gardner investigation—the biggest property crime *of any kind* in the history of the United States and the world's highest-profile art crime—was spearheaded not by the FBI Art Crime Team, but by the chief of the local bank robbery/violent crime squad in Boston.

It was, of course, the case of this supervisor's career, and he spent a great deal of time making sure no one took it away. He didn't like me, probably because of my reputation for taking chances, moving swiftly, doing things without waiting for written approval, risks that might jeopardize his career. He'd already tried to throw me off the case, writing a lengthy and outrageous memo questioning my integrity, a memo that he'd since withdrawn. Although I was back on the case, the supervisor had still insisted on inserting one of his Boston-based undercover agents into the mix. This was the hard-boiled sullen Irish American on the boat camped on the curved couch, fixated on his text messages. I found his odd presence a distraction, an unnecessary ingredient that threatened to spook the savvy Sunny and Laurenz.

The FBI supervisors in Miami and Paris were better than the one in Boston, but not by much. The Miami agents seemed more comfortable chasing kilos of cocaine than a bunch of fancy paintings, and dreamed of enticing Sunny into a drug deal, creating yet another distraction. The FBI's liaison in Paris was too focused on keeping his French police counterparts satisfied, and knew they would be happy only if the arrests occurred in France, where they could make a big splash. The French commander had even called me the day before the yacht sting to ask if I could cancel the meeting. He needed time, he said, to insert a French undercover agent on the boat, and asked me to play down my role as the primary art expert. I'd stifled the impulse to ask why I should take orders from a French cop about an American operation in Florida. Instead, I simply told him we couldn't wait.

Undercover stings are stressful enough without meddling from people who are supposed to have your back. You never know if the bad guys have bought in to your rap, or are laying an ambush. One slipup, one off-key comment, and a case can be lost. In the world of high-end art crime, where you are buying paintings worth ten or twenty or a hundred million dollars, the seller expects the buyer to be a true expert. You have to project an image of expertise and so-phistication that comes with years and years of training. It can't be faked. In this case, we were dealing with people with Mediterranean mob connections, humorless wiseguys who didn't just kill snitches and undercover cops. They murdered their families, too.

After the strawberry-eating contest wound down and I "sold" the paintings to the Colombian in a drawn-out dog-and-pony show, the yacht began a slow return to the dock. I strolled out to the stern, alone with half a glass of champagne, and turned to face the brisk sea air. I needed it. I'm generally a mellow, optimistic guy—I *never* let the little stuff get to me—but lately I'd been irritable. For the first time an undercover case was keeping me awake at night. Why was I risking my life and my hard-won reputation? I had little left to prove and a great deal to lose. I knew Donna and our three kids could feel the stress. We were all watching the calendar. In sixteen months, I'd be eligible for retirement with a full government pen-sion. My supervisor in Philadelphia was an old buddy who'd look the other way if I coasted through that final stretch. I could teach undercover school, hang out with the family, sketch out a consulting career, groom a young FBI agent as my replacement.

The Pelican slowed as it neared the causeway, and I could just make out the dock, the Rolls waiting by the canopy.

My thoughts skipped back to the missing masterpieces and their intricate empty frames, still hanging in place at the Gardner, some seventeen years after the foggy March night in 1990 when two men dressed as policemen had outwitted a pair of hapless guards.

I studied Sunny and Laurenz, chatting by the bow. They were looking out across the Miami skyline at the dark afternoon clouds and the thunder boomers closing in from the Everglades. The fat

Frenchman and his finicky rich friend presented the FBI's best break in the Gardner case in a decade. Our negotiations had moved beyond the exploratory phase. We appeared close on price and we were already discussing the delicate logistics of a discreet cash-for-paintings exchange in a foreign capital.

Yet I still found it tough to read Sunny and Laurenz. Did they believe our little act on the yacht? And even if they did, would they really follow through on the promise to lead me to the paintings? Or were Laurenz and Sunny plotting an elaborate sting of their own, one in which they would kill me once I flashed a suitcase of cash? And, assuming Sunny and Laurenz could produce the Vermeer and Rembrandts, would FBI and French supervisors really let me do my job? Would they let me solve the most spectacular art theft in history?

Sunny waved at me and I nodded. Laurenz went inside and Sunny came over, a nearly empty glass of champagne in his hand.

I put my arm around Sunny's shoulder.

"*Ça va, mon ami?*" I said. "How're you doing, buddy?"

"*Très bien*, Bob. Ver-r-r-ry good."

I doubted it, so I lied too. "*Moi aussi.*"

CHAPTER 2

CRIMES AGAINST HISTORY

Courmayeur, Italy, 2008.

FOR SECURITY, THE UNITED NATIONS MADE THE reservations as discreetly as possible—one hundred and six rooms in an affluent Italian ski resort at the foot of Western Europe's tallest peak, Mont Blanc. The International Conference on Organized Crime in Art and Antiquities was timed to span a slow weekend in mid-December, between the Noir Film Festival and the traditional opening of ski season. The U.N. took care of everything. It arranged for flights from six continents, gourmet meals, and transport from airports in Geneva and Milan. By the time the buses left the airports early Friday afternoon, there was already a foot of fresh powder on the ground, and the drivers wrapped chains around thick tires before they climbed into the Alps. The buses arrived by dusk, bearing the world's leading experts on art crime, jet-lagged but eager to convene the first such summit of its kind.

I arrived the night before the conference began, catching a ride from Milan to Courmayeur with a senior U.N. official who organized the meetings. She invited me to dine early with Afghanistan's Oxford-trained deputy justice minister, and we sat by a table where we could overhear a senior Iranian judge holding forth with a Turkish cultural minister. After dinner, I made my way to the bar, in search of old friends.

I ordered a Chivas and dug into my pocket for a few euros. Through the growing crowd, I recognized Karl-Heinz Kind, the lanky German who leads Interpol's art crime team. He cradled a milky cocktail and spoke with two young women I did not know. By the fireplace, I saw Julian Radcliffe, the prim Brit who runs the world's largest private art crime database, the Art Loss Register. He had the ear of Neil Brodie, the famous Stanford archaeology professor. My drink arrived and I pulled a list of participants from my pocket. No surprise, the Europeans dominated, especially the Italians and Greeks. They always devote significant resources to art crime. I studied the less familiar, more interesting names and titles—an Argentine magistrate, the Iranian judge I'd seen earlier, a Spanish university president, Greece's top archaeologist, a pair of Australian professors, the president of South Korea's leading crime institute, and government officials from Ghana, Gambia, Mexico, Sweden, Japan, all over. A dozen Americans were on the list too, but reflecting our nation's lukewarm commitment to art crime, almost all were academics. The U.S. government sent no one.

I'd just retired from the FBI and now ran an art-security business with Donna. The United Nations had invited me to speak at this conference because, unlike any of the other participants, I'd spent twenty years in the field as an art crime investigator. The other speakers would cite statistics and notions of international law and cooperation, presenting position papers on topics I knew well—like the oft-cited estimate that art crime is a $6-billion-a-year business. The United Nations had asked me to go beyond such academic and diplomatic talk—to explain what the shady art underworld is really like, to describe what kinds of people steal art and antiquities, how they do it, and how I get it back.

Hollywood has created a dashing, uniformly bogus portrait of the art thief. In movies, he is Thomas Crown—the clever connoisseur, a wealthy, well-tailored gentleman. He steals for sport, outfoxing, even seducing, those who pursue him. The Hollywood thief is Riviera cat burglar Cary Grant in *To Catch a Thief,* or Dr. No in the first James Bond movie, Goya's stolen *The Duke of Wellington* hanging in his secret underwater lair. The Hollywood art crime hero is Nicolas Cage, descendant of a Founding Father in *National Treasure,* solving riddles, recovering long-lost treasures. He is Harrison Ford as Indiana Jones with fedora and bullwhip, deciphering hieroglyphics, saving the universe from Nazis and commies.

Plenty of art thefts *are* spectacular, the stuff of movies. In the Boston heist, the Gardner thieves tricked the night watchmen with a ruse and bound them eyes to ankles with silver duct tape. In Italy, a young man dropped a fishing line down a museum skylight, hooked a $4 million Klimt painting, and reeled it up and away. In Venezuela, thieves slipped into a museum at night and replaced three Matisse works with forgeries so fine they were not discovered for sixty days.

But art theft is rarely about the love of art or the cleverness of the crime, and the thief is rarely the Hollywood caricature—the reclusive millionaire with the stunning collection, accessible only by pressing the concealed button on the bust of Shakespeare, opening the steel door that reveals the private, climate-controlled gallery. The art thieves I met in my career ran the gamut—rich, poor, smart, foolish, attractive, grotesque. Yet nearly all of them had one thing in common: brute greed. They stole for money, not beauty.

As I said in every newspaper interview I ever gave, most art thieves quickly discover that *the art in art crime isn't in the theft, it's in the sale.* On the black market, stolen art usually fetches just 10 percent of open-market value. The more famous the painting, the harder it is to sell. As the years pass, thieves get desperate, anxious to unload an albatross no one wants to buy. In the early 1980s, a drug dealer who couldn't find anyone to buy a stolen Rembrandt worth $1 million sold it to an undercover FBI agent for a mere $23,000. When undercover police in Norway sought to buy back

The Scream, Edvard Munch's stolen masterpiece known around the world, the thieves agreed to a deal for $750,000. The painting is worth $75 million.

Master paintings and great art have always been considered "priceless," but it wasn't until the mid twentieth century that their dollar value began a steep climb. The era opened with the 1958 sale of a Cézanne, *Boy in Red Vest,* for $616,000 at a Sotheby's black-tie auction in London. The previous record for a single painting had been $360,000, and so the sale drew widespread press coverage. By the 1980s, when paintings began selling for seven figures or more, almost every record sale drew front-page headlines, imparting celebrity status to long-dead artists, particularly the Impressionists. Prices continued to spiral upward, approaching nine figures. In 1989, the J. Paul Getty Museum in Los Angeles paid a then-shocking $49 million for van Gogh's *Irises.* The following year Christie's auctioned another van Gogh, *Portrait of Dr. Gachet,* for $82 million, and by 2004, Sotheby's was auctioning Picasso's *Boy with a Pipe* for a jaw-dropping $104 million. The record was shattered again in 2006 by the music mogul David Geffen, who sold Pollock's *No. 5, 1948* for $149 million and de Kooning's *Woman III* for $137.5 million.

As value rose, so did theft.

In the 1960s, thieves started swiping Impressionist works from the walls of museums along the French Riviera and from cultural sites in Italy. The greatest was the 1969 theft in Palermo of Caravaggio's painting *Nativity with San Lorenzo and San Francesco.* Such heists continued into the '70s, but they spiked after the stunning van Gogh sales in the '80s and '90s.

The audacious 1990 Gardner theft—eleven stolen masterworks, including pieces by Vermeer and Rembrandt—marked the beginning of a bolder era. Thieves began striking museums across the globe, stealing more than $1 billion worth of paintings from 1990 to 2005. From the Louvre, they removed a Corot during a busy Sunday afternoon. At Oxford, they swiped a Cézanne in the midst of a New Year's Eve celebration. In Rio, they took a Matisse, a Monet, and a

Dalí. Bandits in Scotland posing as tourists stole a da Vinci master-piece from a museum-castle. The Van Gogh Museum was hit twice in eleven years.

Feeling the swirl of jet lag, I drained my Scotch and headed up to my room.

The next morning, I arrived in time to get a decent seat for the opening remarks in the hotel conference center. Cradling my program and a cup of thick Italian coffee, I listened to the translation of the first speaker through wireless headphones. Stefano Mana-corda of the Seconda Università di Napoli, a prominent Italian law professor with wild black hair and a wide purple tie, shuffled his notes and cleared his throat. He began with a blunt assessment that set the stage for the weekend meeting.

"Art crime is a problem of epidemic proportions."

He's right, of course. The $6-billion-a-year figure is probably low, the professor said, because it includes statistics supplied by only a third of the 192 member countries of the United Nations. Art and antiquities theft ranks fourth in transnational crime, after drugs, money laundering, and illegal arms shipments. The scope of art and antiquity crime varies from country to country, but it's safe to say that art crime is on the rise, easily outpacing efforts to police it. Everything fueling the legitimate global economic revolution—the Internet, efficient shipping, mobile phones, and customs reforms, particularly within the European Union—makes it easier for criminals to smuggle and sell stolen art and antiquities.

Like many international crimes, the illegal art and antiquity trade depends on close ties between the legitimate and the illegitimate worlds. The global market for legitimate art tops tens of billions of dollars annually, with roughly 40 percent sold in the United States. With so much money at stake, hot art and antiquities attract money launderers, shady gallery owners and art brokers, drug dealers, shipping companies, unscrupulous collectors, and the occasional terrorist. Criminals use paintings, sculptures, and statues as collateral to finance arms, drug, and money-laundering deals. Art and antiquities, particularly pieces as small as a carry-on suitcase, are easier to smuggle than cash or drugs and their value easily converts in any currency. Stolen art is tough for customs agents to spot because art and antiquities moving across international borders don't scream contraband the way drugs, guns, or bundles of cash do. Most stolen and looted pieces are quickly smuggled over borders, in search of new markets. Half the art and antiquities recovered by law enforcement is recaptured in another country.

Museum heists may grab the big headlines, but they represent only a tenth of all art crime. Statistics presented by the Art Loss Register in Courmayeur showed that 52 percent of all pilfered works are taken from private homes and organizations with little or no fanfare. Ten percent are stolen from galleries and 8 percent from churches. Most of the rest is spirited away from archaeological sites.

As another diplomat droned on about a rarely used codicil in some fifty-year-old treaty, I studied the Interpol figures in my conference packet. When I reached a chart on the geographic distribution of art thefts, I did a double take and took off my translation headphones: Interpol's statistics asserted that 74 percent of the world's art crime occurs in Europe. Seventy-four percent! That's not likely, by a long shot. In reality, the numbers demonstrate only which nations keep good statistics—and this in turn may reveal the extent to which some nations truly care about policing art crime. The disparity between national art crime teams can be staggering. The French national art crime squad employs thirty dedicated officers in Paris and is led by a full colonel of the Gendarmerie Nationale. Scotland Yard deploys a dozen officers full-time and has deputized professors of art and anthropologists, partnering them with detectives investigating cases. Italy probably does the most. It maintains a three-hundred-person art and antiquity squad, a highly regarded, aggressive unit run by Giovanni Nistri, a general of the Carabinieri. In Courmayeur, General Nistri disclosed that Italy fights art crime using some of the same resources our DEA uses to fight drugs—it deploys helicopters, cybersleuths, and even submarines.

In the early afternoon, one of the top U.N. officials at the summit, Alessandro Calvani, urged other nations to follow Italy's example, suggesting a worldwide public relations campaign to educate people about the loss of history and culture art crime causes. He pointed to the successes of public education campaigns that focused attention on tobacco, land mines, HIV, and the human rights abuses associated with the diamond trade. "Governments were finally forced to act because of strong public opinion," he said. "A lot of people don't think art crime is a crime, and without that feeling you can't generate a groundswell."

That's certainly the case in the United States. Nationwide, only a handful of detectives works art crime. Despite the front-page play and prominent television coverage each large art heist triggers, most police agencies don't dedicate proper resources to investigate. The LAPD is the only American police department with a full-time art crime investigator. In most cities, general purpose theft-squad detectives simply offer a reward and hope thieves are tempted. The FBI and U.S. Immigration and Customs Enforcement have jurisdiction over art crime but expend few resources to police it. The FBI's art crime team, created in 2004, employed only one full-time undercover agent—me. Now that I've retired, there is no one. The art crime team still exists—it's managed by a trained archaeologist, not an FBI agent but turnover is rampant. Almost all of the eight art crime team members I trained in 2005 had by 2008 already moved to other jobs, eager to advance their careers. I didn't begrudge them that, but it made it impossible to create a trained cohesive unit or build institutional memory.

The United States wasn't the only country at the conference that was urged to do more. With a few notable exceptions, art crime simply isn't a priority for most nations. As one of the Italians told the summit: "What we have is a paradigm of collective delinquency."

After lunch—turkey scaloppine, *zuppa di formaggio,* a light rosé—we heard from a pair of Australian academics who provided an overview on looting. The subject matter wasn't new to me, but I was pleased to see them offer a non-Western perspective at this Euro-centric gathering. It's folly to try to address a global problem without taking into consideration cultural differences. In some Third World countries, the illicit art and antiquities trade is quietly accepted as a way to boost the economy. Semi-lawless, war-torn regions have long been vulnerable. In Iraq, antiquities are one of the few indigenous, valuable commodities (and easier to steal than oil). In less dangerous but developing countries like Cambodia, Ethiopia, and Peru, where looters have turned archaeology sites into moonscapes, local governments don't view every excavation as a crime against history and culture. Many view it as an economic stimulus. As the professors noted, the diggers are indigenous and unemployed, desperate to convert rubble from dead ancestors' graves to food for starving families. At the conference, this perspective triggered hand-wringing from politically correct diplomats, bemoaning corrupt local officials who take bribes. So much so that I had to snicker when Kenyan National Museum director George Okello Abungu rightly rose to chastise the group. "Don't be so quick to judge the corrupt customs man," he said. "Remember who bribes him: the Westerner."

Art and antiquity crime is tolerated, in part, because it is considered a victimless crime. Having personally rescued national treasures on three continents, I know firsthand that this is foolishly nearsighted. Most stolen works are worth far more than their dollar value. They document reflections of our collective human culture. Ownership of a particular piece may change over decades and centuries, but these great works belong to all of us, to our ancestors and to future generations. For some oppressed and endangered peoples, their art is often the only remaining expression of a culture. Art thieves steal more than beautiful objects; they steal memories and identities. They steal history.

Americans, in particular, are said to be uncultured when it comes to high art, more likely to go to a ballpark than a museum. But as I tell my foreign colleagues, the statistics belie that stereotype. Americans visit museums on a scale eclipsing sports. In 2007, more people visited the Smithsonian Institution museums in Washington (24.2 million) than attended a game played by the National Basketball Association (21.8 million), the National Hockey League (21.2 million), or the National Football League (17 million). In Chicago, eight million people visit the city's museums every year. That's more than one season's attendance for the Bears, Cubs, White Sox, and Bulls combined.

As the agenda inched toward my presentation, I realized that I could place each of the speakers into one of three boxes—academic, lawyer, or diplomat. The academics spouted the statistics and theory diagrams. The lawyers offered deathly dull, law review–style histories of international treaties related to art theft. The diplomats were completely useless. They seemed harmless enough, encouraging genteel cooperation. Yet they seemed to have two true goals. One: offend no one. Two: craft a bland statement for submission to a U.N. committee. In other words, no action.

Where was the passion?

We love art because it strikes a visceral chord in everyone, from the eight-year-old kid to the octogenarian. The simple act of putting paint on canvas or transforming iron into sculpture, whether by a French master or a first-grader, is a marvel of the human mind and creates a universal connection. All art elicits emotion. All art makes you feel.

This is why, when a work of art is stolen or an ancient city is stripped of its artifacts and its soul, we feel violated.

As I waited for the Interpol chief to wrap up so I could begin my presentation, I looked out across the room at all the dignitaries. The heavy snow was now piled as high as the windows. I began to daydream. *How,* I wondered, *did the son of a Baltimore orphan and a Japanese clerk wind up here, as his country's top art crime sleuth?*

PROVENANCE

CHAPTER 3

THE MAKING OF AN AGENT

Baltimore, 1963.

"JAP!"

I'd heard it before, but the slur from the large white woman with an armful of groceries hit me with such force, I stumbled. I squeezed my mother's hand and dropped my eyes to the sidewalk. As the woman brushed past, she hissed again.

"Nip!"

I was seven years old.

My mother, Yachiyo Akaishi Wittman, did not flinch. She kept her gaze level and her face taut, and I knew that she expected me to do the same. She was thirty-eight years old and, as far as I knew, the only Japanese woman in our working-class neighborhood of two-story brick starter homes. We were newcomers, having moved from my mother's native Tokyo to my father's Baltimore a few years earlier. My parents had met in Japan during the last months of the Korean War, while Dad was stationed at the Tachikawa U.S. air base, where Mom was a clerk. They married in 1953 and my older brother, Bill, was born the same year. I was born in Tokyo two years later. We inherited my mom's almond eyes and thin build, and my father's Caucasian complexion and wide smile.

Mom didn't speak English well, and this isolated her, slowing her assimilation in the United States. She remained mystified by basic American customs, such as the birthday cake. But she certainly recognized and understood the racial slurs. With memories of World War II still raw, we had neighbors who'd fought in the Pacific or lost family there. During the war my American dad and my Japanese mom's brothers had served in opposing armies. Dad dodged kamikazes driving a landing craft that ferried Marines to Pacific beaches; one of Mom's older brothers died fighting Americans in the Philippines.

My parents sent my brother and me to proper Catholic schools in Baltimore, but surrounded us with all things Japanese. Our cabinets and shelves overflowed with Japanese ceramics and antiques. The walls were covered with woodblocks by Hiroshige, Toyokuni, and Utamaro, the Japanese masters who inspired van Gogh and Monet. We ate dinner on a table crafted from dark Japanese mahogany and sat on funky curved bamboo chairs.

The overt racism that we encountered enraged my father, but his anger rarely flared in front of me. Dad didn't talk about it much and I knew he'd faced far greater hardship as a kid. When he was three or four years old, his parents died one after the other, and he and his older brother, Jack, became wards of Catholic Charities. At St. Patrick's Orphanage, my dad learned to fend for himself. When forced to participate in chorus, he sang loudly off key. When unjustly persecuted by a brutal male teacher, he socked the man in the nose. Dad quickly became too much for the nuns to handle, and they shipped him to a foster home, separating him from his brother. Dad bounced from family to family, more than a dozen in all, until he turned seventeen, old enough to join the U.S. Navy, in 1944.

As I moved through elementary school and junior high in the 1960s, I followed the daily struggles of the civil rights movement in the papers and on television. The FBI and its special agents always seemed involved. They protected victims of racism and prosecuted the bigots and bullies. I asked my mother about the FBI agents and she said they sounded like honorable men. On Sunday nights in the

late 1960s, my mom, dad, brother, and I gathered by our new color
television to watch episodes of *The F.B.I.*, the no-nonsense series
starring Efrem Zimbalist Jr., with scripts personally approved by
J. Edgar Hoover. On TV, the FBI always got its man, and the agents
were noble protectors of justice and the American way. At the end
of some shows, Zimbalist asked for the public's help to solve a
crime, a sort of precursor to *America's Most Wanted*. I loved it. We
rarely missed an episode.

One of our neighbors, Walter Gordon, was a special agent in
the FBI's Baltimore division. When I was ten years old, he was the
coolest man I knew. Mr. Gordon wore a fine suit, shined shoes, and
crisp white shirt every day. He drove the nicest car on the block,
a bureau-issue late-model green two-door Buick Skylark. People
looked up to him. I knew that he carried a gun, but I never saw it,
only deepening his G-man mystique. I hung out with three of his
sons, Jeff, Dennis, and Donald, playing stoopball in their front yard
and trading baseball cards in their basement. The Gordons were
genuinely kind people who embraced our struggling family without
making it feel like charity. When I turned eleven, Mrs. Gordon heard
that I had never had a birthday cake. So she baked one for me, layered with dark chocolate. Years later, when Mr. Gordon heard that
my dad had opened a new seafood restaurant, he began to bring
fellow agents there for lunch, even though it was out of the way, in a
sketchy part of town near the Pimlico racetrack. I knew Mr. Gordon
didn't come for the food. He came to bring paying customers to
help a neighbor.

The restaurant, a short-lived enterprise called Neptune's Galley,
was only one of my dad's many start-up businesses. Whatever the
venture, Dad was always boss-owner and a gregarious guy, never
cheap, but we struggled to build savings and financial stability. He
opened a home-remodeling company, raced second-tier Thorough-
breds, created a college catalog business, and wrote a book on how
to win the lottery. He ran unsuccessfully for city council and opened
an antiques storefront on Howard Street called Wittman's Oriental

Gallery. That business was among his most successful and satisfying. My dad figured I'd join him in his business ventures and my mom hoped I would become a professional classical pianist. (I was accomplished in high school, but I soon discovered I wasn't good enough to make a career of it.)

By the time I entered Towson University in 1973—as a part-time night student, taking classes as I could afford them—I knew what I wanted to be: an FBI agent. I kept these plans to myself. I'm the kind of guy who doesn't like to talk much about what he's going to do until he does it. I guess the trait comes from my mom's Japanese heritage. Besides, I didn't want to disappoint my parents.

Still, my view of the FBI had matured. The job now seemed not only interesting but sensible, responsible yet thrilling. I liked the notion of protecting the innocent, investigating cases, working as a policeman whose main weapon is his brain, not his gun. I also liked the idea of serving my country, and still felt guilty that the Vietnam draft lottery had ended the year before I turned eighteen. And after years of watching my dad struggle as a small businessman, I also could not ignore the promise of a stable government job with guaranteed benefits. Another allure was an agent's sense of honor, or *gedi* in Japanese. The little I knew about FBI agents came mostly from watching Mr. Gordon and from television. But it seemed like an honorable profession and a good way to serve my country. After I graduated from Towson, I called the FBI and asked for a job.

I excitedly told the agent who took my call that I met each of the FBI's requirements. I was twenty-four years old, a college graduate, a U.S. citizen, and had no criminal record.

That's nice, kid, the agent said as kindly as he could. "But we like our applicants to get three years' real-world work experience first. Give us a call then." Discouraged, I moved to Plan B: the Foreign Service, figuring I could work for the State Department and travel for three years, then transfer to the FBI. I took the exam, but didn't get the job. Apparently, I didn't have enough political juice.

The same year, my brother Bill and I joined my dad in a new

business, a monthly agricultural newspaper called *The Maryland Farmer*. Neither my dad nor I knew anything about journalism or farming, but the paper was 75 percent ads anyway—for fertilizer, seed, dairy products, tractors, anything a farmer might need. Our advertisers were as big as Monsanto and as small as a local general store. I had never set type or written a headline, and I couldn't tell the difference between an Angus and a Holstein. But I quickly learned how to do all of those things. I also learned the art of listening. I met with farmers, judged farm show contests, wooed corporate executives, and got to know career bureaucrats. I wrote stories, edited them, sold ads, designed headlines, supervised copy as it was punched into the big Compugraphic machine, and used an X-Acto knife to paste it all onto the page. We did fairly well, and by 1982, Wittman Publications had expanded to four states. I traveled extensively, perhaps a hundred thousand miles a year, learning how to sell a product, and more important, to sell myself, a skill that would become essential years later when I worked undercover. I mastered the most important lesson of sales: If someone likes the product, but doesn't like you, they won't buy it; if, on the other hand, they're not crazy about the product, yet they like you, well, they may buy it anyway. In business, you have to sell yourself first. It's all about impressions.

On the road, I learned how to manipulate—how to make cattlemen, peanut farmers, tobacco growers, and lobbyists believe this city boy cared about their issues. But I didn't *really* care. I still longed to join the FBI. And after eight years of constant deadlines, weekly scrambles to find advertisers, and managing banal disputes between reporters and advertising salesmen, the job got old.

One October evening, after another frantic day at the office, I headed out to blow off some steam and grab a good dinner. I made my way to a trendy new restaurant in the city, a place where I knew I could grab a great bowl of lobster bisque and catch Game Four of the American League Championship Series, the Orioles versus the Angels. My bisque arrived and hit the spot; I'd been so busy that day I'd missed lunch. The Orioles jumped out to a three-run lead in the fourth inning, but at the bar, a blond woman kept bobbing up and down, blocking my view of the television. I found it irritating. But during the fifth inning, she turned slightly and I caught her profile. Wow. This woman was a radiant beauty with a smile that made me forget the game. I introduced myself, tried to stay cool. We spoke for an hour and she finally agreed to give me her number. Her name was Donna Goodhand, and she was twenty-five years old, a dental office manager with a bright sense of humor. On the rear of her white 1977 Malibu Classic was a bumper sticker that said, IGNORE YOUR TEETH AND THEY WILL GO AWAY. I liked her style, and I thought I'd acted suavely during our first encounter. Later, she would confide that she hadn't seen it that way—she originally found me pushy, obnoxious. By her account, I rescued myself on our third date, when I took her to my parents' home and serenaded her with "Unchained Melody" on the piano. We married two and a half years later.

In the mid-1980s, Donna and I had two young sons, Kevin and Jeffrey. We lived in a tiny townhouse and, because my newspaper business was too small to provide medical benefits, Donna worked full-time for the Union Carbide Corporation.

One day in 1988, Donna showed me a newspaper ad that said the FBI was hiring. I played it cool and shrugged, careful not to raise expectations, still embarrassed by the post-graduation call. But my mind drifted back to the notions of service, honor, independence, Mr. Gordon and Efrem Zimbalist Jr. I also knew I didn't have much more time. I was thirty-two years old. The FBI stopped taking new agents at age thirty-five. Without telling Donna, I took the aptitude test at the FBI offices in Baltimore. I figured if I failed, I wouldn't tell anyone and that would be it. A few months later, an FBI agent showed up at the newspaper and asked to see me. I took him into my private office and we sat down. He was thin, tall, and wore large round glasses with thick lenses. He wore a cheap light-brown sport coat and blue trousers. The agent was there to check my background, but we also talked a lot about what it was like to be an agent. He was a good salesman. Then again, I was an easy sell.

". . . And so, in just a few months, if you became a special agent, you could find yourself driving a high-powered car with a shotgun on the side of a mountain or on an Indian reservation, and you might be the only law around for thirty miles . . ."

That sounded pretty cool. Working alone, supervising no one. Carrying a shotgun. Representing the U.S. government. Protecting the innocent, prosecuting evil. The only law around for miles.

The agent looked me over once more. "Let me ask you something." He pointed through the door to my newspaper employees scurrying to put out the next edition. "Why do you want to leave all this? You make $65,000 and you're the boss, the owner. In the FBI, you'll start at $25,000 and be told what to do, where to live."

I didn't hesitate. "Easy choice. I've always wanted to be an FBI agent."

We shook hands.

There was one more test—the FBI's physical training test, a complexly scored series of exercises—running, pull-ups, push-ups, sit-ups. I was thirty-two years old, and had to train to pass. That summer, every evening after work, I hit the local track. The whole family joined me, Donna pushing baby Jeffrey in an umbrella stroller as toddler Kevin ran behind her. I passed and won entrance to the FBI Academy. On the Sunday of Labor Day weekend 1988, we drove to Donna's parents' home on the Chesapeake Bay to celebrate Kevin's fourth birthday and my entrance into the FBI. We lined six picnic tables side by side—sixty friends, neighbors, and family members munching burgers and hot dogs, cracking large steamed crabs, sipping chilled Budweiser by the bay. There were toasts, hugs, and family photos. It was bittersweet. The next day, I piled into Donna's aging Malibu, left my family, and headed to Quantico, Virginia, to report for the fourteen-week FBI Academy.

From the first day, I was struck by how much each of my fifty classmates had in common. We were mostly conservative, roughly thirty years old, patriotic, clean-cut. I was also struck by the fact that unlike me, most recruits came to the Academy with a law-enforcement background. They were ex-soldiers and former policemen, people who embraced military bearing and physical contact. They enjoyed boxing, wrestling, kicking, handcuffing and firing weapons, taking pepper spray in the face as part of a manly right of passage. I didn't share their macho creed. While I understood that my job might be dangerous, and I stood willing to sacrifice myself to save a civilian or a fellow agent, that didn't mean I would do something stupid. I always scored well on FBI written tests because I knew the correct answer in most scenarios was to call for backup, not to play hero. *Question: Two armed men rob a bank, fire at a police officer, and duck into a home. What do you do? Answer: Call for backup and the SWAT team.* The military might be willing to accept some losses, but in law enforcement there is no such thing as an acceptable loss. The physical training at the academy was necessary, but I found it something to endure, not embrace. Thankfully, my dorm roommate, Larry Wenko, shared my view. Larry came up with a mantra that helped us get through the hellish fourteen weeks: *Here to Leave.*

In our final weeks at the academy, we received our postings. Donna and I had hoped for Honolulu. We got Philly.

It was not a choice assignment. In 1988, Philadelphia was grimy, expensive, and a decade away from making its great comeback. I tried to make the best of it, lamely reminding Donna that Philadelphia was only ninety minutes from our relatives in Baltimore. She laughed and bit her tongue. We both knew we weren't moving to Philadelphia for its location or quality of life. We moved to Philadelphia so I could pursue my dream.

We didn't realize how fortuitous the FBI's choice would be. Philadelphia is home to two of the nation's best art museums and one of the country's largest archaeology collections.

The month I reported for duty, two of them were robbed.

CHAPTER 4

MASK OF THE MAN WITH THE BROKEN NOSE

Philadelphia, 1988.

THE FIRST THIEF HIT THE RODIN MUSEUM, AN ELE-gant building dedicated to the French artist who sparked the Impressionist movement in sculpture.

The museum holds the largest collection of Rodin's work outside of Paris and sits prominently on the northwestern edge of Philadelphia's grand boulevard, the Benjamin Franklin Parkway. The Rodin is managed by its sprawling neighbor, the Philadelphia Museum of Art, which boasts paintings by Dalí, Monet, van Gogh, Rubens, Eakins, and Cézanne. In pop culture, the Philadelphia Museum of Art is better known as the spot where Sylvester Stallone jogged up seventy-two steps in the movie *Rocky*. It's an exhausting climb. The flat terrain in front of the Rodin Museum, on the other hand, is far more hospitable. The only barrier between the museum and the parkway is a lovely courtyard anchored by a six-and-a-half-foot-tall cast of the artist's most famous work, *The Thinker*.

On November 23, 1988, a troubled young man entered the Rodin Museum at 4:55 p.m., five minutes before closing time. The winter sun had already set, and the museum was nearly empty. The man wore blue jeans, white sneakers, a dark T-shirt, and a long gray tweed overcoat. His dirty blond hair fell below his shoulders, and the guards at the door figured he was an art student. The lone cashier at the tiny gift shop did not notice the man until he spoke.

"This is business!" the bandit announced as he drew a .25-caliber Raven pistol, a Saturday night special with a worn wooden grip. "On the floor, I say!" He pointed the shiny silver barrel at the guards, but the weapon was so small and the man spoke so theatrically that the guards hesitated. Was this an act? A prank? Was this guy unhinged? He spoke with the lilt of a British accent, but was clearly American. With his hair slicked back and his high cheekbones, he looked a little like James Dean. When no one moved, the man fired a shot into the wall.

The guards dropped to the floor.

The thief kneeled down, the weapon trembling in his left hand, and handcuffed each guard. He moved to the Rodin sculpture closest to the front door, *Mask of the Man with the Broken Nose,* a ten-inch-high bronze of a bearded middle-aged man with a weathered face, and snapped it from its marble podium. He turned and dashed out the front door, cradling the sculpture like a football, through the museum courtyard and past *The Thinker.* When the thief reached the edge of the museum grounds at the Ben Franklin Parkway, he turned west toward the art museum, disappearing into the maze of rush-hour traffic.

It was my first month as an FBI agent.

On its face the heist seemed like a simple, stupid, uncivil act. How ironic that my work on the investigation would open worlds I had never considered—the struggles of one of Impressionism's most significant artists, the dream of a Roaring Twenties tycoon who sought to share an artist's extraordinary beauty with his fellow Philadelphians, and the hopeful, often hapless mind of the art thief. Looking back, I see now that it sparked an interest I would turn into a career. But during my first month on the job, I was focused on more basic tasks, like remembering to take my radio with me on stakeouts.

Back then, the FBI didn't have full-time art crime investigators.

In fact, the theft of art and antiquities from museums wouldn't become a federal crime until 1995. The theft of an object of art or cultural significance was treated like the theft of any valuable piece of property. The property-theft squad handled it. Usually, the FBI didn't become involved in art crime cases unless there was evidence that a stolen piece was carried across a state line, a federal crime. But in Philadelphia, there was one guy, a respected agent named Bob Bazin, who liked to work museum cases. He worked closely with the Philadelphia police, and they often consulted with him on thefts. I got lucky. When I graduated from the Academy and reported for duty, I was assigned to partner with Bazin.

Not that Bazin wanted me, or any other rookie. Veteran agents called us "Blue Flamers" because in our first months we were so eager to please that we were said to have blue flames shooting from our asses. Bazin liked to work alone and, at least on the surface, acted as if he couldn't be bothered to train a neophyte. I suspected he was suspicious of my background. My brief years in the Japanese antiques business with my dad hardly qualified me as an art expert. Worse, most FBI rookies are former cops, soldiers, or state troopers. I was a geeky former ag-journalist. Bazin was a bear of a man, not tall, but burly, and a no-nonsense investigator who'd spent years on the street hunting bank robbers and fugitives. He had an unfailing, enduring loyalty to the FBI and worked diligently on any assignment. That included taking me on.

I settled into an empty desk next to Bazin. The FBI occupied two floors in the central federal building in Philadelphia, part of a red-brick judicial complex two blocks from Independence Hall. The property-theft squad worked in a bullpen in a corner of the eighth floor. On my first day, I went to the supply closet and grabbed a couple of pads, pens, and a handful of blank forms. Bazin patiently watched me arrange them on my desk. When I finished, he caught my eye. "How do you plan to carry all that on the street?"

I didn't know. "They didn't tell us at the Academy," I said lamely.

Bazin growled. "Forget all that shit. The Academy is Disneyland."

He reached behind his desk, pulled out a weathered tan brief-case, and threw it at me. He told me to fill the case with the essential FBI forms I would need to conduct investigations—forms to execute search warrants, read people their rights, make hidden audio recordings, and seize property.

"Take it with you everywhere you go, every day, every case," Bazin said. My new partner stood. "C'mon, we're not going to solve any crimes sitting around here," he said. "We'll start after lunch."

After a couple of hoagies, we drove fifteen blocks to the Rodin Museum. Bazin asked all the questions, and I took detailed notes. We didn't learn much more than the city police detectives had, and I couldn't tell what Bazin was thinking as we drove back to the squad room. I wondered—but did not dare ask—why the thief had chosen *The Man with the Broken Nose*. Perhaps he picked it because it was located so close to the front door. Maybe he was attracted by the sculpture's shiny nose—for years, curators had allowed museum patrons to rub it for good luck, and the bronze had acquired a bright patina. With few leads to investigate, I tried to make myself useful. I quietly read up on Auguste Rodin and *The Man with the Broken Nose,* or *L'Homme au Nez Cassé.*

Mask of the Man with the Broken Nose was Rodin's first important work, and it is not an overstatement to say that it was revolutionary, as it led him to redefine the world of sculpture, moving it beyond photographic realism, much as fellow Impressionist Claude Monet transformed painting. In many ways, Rodin's task was tougher. Painters like Monet expressed themselves by deft use of color and light. A sculptor like Rodin worked in monotones on a three-dimensional surface, manipulating light and expression with lumps and creases in plaster and terra-cotta molds. The turning point for Rodin, and indeed for art history, began in 1863, when he was twenty-four, the year his beloved sister died.

Distraught over Maria Rodin's death, Rodin abandoned his fledgling career as an artist. He turned away from family and friends and toward the church. He even took to calling himself Brother Augustin.

Fortunately, a priest recognized that Rodin's true calling was art, not religion, and he put him to work on church projects. This led to design jobs for Parisian general contractors and the sculptor and painter Albert-Earnest Carrier-Belleuse, known for his sculpture of figures from Greek mythology. On the side, Rodin resumed his own work.

He rented his first studio, a horse stable on the Rue Le Brun, for ten francs a month. The place was raw, one hundred square feet of workspace, a slate floor with a poorly capped well in a corner. "It was ice cold," he wrote years later, "and penetratingly damp at all seasons of the year." In a rare photograph from this formative period, Rodin wears a top hat, frock coat, and scraggly goatee, his unkempt hair swept across his ears. He looks confident.

Rodin's new pieces were not meant to be realistic; they were designed to impart deeper, sometimes multiple meanings. Before his sister's death, Rodin sculpted people close to him—family, friends, women he dated. Now he turned outward, to sculpt the common man. He was too poor to afford to pay models, and he grabbed volunteers where he could, including the handyman who cleaned his stable-studio three days a week. Rodin described this handyman as "a terribly hideous man with a broken nose." He was Italian and went by the nickname Bibi, which was the nineteenth-century French equivalent of Mac or Buddy. "At first I could hardly bear to do it, he seemed so dreadful to me. But while I was working, I discovered that his head really had a wonderful shape, that in his own way he was beautiful. . . . That man taught me many things."

Rodin worked on the piece on and off for eighteen months. He stored it in the stable, which he could not afford to heat, and covered it only with a damp cloth to keep the terra-cotta from drying out. Rodin's complex sculpture of a handyman came to resemble a Greek philosopher. It was at once a portrait of an everyman and a superman. It was a portrait of a man and of his times, and a portrait of humanity. It offered a new way for Rodin, a way toward the truth.

Then something extraordinary happened.

One winter night in 1863, the temperature plunged below freezing and the terra-cotta mold froze. The back of its head split off, fell, and shattered. Rodin studied the mask that remained. It seemed to accentuate the creases and the texture of Bibi's face, his broken nose and the man's inner agony. The half-finished nature of the work, Rodin concluded, added depth. He had discovered a new form of sculpture, one he would employ again and again.

"The mask determined all my future work," Rodin recalled. "It was the first good piece of modeling I ever did."

The Salon was not impressed. The state-sponsored umbrella organization of artists and critics who controlled the most sought-after exhibition space was a conservative crew. In 1864, they were not ready to accept Impressionist art of any kind. Rodin would not necessarily have cared, if the Salon were not so influential, at least economically. The wealthiest buyers, including the Republic of France, were reticent to purchase art not exhibited at the Salon. It would take eleven years before the Salon would accept work by Rodin, Monet, or any of their Impressionist colleagues.

In 1876, *Mask of the Man with the Broken Nose* made its American debut in Philadelphia, as part of a French exhibition in Fairmount Park celebrating the American centennial, a milestone cultural event that led to the founding of the city's art museum. For Rodin, the show was a disappointment. He won no prizes, and his work apparently garnered no publicity.

A half century later, an American visionary brought Rodin back to Philadelphia in style.

Jules E. Mastbaum was a self-made movie tycoon who seized on the potential of the cinema-house business in the early 1900s. He turned the moviegoing experience into an entertainment venue that was at once glamorous and accessible. By the early 1920s, as Hollywood began to boom, Mastbaum owned more movie houses than anyone in the United States. Mastbaum named his business the Stanley Company of America in honor of his dead brother, and in scores of midsized cities and towns across America, the local Stanley

Theaters, many with grand staircases and lavish decor, became a prime social spot. The most extravagant theater in the chain was built in Philadelphia; it was a 4,717-seat theater with room for a sixty-piece orchestra, a French Empire/Art Deco monstrosity adorned with marble, gold leaf, leaded glass, tapestries, paintings, statues, three balconies, a Wurlitzer organ, and the largest crystal chandelier in the city.

In 1923, some six years after Rodin's death, Mastbaum visited Paris on an extended vacation and became entranced with the French sculptor. He began to buy up bronze castings, plaster studies, drawings, prints, letters, and books, and shipped them home to his beloved Philadelphia. His collection soon included pieces from every period of Rodin's life. In addition to *The Thinker* and *Mask of the Man with the Broken Nose,* Mastbaum brought back *The Burghers of Calais, Eternal Springtime,* and the complex piece Rodin spent the last thirty-seven years of his life crafting, the enormous sculpture *The Gates of Hell.* Mastbaum always intended to share his collection with the public, and three years after he began his collection he hired two prominent French neoclassical architects, Paul Cret and Jacques Gréber, to design a building and gardens on a city-donated plot of land on the parkway. In front of the museum courtyard, they erected a facade of the same French château that Rodin had created outside his country estate in his later years. Designed by Jacques Gréber as part of the museum's overall plan, the Rodin Gardens have remained a calm respite from the clatter of the city, even as the Ben Franklin Parkway landscape morphed over the years.

Mastbaum died unexpectedly in 1926, but his widow finished the project and donated it to the city. The museum opened in 1929 to rave popular and critical reviews. "It is a jewel which shines on the breast of a woman called Philadelphia," one newspaper gushed. Today, the museum seems small and subtle, especially given its big brother on the hill, the art museum. But its intimate size and wide scope make it unusually accessible. Visitors are encouraged to partake in the lone interactive exhibit—rubbing the nose of the *Mask of the Man with the Broken Nose,* and wishing for the same kind of good luck the sculpture brought the artist.

In the months that followed the 1988 theft, Bazin and I could have used some of that luck.

With so few clues, we did what any cop does when he comes up empty: We offered a reward. The museum and its insurance company put up $15,000 and we got the local newspapers and television stations to publicize it. The tips flew in, and as always, almost all were wrong. We dug through each one anyway. About a month later, we received a call from a Philadelphia man who knew things about the crime that had not been publicized—like the thief's flamboyant monologue. He also seemed to know a lot about the man he fingered, Stephen W. Shih. The suspect was twenty-four years old, slightly older than the college student described by the guards, but our informant insisted that he was our man. The rest of the physical appearance seemed to match, and—get this—Shih was working as a $400-a-day stripper to pay the rent. He was unusually handsome. And theatrical!

We figured we had our man, but we needed more than a tip to arrest Shih or search his home. We needed solid evidence, and Bazin moved cautiously. He explained that if we simply confronted Shih and tried to intimidate him into confessing, it might backfire. He might clam up and ditch or destroy the Rodin. This has happened several times in Europe as the police have closed in on thieves. In one infamous case, the mother of a Swiss man suspected of a dozen museum thefts dumped more than one hundred paintings in a lake, destroying not only the evidence but also irreplaceable works of art. Our primary goal, Bazin reminded me, was to recover the sculpture. Our job was to save fragments of history, messages from the past. If, in the process, we busted the bad guy, that would be a bonus.

Bazin came up with a simple plan: Show the guards a photo lineup of Shih and seven guys who looked like him. If the guards ID'd him, we'd have enough to move in. First, we needed a photo of

Shih. That was grunt work, and it fell to me. Bazin sent me out with the FBI photographer in the surveillance van. He instructed me to sit on Shih's house, snap surreptitious pictures, and radio back when I had accomplished my mission.

I learned two painful lessons that week. First: Dress warmly in February in Philadelphia, even if you plan to spend the day inside an undercover van. To maintain cover on stakeout, you have to switch the engine off, and that means no heat. The chief FBI photographer who accompanied me arrived well bundled. After an hour, despite my rookie exuberance, I started shivering like a fool. The photographer's breath floated through the sub-freezing air as he laughed. My second mistake was leaving my FBI radio on my desk, naively figuring I could use the one in the van dashboard. After a few mind-numbing hours, Shih came out and we got our picture. I flipped on the van radio to make the call, but the radio battery was dead. We drove around the block to the spot where Bazin was waiting for us with another agent, ready to move in if we radioed for backup. I knew he would let me have it for forgetting the handheld radio, and he did.

When we got back to the office, I saw my radio standing upright on his desk. Lesson learned. I'd never again be so casual or make an assumption about an undercover operation.

For comparison's sake in the photo lineup, the FBI photographer and I set out again to find seven men who looked like Shih. We couldn't use mug shots; the pictures had to be similar—candids shot from a distance. I figured the task would take a day. Like a lot of things in law enforcement, it took us a lot longer than it should have. To get it right—to find pictures so similar that no judge would ever throw the case out—it took two weeks. When we laid out the photos for the museum guards, each picked Shih. Bazin told me to open my briefcase and start the paperwork.

Because Shih was armed and might have the sculpture stashed in his house, we hoped to confront him elsewhere. We called our tipster back. Did he know when Shih might leave home? As a matter of fact, he said, he did: At 11 a.m. Thursday, the stripper-cum-art-thief would travel to a building at Twelfth and Walnut streets, a teeming downtown corner. It wasn't ideal—an armed daylight take-down on a busy intersection three blocks from City Hall—but it was the best we had.

It was bitterly cold that March morning, which was fortunate because it made it easy for us to hide our vests and weapons under thick overcoats. Bazin, sitting in one of four undercover cars parked at the lip of the intersection, had "the eye"—he was closest and would give the order to move in. A handful of FBI agents strolled casually down each of the four streets. A dozen city cops were positioned a block away, ready to pounce or block all escape routes. I sat in a parked undercover car half a block away from Bazin, coordinating the radio traffic with a car unit (and a handheld backup radio in the glove box). The agent sitting next to me carried one of the world's most powerful personal machine guns, an MP5.

Two minutes before eleven, Bazin's voice came over the radio. "We think we have our suspect. He is not alone. With a female. I'm behind him." The agent beside me turned the ignition and put the car in drive. Bazin gave the signal, calmly. "All units: Move in. Move in, now." We lurched forward fifty feet and braked hard in front of Bazin, who already had Shih spread-eagled against the wall. I jumped out awkwardly, constricted by my vest, and held my gun in my best Quantico-style position. Bazin pulled the .25-caliber Raven from Shih's pocket. He emptied the magazine. One round was missing.

We had Shih, but not the Rodin, and he wouldn't talk. We searched his room and found an address book with the name of a well-known antiques dealer. The dealer suggested that we talk to Shih's mother. We did, and she gave us permission to search her place. In the basement, wrapped in newspaper under a tarpaulin hidden beneath a pipe by the water heater, we found *The Man with the Broken Nose,* undamaged.

Shih was charged in state court, pleaded guilty, and was

sentenced to seven to fifteen years in prison. Although we solved the case, it was not yet a federal crime to steal something of value from a museum, reflecting Congress's belief that art crime was not a priority. Within the FBI's Philadelphia Division, Bazin's interest in art theft was considered informal, an interesting sidelight, a hobby. It wasn't that other agents denigrated what Bazin did. It was just that most didn't care. They were too busy chasing bank robbers, mobsters, corrupt politicians, and drug dealers. Thefts from U.S. museums were treated as isolated cases—and, like the Rodin heist, one-piece jobs, pulled off by loners or losers. As the eighties drew to a close, art thefts made news as oddities, not as outrages.

In March 1990, all that changed. Thieves hit the Isabella Stewart Gardner Museum in Boston, and made off with a bounty that dwarfed every other art crime in American history.

I was not involved in the initial Gardner investigation.

I was too busy recuperating and mourning a loss. I was also looking for a good defense lawyer.

CHAPTER 5

THE ACCIDENT

Cherry Hill, New Jersey, 1989.

"SIR? ARE YOU ALL RIGHT, SIR? SIR?"

The voice in my left ear sounded firm, polite. My eyes bolted open and I found myself staring at the gray seat belt across my chest. I lifted my chin and stared through a cracked windshield. I could see we'd hit a tree, and it had split the front bumper. Instinctively, I checked my hands for blood. Nothing. *Wow, that wasn't so bad. And . . . I'm alive!* I switched off the ignition. I looked to my right to check on my partner and best friend, Denis Bozella. His seat was wedged backward and nearly flat. Denis was moaning.

"Sir? Sir?" It was that voice again. "Sir? What's your name, sir?"

I turned slowly to my left. A Cherry Hill cop leaned in the window. "Bob," I said. "I'm Bob. Bob Wittman."

"OK, sit tight, Bob. We're going to get you out," the cop said, warming his hands on his breath. The paramedics and firefighters were only a few minutes away, he said. They were going to have to use the Jaws of Life to get us out. "We're going to take the roof off and give you a convertible for free."

I grunted and tried to get a better look at Denis. I started to unbuckle my seat belt and winced at the pain in my left side. I wheezed. I tried to lift the door handle, but it was jammed. Frozen air blew through the broken windows. I closed my eyes and thought about Donna. In the distance, I could hear a siren. Jesus, it was cold.

I heard Denis moan again. I turned but I couldn't see his face. "Denis? . . . Denis? Can you hear me, buddy?"

He spoke weakly. "What happened?"

"A car cut us off."

"My chest hurts. I'm not going to die, am I?"

"No!" I caught the panic in my voice and calmed myself. "We'll both be fine, partner. We're gonna be fine."

I held his hand. I heard more sirens and closed my eyes.

The day had begun with such promise.

IT HAD BEGUN an hour before dawn, as I drew myself out of bed, careful not to disturb Donna or our two sons, nursery-schoolers obsessed with counting the final days until Christmas. Overnight, a light snow had laid a fresh thin layer across the frozen remnants of a week-old storm. I showered, made coffee, and put on my uniform—dark suit, white shirt, dark tie, leather holster, and .357 Smith & Wesson snub-nosed revolver. As I walked toward the front door I smelled the piney evergreen of the Christmas tree. I plugged in the white tree lights.

I was my happiest in years. I had a dynamic wife, two healthy boys, and a dream job with civil service protection and benefits. Donna loved our three-bedroom home nestled in the Pine Barrens, the burnt orange Southwestern decor, the half-hour drive to the Jersey shore. We'd just celebrated the first anniversary of my first FBI post. Like most rookies, I'd been shifted between squads every few months to get a feel for different work. In the summer, I'd moved from the property theft squad, where I'd partnered with Bazin, to the public corruption squad, where I was paired with Denis. A rising star with brown curly hair and piercing green eyes, he was an extrovert from the hills of western Pennsylvania. His rakish charm easily won over fellow agents, supervisors, prosecutors, witnesses, and the ladies. We bonded when we spent several months prepping for a high-profile police corruption trial, sometimes babysitting witnesses in hotel rooms. It was nearly 24/7 work. You drove the witnesses everywhere, took them to breakfast, lunch, and dinner, to prosecutors' offices and the courthouse. Denis and I both liked to play piano, and sometimes after work I'd give him an informal lesson. Lately, I was teaching him Jackson Browne's "The Load-Out/Stay."

At 7:30 a.m., I kissed Donna, promised to be home for dinner, and stepped carefully out onto our frozen driveway. Balancing a second cup of coffee and Bazin's old briefcase in one hand, I ducked into my bureau car, a 1989 silver Ford Probe. I flipped on the defroster and rock station WMMR.

That morning, I was headed to Denis's house to give him a ride to work—his FBI car was in the repair shop again. It was great to spend time with him, even if it meant inching through South Jersey traffic. Denis had recently been promoted to Washington to serve on the U.S. Attorney General's protective detail and I would miss him when he left in January.

When I got to Denis's house, he slipped into the front seat as the first chords of the song "Panama" by Van Halen began to jam on the radio, and he cranked it up. I recall this vividly, because it was the day that the United States invaded Panama. We both enjoyed the joke. I sang and drove. Denis played air guitar.

The corruption squad's annual Christmas party was that afternoon at a bar in Pennsauken, New Jersey. We would drive into Philly, then after work head to the party. It would be a good day. At the office, we squeezed in a day's worth of paperwork in time to make it to the party by 2 p.m. We met everyone at a place called The Pub, a sprawling South Jersey landmark at the foot of a triangle of busy highway ramps and arteries. A former speakeasy, The Pub had evolved into a large restaurant, an oversized Swiss chalet with medieval flair—swords and shields on the walls, burgundy carpet, simple brown wooden chairs and tables. The Pub's size, location, and bland grub made it a perfect place for an office party. We spent two hours exchanging gifts and talking shop. There was typical ribbing, but this was the corruption squad, a buttoned-down crew, so they kept it light. When we finally paid the bill, most of us wandered over to the bar for a beer. Denis was up for more and he tried to move the party to a bar called Taylor's for a drink or two. He was single and tried to hit free happy-hour buffets whenever he could. It was nearly 7 p.m. and I wanted to go home, but I figured this might be the last time I could hang out with Denis before he moved. I found a pay phone and let Donna know I would be late.

Taylor's Bar and Grille isn't much—a suburban sports bar in a strip mall near the edge of the abandoned Garden State Race Track. But it was packed. I forced my way to the bar, grabbed my second beer of the evening, and found a table. Denis and a fellow agent hit the buffet. Soon, Denis was talking up a cute woman named Pamela. I felt like a third wheel.

By 9:30 p.m., Denis was still dancing with Pamela and I was way overdue at home. I pulled Denis aside. "Buddy, I gotta get back. You ready to go?"

"Look, not yet," he said. He pointed to Pamela with his eyes. "If that works out, I won't need a ride. I need to find out, so I need you to stick around."

We went back and forth like this for another hour. Denis was having fun, dancing, drinking shots of tequila with Pamela. He brought me another beer and shot me a grin. I gave him a look that said, "Let's go." Around 11 p.m., I'd had enough. I grabbed our coats, took Denis by the arm, led him off the dance floor to the car. He didn't resist.

It was only one hundred yards from Taylor's to Race Track Circle, but this was South Jersey, land of jug-handles, no left turns, and Jersey barriers, so you could only get there by going in the opposite direction and making a series of winding right turns. By the time we reached the circle, Denis was asleep. I slowed as I approached the circle, and as I did, a bright white light flashed in my rearview mirror.

There was a two-inch-high concrete curb at the foot of the circle, channeling traffic to the right, but I was distracted by the light and didn't see this curb. The car hit the curb at about thirty-five miles an hour, and the steering wheel vibrated violently, throwing my hands into the air. When I regained the wheel a second later and tried to turn into the circle, I got no response. We were airborne.

We landed just before the edge of the circle, hurtled into the oval interior, skidded sideways, and flipped, left wheels over right. When the car's roof slammed down on my head, everything went black.

At Cooper University Hospital, Denis and I were rolled into the same trauma room and a surgeon drew blood from our shoulders. The doctor asked me if I had had anything to drink. It was important, she said, for me to tell the truth, because they were going to administer pain medication. I thought back to my first beer at The Pub early in the afternoon. "Probably four or five beers over eight hours." She nodded.

I looked over at Denis. There was a little blood on his cheek, but he didn't look too bad. Denis caught my eye. "Am I going to be OK?" he mumbled.

I really didn't know. "It's OK, buddy. You're going to be fine, partner."

They wheeled Denis away.

The nurse told me I had four broken ribs, a concussion, and a punctured lung. The doctors performed a thoracostomy, cracking open my chest and inserting a tube into my damaged lung, draining fluid from my chest. About an hour later, I found myself lying in a recovery room, a plastic tube in my left side, surrounded by nurses, a doctor, and my FBI supervisor. I asked about Denis and they said he was still in surgery.

"You guys are lucky," the doctor said. "Your injuries aren't life threatening." He pointed to the bed next to mine. "Your friend will be back soon."

Medicated, I drifted off.

Three hours later, I woke with the hard winter sun. I felt foggy, sore, confused. I reached up to my head and felt small pieces of windshield glass matted in my hair, a walnut-sized lump on the right side of my skull. I saw a nurse chatting with a female FBI agent and my wife by the door. Donna turned her bloodshot blue eyes to mine. She offered a nervous smile. The bed beside me was empty.

I winced as I spoke. "Where's Denis?"

The ladies glanced at the floor.

"Where's Denis?"

"He's not here," the nurse said.

"When is he coming up? He's still in the OR?"

The nurse hesitated and the agent stepped forward. "Denis didn't make it. He died."

"What . . . what? . . ." My chest burned. My throat constricted. I coughed and the nurse stepped toward me. They'd told me he was going to make it! What was it the doctor had said? *"The injuries are not life threatening."* Yes, those were his exact words. *Not life threatening.*

Donna crossed to my side. She held me and we cried.

"He had a ruptured aorta," the nurse said, carefully. "He came back from surgery and then it ruptured around 4 a.m. We couldn't stop the bleeding." I sat mute for a few seconds and stared into her eyes. I think she felt compelled to fill the silence. "It's common in this kind of accident," the nurse said. I suppose she thought she was being helpful. I felt devastated.

I floated through eight days in the hospital, trying to lose the pain. Denis was buried while I was there. Fellow agents called with updates describing the funeral, but it was hard to focus. I thought about Denis's family.

Before I left, a psychiatrist came to see me. I don't remember the conversation, but years later I came across his handwritten notes: "Patient has feelings of guilt, anguish, chagrin, and humiliation. He feels solidly supported by wife, staff here, coworkers, and bosses. . . . Acute posttraumatic stress disorder . . . acute grief."

A few days later, a reporter called me in my hospital room. She wanted to know if I had any comment on the investigation, or about the blood-alcohol results.

"What are you talking about?"

She told me the local county prosecutor was considering drunk-driving manslaughter charges against me. The prosecutor claimed that my blood alcohol level was .21, more than twice the legal limit. I told the reporter I had no comment. I hung up and tried to digest what she'd said. The blood test results sounded absurd. A beer every two hours over eight hours didn't get you to .21. It probably didn't even get you to .04. My mind raced for an explanation. Obviously, there was a mistake in the blood test. But where? And how? More important, could I prove it?

Five months later, the grand jury filed formal charges. While my FBI colleagues and supervisors appeared sympathetic, I figured my career was over. Worse, I agonized over Denis's death. Why was I the one who survived? My driving error meant the death of my best friend. Now it threatened to tear away my job and my freedom. What would Donna and the kids do if I was sent to prison?

Facing a hard five-year sentence, I resolved to fight. I drew strength from the comforting familiar in my life—my family and my fledgling career, everything good I knew. Friends and colleagues were supportive, but a few urged me to consider a plea bargain. I couldn't do it. As difficult as it was to accept that Denis died when my hands were on the wheel, my tortured heart told me he would want me to be forgiven—and his parents made it clear they didn't hold me responsible, even urging authorities to drop the charges. But the prosecutor's position was clear, so I hired a top-shelf criminal defense lawyer, Mike Pinsky, and he put his private investigators to work. Pinsky had a reputation for winning tough cases at trial. He was probably best known for winning not-guilty verdicts for a mobster accused of murder and a county clerk facing a bribery rap. Like me, Pinksy also had a reputation for being brutally frank. During our first meeting, we laid our cards on the table.

I asked him how he could represent mobsters, people he knew had done terrible things, including murder. How could he be so friendly with them?

Pinsky moved from behind his desk and took the chair beside me. He smiled.

"Bobby, let me tell you a little secret," he said. "Appearances can be deceiving. It's really all about perceptions, not friendships. These wiseguys call me all the time and say, 'Mike, I got a parking ticket. Mike, I got a speeding ticket. Take care of it, will you?' And I say, 'Sure, no problem, I'll take care of it.' And you know what I do? I take the tickets and I pay them with my own money! Then later, much later, I bill them for it from some other case. They think I've got some sort of power and can fix their tickets. And I let them think that. It's legal and it's good for business."

He leaned close.

"Bobby, I want to be clear about something in your case," he said. "Before we proceed I want to make sure you understand exactly what's at stake. If we go to trial, it may take years. It will certainly cost tens of thousands of dollars in legal fees and investigative expenses. There is no way to prepare for the strain this will put on your family, your marriage, and your job. And in the end, you could still lose and go to prison. You're an FBI agent. You know that if you go to trial and are convicted, instead of pleading guilty at the beginning, the judge will give you a *much* longer sentence."

I didn't hesitate. "Mike, I'm innocent."

CHAPTER 6

LEARNING TO SEE

Merion, Pennsylvania, 1991.

I PILOTED MY DINKY BUREAU PONTIAC SLOWLY DOWN
North Latches Lane, a wide side street framed by graceful oak
trees and gated stone mansions in the heart of Philadelphia's upper-
crust Main Line. I checked my hand-scrawled directions and followed North Latches until I arrived at a black wrought-iron gate
with a discreet sign that said THE BARNES FOUNDATION. I pulled to
the guardhouse and rolled down my passenger window.

The guard carried a clipboard. "Can I help you?"

"Hi. Bob Wittman. I'm here for the class."

He checked his list and waved me in.

I was early and when I found a parking spot I sat in the car for
a few moments. I gripped the steering wheel and exhaled. It was a
crisp fall afternoon, almost two years after the accident, and I was
still awaiting trial on the manslaughter charges. Pinsky wasn't worried about delays, because it gave us time to get to the bottom of the
screwy blood-alcohol test. Every few weeks, the lawyer would mail
me a stack of documents related to the case—a pleading, a medical
record, a private investigator's witness interview. I'd quickly scan
whatever Pinsky sent me, but I found it incredibly stressful to read
investigative records about myself. It was even harder to read the

cold, clinical medical assessments about Denis. Sometimes, I would open the long legal envelope from Pinsky, stack the papers on the kitchen table, and just stare at them.

Thank God I was working. The FBI, following an internal investigation, cleared me and put me back on the street. For a while, I worked with the drug squad. We seized cash, cocaine, and Corvettes, and locked up some pretty dangerous guys. I backed up undercover agents who risked their lives in hotel-room stings. I ducked gunfire from a couple of thugs during my first shoot-out. But drug cases weren't for me. I doubted we were making a big difference. Most people I met on the streets sold drugs because they couldn't make it any other way; they did it to survive. The way I saw it, drugs were a social problem, not a law-enforcement problem. I asked to return to the property theft squad, and soon I was working art crime again with Bazin. It was good to be back.

Within a few months, Bazin and I recovered a set of two-foot-high tomes by eighteenth-century British wildlife artist Mark Catesby, books of sketches worth $250,000 and as impressive as any by John James Audubon. Rescuing such beautiful books meant so much more to me than busting some sad sack in a crack house. Bazin told me that if I was serious about making art crime a career, I should consider taking a class at the Barnes, an appointment-only museum in the suburbs I knew only by its reputation as a treasure trove of Impressionist art. I said OK and Bazin set it up.

As I got out of my car and headed to my first class that afternoon, I didn't know what to expect.

I made my way to the intimidating grand entrance—six marble steps, four Doric columns, and two large wooden doors framed by a remarkable wall of rust-colored Enfield ceramic tiles, each centered with a relief of a tribal mask and crocodile by the Akan peoples of the Ivory Coast and Ghana. As I would soon learn, every arrangement at the Barnes carried meaning. The entrance theme represented the debt modern Western art owes tribal Africa.

I stepped inside, signed in at the security desk, and stepped into the first gallery, an outrageous room jammed with a collection of masterpieces unrivaled by any one room in any gallery in Europe. On the wall in front of me, surrounding a thirty-foot window, hung three works with a combined worth of half a billion dollars. To the right was Picasso's heroic *Composition: The Peasants,* a striking rendering of a man and a woman with flowers presented in deep hues of rust and persimmon, accented with a splash of carmine. To the left was Matisse's *Seated Riffian,* a larger-than-life oil on canvas. It depicted a fierce-looking young man from the mountains of Morocco, his face rendered in bold Mediterranean hues. Rising above it all, reaching for the ceiling, was the Matisse masterpiece *The Dance,* a forty-six-foot-long mural with lithe figures in salmon, blue, and black, dancing joyously. I looked to my right and the room continued to overload my senses. *The Card Players,* a Cézanne in muted denim hues highlighted by the artist's signature folds in the players' overcoats, hung below Seurat's much larger *Models,* which depicted demure nudes in a firework of color, the figures formed by millions of dots in the pointillist style.

A set of twelve folding chairs was arranged on a parquet floor in the center of the great room. Each student received writing paper, a pencil, and a copy of a thick book with a canary cover, *The Art in Painting,* by our benefactor, Dr. Albert C. Barnes. As we were warned in our letter of invitation, the museum doors were locked at precisely 2:25 p.m. The lecture began promptly at 2:30 p.m.

Our teacher, Harry Sefarbi, was an elderly gentleman with large round glasses and short wisps of white hair behind his ears. He was entering his fourth decade teaching art at the Barnes, having been trained by Barnes himself in a class just like mine in the late 1940s. Mr. Sefarbi, as he liked to be called, began with a little history lesson about Barnes.

Born to working-class parents in Philadelphia in 1872, Barnes excelled in public high school and had earned his M.D. from the University of Pennsylvania by age twenty. He developed a wide range of interests, and became a student of the pragmatist movement, which later served as a foundation for his commonsense, everyman philosophy about art. Barnes studied chemistry and pharmacology at the University of Berlin, and returned with a German colleague at the turn of the century to open a lab in Philadelphia. Together, they invented a new antiseptic silver compound called Argyrol, a treatment for eye inflammation. The medicine dominated the medical market for the next forty years, making Barnes a millionaire many times over. He began to travel extensively and soon became an art collector, joining the legion of rich and cultured Americans, including Jules E. Mastbaum and Isabella Stewart Gardner, who sailed to Europe to snap up Old Master and Impressionist works at relatively bargain prices. By any measure, public or private, national or international, the number and quality of Impressionist and Modern paintings Barnes acquired was astonishing: 181 works by Pierre-Auguste Renoir, 69 by Paul Cézanne, 59 by Henri Matisse, 46 by Pablo Picasso, 21 by Chaim Soutine, 18 by Henri Rousseau, 11 by Edgar Degas, 7 by Vincent van Gogh, and 4 by Claude Monet.

Barnes sought to bring his love of high art to others. He began with his employees, hanging valuable works in his factory and offering free art and philosophy classes. When he decided to build himself a new home on a twelve-acre plot just outside the city limits, he hired Paul Cret, the Frenchman who had laid out the Benjamin Franklin Parkway and designed Philadelphia's Rodin Museum, and instructed him to build an art gallery beside the house.

This would not be a museum, Barnes declared, but a laboratory for learning. Each of the twenty-three galleries would be a classroom, and each of the four walls in each gallery would be a blackboard with a lesson plan. It was central to Barnes's plan to make art accessible and understandable to the masses.

Barnes believed that one could only come to appreciate and understand art by viewing it firsthand. Most Americans began at a disadvantage, he believed, because they held preconceived Western notions of art, likely learned (subconsciously or not) from ivory tower academics. The best way to understand art was to look at a painting, compare it to what you saw next to it, and come to your own conclusions. Which is why Barnes arranged his galleries like no other—masterpieces beside the mediocre, Old Masters next to Impressionists, African near European, tribal juxtaposed with Modernists. To emphasize shapes, he arranged three-dimensional objects—often simple metalwork and basic kitchen utensils beside paintings. On the floor along the walls, Barnes set up furniture, candles, teapots, and vases. He called these unorthodox and controversial layouts "wall ensembles," and they were designed to help students see patterns, shapes, and trends you can't teach in books. He wanted classes to be democratic, a place where free discussion was encouraged.

Study the overstuffed walls and discover two chairs that match the female derriere in a set of Renoirs, or an African mask that matches the shape of a man's face in a Picasso painting. Notice a wooden trunk that mimics shapes in Prendergast and Gauguin paintings. Ponder the significance of a set of soup ladles straddling a series of Old Master paintings, or a pair of ox shoes hanging over a pair of Soutines. Chuckle when you realize the theme of a corner gallery is elbows.

Barnes always kept you guessing, thinking. He hung Matisse's iconic *The Joy of Life,* considered the first painting of the Modern art era (and the one a conservative French critic famously labeled "beastly") in a stairwell.

I got a kick out of Barnes's life story, his egalitarian values and eclectic galleries, each filled with jaw-dropping art. But I dreaded my first homework assignment: the first few chapters of *The Art in Painting,* the 521-page treatise Barnes wrote in 1925. The canary-covered book felt as heavy as a brick and I feared the words would be as dense and intimidating. But when I cracked the first chapter, I was pleasantly surprised. The writing was, as I suspected, erudite, but Barnes's unpretentious, workmanlike philosophy struck a chord. He wrote that his method for studying art presented "something basically objective to replace the sentimentalism, the antiquarianism, sheltered under the cloak of academic prestige, which make futile the present courses in art universities and colleges." In other words, Barnes devised a method for his students to think for themselves, to resist the urge to simply accept the prevailing and often pretentious sentiments of so-called experts. Barnes seemed like my kind of guy.

"People often suppose that there is some secret about art, some password which must be divulged before they can discover its purpose or meaning," Barnes wrote. "Absurd as such an idea is, it contains the important truth that seeing is something which must be learned, and not something which we all do as naturally as we breathe." He called this "learning to see."

First and foremost, Barnes taught that all art is based on the work of previous generations. "A person who professes to understand and appreciate Titian and Michelangelo and who fails to recognize the same traditions in the moderns, Renoir and Cézanne, is practicing self-deception," Barnes wrote. "An understanding of early Oriental art and of El Greco carries with it an appreciation of the contemporary work of Matisse and Picasso. The best of the modern painters use the same means, to the same ends, as did the great Florentines, Venetians, Dutchmen, and Spaniards."

The purpose of art is not to create a literal, documentary-style reproduction of a scene from real life. "The artist must open our eyes to what unaided we could not see, and in order to do so he often needs to modify the familiar appearance of things and so make something which is, in the photographic sense, a bad likeness." The greatest artists teach us how to perceive through the use of expression and decoration. They are scientists, manipulating color, line, light, space, and mass in ways that reveal human nature. "The artist gives us satisfaction by seeing far more clearly than we could see for ourselves."

A great painting should be more than a sum of technical beauty. At the Barnes, we were taught to look for delicacy, subtlety, power, surprise, grace, firmness, complexity, and drama—but to do so with a scientist's eye. This was an important point. As an art crime investigator, or an undercover agent posing as a collector, I would have to evaluate and expound upon a wide variety of art, regardless of whether I liked a particular piece.

For the next year, I spent four hours a week in class with ten other students. Each week, we gathered in one of the Barnes's twenty-three galleries, just a few feet from the three or four masterpieces we would study that day. As our teacher outlined the finer points of composition, palette, makeup, and light, I drank it in. I wasn't only listening to the teacher—sometimes I learned more by tuning out and just staring at a wall ensemble. At the Barnes, I didn't learn how to identify a fake or a forgery, but I trained my eye to discern a good painting from a bad one. I learned how to tell the difference between works by Renoir and Manet, or Gauguin and Cézanne— and more important, how to confidently explain in detail these differences and patterns. It's not as hard as you might think, certainly not for a trained art historian or curator. But it's not the kind of thing most police officers know. As I would learn years later, it's not even the kind of thing most art thieves know.

My Barnes experience couldn't have come at a better time, personally or professionally. I remember walking through the second-floor gallery one day, depressed about the indictment, stressed about lawyer bills and the thought of leaving Donna and the kids for prison, when I came upon Renoir's *Mussel Fishers at Berneval*. The painting stopped me. A young mother and children along a sienna seashore. Smiling sisters holding hands. A boy with a basket of mussels. An indigo sky. I moved closer. I cocked my head and followed a brushstroke out to sea. The painting felt warm, soothing. It evoked images of a quieter, simpler time, when playing on the shoreline coupled with picking mussels for a fresh dinner were enough to bring joie de vivre.

Young kids and a mom at the shore. A family. My family.

I found a bench, sat down, and exhaled.

* * *

THE BARNES CLASSES only deepened my interest and appreciation for art, and I couldn't help but approach my art crime cases with new enthusiasm and perspective. While I was still enrolled at the Barnes, Bazin and I got a break on an old case, a 1988 heist from the prestigious University of Pennsylvania Museum of Archaeology and Anthropology. Inside its ninety-foot rotunda, the Penn Museum showcases one of the nation's foremost collections of Chinese antiquities. Late one winter evening, thieves lifted the Chinese exhibition's most significant piece, a fifty-pound crystal ball from the Imperial Palace in Beijing, from its place of honor in the center of the rotunda. The perfect sphere, which projects a person's image upside down, once belonged to the Dowager Empress Cixi, and is the second largest such orb in the world. Hand-crafted during the nineteenth century, the crystal ball represented a triumph of skill and patience, a year's worth of an artist's labor with emery and garnet powder and water. The burglars who took the orb also swiped a five-thousand-year-old bronze statue of Osiris, the Egyptian god of the dead. Museum officials figured it was the work of amateurs, but the pieces seemed to vanish without a trace.

Now, three years later, a museum official was calling Bazin to say a former curator had spotted the Osiris statue for sale at one of the jumble of eclectic shops on Philadelphia's South Street. We rushed over and pressed the proprietor for details. He told us that he'd bought the $500,000 bronze statue for $30 from "Al the Trash Picker," a homeless man who trawled the streets with a shopping cart, looking for junk. We found Al and he quickly told us that he'd gotten the statue from a man named Larry, who happened to live a few blocks from the store. Bazin and I went to see "Larry."

Larry was a compact man with a South Philly attitude and a flimsy story. "I dunno, man, it just showed up in my mudroom a few years ago," Larry offered, lamely suggesting that a friend probably dropped it off and forgot about it. We countered with the textbook good-cop, bad-cop routine. Bazin stomped, glowered, and threatened to arrest him if he didn't tell us "the truth." When Bazin stormed out, I spoke softly to Larry, confiding that we wouldn't charge him if he helped us out. When that didn't work, I went out to tell Bazin.

"Why did you walk out so quickly?" I said.

He shrugged. "I'm hungry, I want to get lunch."

I kept a straight face, and we went back inside to see Larry. I tried the direct approach.

"Was there anything else that you just happened to find when you found the statue?"

"Anything else, like what?"

"A glass ball."

"A glass ball? Yeah, yeah. It was a big heavy thing, but I thought it was one of those lawn globe things. It was pretty ugly, so I just left it in the garage for about a year. Then I gave it away."

As nonchalantly as I could, I uncapped my pen and drew my notebook. "Gave it away?" I said. "To whom?"

"Kim Beckles. My housekeeper. For her birthday, September 1989. She was into crystals and pyramids and stuff like that. She joked that she was a good witch."

I told Larry to call Beckles, to say that he'd just learned that the crystal might be valuable, and that he was sending a couple of appraisers over to take a look. "Tell her that if you sell it, you'll split the money, OK?"

Larry made the call and we headed for the witch's house in Trenton, New Jersey. As soon as we arrived, we dropped the ruse. I banged on the door and yelled, "Police!" She answered quickly. From Larry's description we were expecting a hag, but Beckles was a lithe beauty, twenty-nine years old, blond curly hair. We showed our badges, explained what we were looking for, and she seemed genuinely surprised. She told us she kept the orb in her bedroom. We followed her upstairs.

I'll never forget the anticipation I felt climbing those stairs. It was the same kind of nervous anticipation I got whenever I went on

a drug raid, or helped collar a fleeing suspect—but better. I felt my
heart pound. I wasn't searching for common drugs or guns. I was
searching for lost treasure.

We found the Dowager's crystal ball on the witch's dresser,
under a ball cap.

When Bazin and I returned the orb to its rightful place under the
rotunda at the Penn museum, I felt as proud of myself as an agent
as I ever had, even though no one was charged with a crime. These
art cases offered a different kind of satisfaction. And because Bazin
and I were the only ones working them, we won a degree of independence rare in the by-the-book world of the FBI.

It didn't hurt, either, that the case made big headlines. The day
before the scheduled FBI press conference, someone leaked the story
to the *Philadelphia Inquirer* and the paper put its exclusive on the
front page. After the press conference, the story made all the evening news programs and appeared in four other papers the next
morning. A few years later, when Bazin and I recovered a long-lost
painting stolen from the Philadelphia Museum of Art, the story
landed on the front page again. Fellow agents who pursued the more
traditional FBI crimes, like drugs and robbery, might not seem too
interested, but journalists appeared eager to write about art crime
and give the stories good play. Each art crime inevitably carried a
"hook," a bit of intrigue, and the public ate it up. The attention was
nice, but most important was that it made our local bosses look
good, making it easier for them to green-light our next art crime case.

I led one other significant investigation while awaiting my trial
in the early 1990s. Violent gangs were hitting high-end jewelry
stores in smash-and-grab heists, bolting into the likes of Tiffany,
Black, Starr and Frost, and Bailey Banks and Biddle in broad daylight, taking hammers and tire irons to display cases, and dashing
off with fistfuls of diamonds and Rolex watches worth tens of thousands of dollars. The hoods came from Philadelphia but had hit
more than one hundred stores in five states. I created and led a special task force that not only won federal indictments against thirty

gang members but also snared the ringleaders who fenced the stolen loot—two corrupt merchants from Philly's Jewelers' Row. Our work made the front page again and I developed long-term sources on Jewelers' Row.

The successes at work were gratifying, but the accident continued to haunt my life. No matter how hard we tried, Donna and I couldn't escape it. It always lingered in the background. Neighbors and friends followed developments regularly in the *Inquirer* and the *Camden Courier-Post*. Most people meant well, but they asked about the case whenever they saw us, and it was awkward—we didn't want to be rude, but we wanted to talk about anything else. Meanwhile, the legal bills and delays piled up. Court hearings were scheduled, then postponed, scheduled, then postponed again. I wanted it all to end, but I feared the result. I was driving myself nuts. I needed an escape, something to occupy my mind.

"I gotta find something to do," I told Donna. "I gotta find a hobby."

"Yes, you do."

I found one in baseball. I coached my sons, Kevin and Jeff, in Little League, and we liked to duck down to Baltimore to see my Orioles play at their new, throwback stadium, Camden Yards. On each trip, we fell into a routine: We arrived early for batting practice, got cheap seats, split a pack of baseball cards, and sometimes stayed late to try to snag autographs. Soon, we started attending baseball card shows, and I recognized a market in the Cal Ripken '82 rookie cards (special Topps edition). The Oriole infielder was hugely popular in Baltimore, but not in Philadelphia. I started driving to card shows and strip mall storefronts near Philly, snapping up as many Ripken cards as possible. I got 'em for about $25 to $50 each. Then I'd drive to shows and events in Baltimore and sell them for $100 or $200 more. The year that Ripken broke the Iron Man record for most consecutive games, I sold the cards for $400. I was making a little extra cash doing something I liked. I thought, *Who knows?* If I lost my job and landed in prison, I'd need a new career when I got out. Inspired, I branched out, trying my hand at Civil War collectibles and antique firearms. I attended shows, scoured newsletters for bargains, and began to buy, barter, and sell. I even put my Barnes experience to work and dabbled in fine art. I bought a few Picasso prints, and spent weekend afternoons wandering through suburban galleries and flea markets. I daydreamed about finding a long-lost Monet and turning a $1,000 investment into $100,000.

Unbeknownst to me, Donna had other things on her mind. She wanted a third child. I wasn't so sure. My future was so uncertain. Donna was adamant. "We have to stop putting our life on hold," she said. Our boys were already four and six. Donna was thirty-five. If we were going to expand our family, now was the time. I nervously agreed. Kristin was born on Thanksgiving Day, and, as it turned out, having a little girl was the best decision we made during those stressful years.

Incredibly, the trial delays continued into 1993, 1994, and beyond. I kept myself as busy as I could with the kids and work, and with my new hobbies and interest in fine art, but every few hours, my thoughts returned to Denis and what lay ahead for me. Each day I crossed the Delaware River on the way to work, I passed New Jersey's Riverfront State Prison at the foot of the Ben Franklin Bridge. It was the place I would be sent if convicted.

One day in 1995, a few weeks before my trial was set to begin, I ran into a member of the prosecution team on South Street in Philadelphia. We had to be careful. We weren't supposed to talk outside of court.

We exchanged pleasantries and an awkward silence followed. We just stood there. Finally, the person said, "How are you holding up?"

How was I holding up? I kept my cool, and answered with a question of my own. As politely as I could, I said, "Why are you doing this?"

What the person said shook me. "Look, we know this is a bad case, but it's just one we have to lose at trial."

The comment shattered my assumption that prosecutors pursued fundamental fairness. As a defendant, I figured the truth, witnesses, and evidence were on my side. It didn't occur to me that government officials would prosecute a case they did not believe in. *We know this is a bad case, but it's just one we have to lose at trial.* I started to stammer a response, but thought better of it, and walked away.

I was forty years old and my hair was gray.

CHAPTER 7

A NEW LIFE

Camden, New Jersey, 1995.

"WILL THE DEFENDANT PLEASE RISE?"
The jurors shuffled into the courtroom, the forewoman gripping the verdict sheet. I tried to catch her eye. The jury had been out only forty-five minutes. The trial was in its ninth day, unbelievably long for a DUI case, but I thought it was going very well. I testified that I drank four or five beers over eight hours. My attorney, Mike Pinsky, ripped the government witnesses apart, and the paramedics who took the stand said I hadn't looked drunk. Pamela, the woman Denis met at the bar, described me as sober, the guy who was clearly his friend's designated driver. The prosecutor stuck to her best evidence—the hospital report showed that my blood alcohol count was .21, so high that I should have had trouble walking, let alone driving.

Fortunately, Pinsky's experts had by then solved the mystery of the blood test. They explained to the jury that when they closely compared Denis's medical records with mine, they found something odd: My alleged blood alcohol content, when calculated to the fifth decimal point, was .21232 and Denis's reading was .21185. It was a difference of just .00047, less than the typical variation found when testing the same vial of blood. This was too close to be a coincidence, my experts testified. Someone at the hospital had mixed up the samples. The standard practice is to test every vial of blood twice—and it looked like someone had tested Denis's blood twice, and assigned one of the readings to me. Our argument was bolstered when our experts discovered that the hospital didn't have a method for securing each sample—there were no procedures to keep a proper chain of custody. One of our experts was the former head of the state police crime lab. On the stand, he spoke definitively: The government's only evidence was worthless.

As the clerk handed the verdict sheet to the judge, my mind raced. Why the quick verdict? Did the jury even take the time to analyze the lab reports? Did they like my lawyer? The prosecutor? Me? A uniformed deputy quietly slipped behind me. What did that mean? Did he plan to take me into custody? Or was he there to protect me?

As the judge unfolded the verdict sheet, the street encounter with that member of the prosecution team flashed in my head—*We know it's a bad case, but it's just one we have to lose at trial.* What if? What if the jury didn't get that?

The judge cleared his throat. "In the case of New Jersey versus Robert K. Wittman, we find the defendant . . . not guilty."

I exhaled deeply and unclenched my fists. I hugged my lawyer. I hugged Donna. I even hugged the prosecutor. The news accounts said I "wept openly." I wanted to hug the judge, too. For after the verdict, he took the unusual step of publicly stating that he agreed with the jury. He called the blood test evidence bogus, concluding: "He lost control and tragically there was an accident and his passenger lost his life. That's an accident."

Donna and I vowed to make a fresh start, and decided to move from suburban New Jersey to suburban Pennsylvania.

I thought about Denis every day.

I spent late nights on the porch, with a tall glass of iced tea, thinking about all I was learning from my ordeal. I had a choice: I could go into a funk of self-pity and ride a desk for the rest of my career—put in forty hours a week, earn a pension, make no waves—or I could come out swinging. Either way, the accident and trial would mark the turning point of my life and my career.

I never seriously considered quitting the FBI, but I did vow that I wouldn't be the same kind of agent anymore. Most law officers I knew were honorable, but some were too focused on putting people away at any cost in order to close a case. It was a dangerous attitude. These guys might say, *Well, maybe he didn't commit the crime I busted him for, but it's OK because this guy's a dirtbag and I'm sure he got away with something else he did do.* I never agreed with that philosophy. Innocence is innocence. I now knew what it felt like to be charged with a crime I hadn't committed, what it did to families, how an innocent person facing trial can feel helpless, alone in the world. I could never knowingly put anyone through that.

I was now a member of a narrow class. Few FBI agents indicted on felony charges take the case to trial. Fewer still win acquittal, and only a handful of those choose to remain with the bureau. I brought a perspective few of my brethren could match. Most agents saw things in black and white; I started seeing shades of gray. I understood that just because someone made a mistake in judgment, it didn't make him evil. Perhaps as important, I also now knew what most suspects, guilty or innocent, truly feared, and what they wanted to hear. My newfound ability to see both sides of a situation—to think and feel like the accused—was invaluable. I knew it would make me a better agent, especially undercover.

But what kind of agent did I want to be?

One evening, I sat alone at my piano and played a Chopin "Fantasie." It was a favorite from my days as a piano performance major in college, but one I had not played in years. As I got lost in the piece, I thought about the rush I'd gotten when we recovered the Chinese orb and Rodin statue, what it felt like to hold history in your hands. My thoughts bounced with the music, and settled on the inspirational pianist Van Cliburn. He always impressed me, the way he came from such lowly roots, and used his insatiable drive and talent to win the Tchaikovsky competition in Moscow at the height of the Cold War, showing unprecedented courage at a time when Americans had little hope of winning anything in Russia. I decided that, like him, I was going to take a chance and channel my energies toward making a difference in the world.

And finally it hit me: I was uniquely positioned to do something about art crime. Here I was, already an FBI agent with a track record of working art crime cases and, in the case of the jewelry-store robberies, leading a team effort that had solved a complex crime. What's more, I'd worked on my own to become a bit of an expert in several fields. In the five-year period between the accident and my acquittal, I'd studied in classrooms as diverse as flea markets and the Barnes, mastering the nuances of everything from collectibles to fine art. While I specialized in baseball cards, Civil War relics, Japanese collectibles, antique guns, and Impressionist art, I knew the knowledge and skills I was honing could be used in almost any medium.

I could now walk into any collectibles, antiques, or fine art forum and mingle and barter with confidence. I knew that a mint condition Mickey Mantle rookie card was worth twice as much as a rookie Joe DiMaggio, that a Custer autograph was far more valuable than one from Robert E. Lee. I could spot a Soutine in a second and explain how his constructive use of color was influenced by Cézanne, and just as easily discuss Boucher's eighteenth-century influences on Modigliani's nineteenth-century nudes. I could explain the difference between *provenance* (the ownership history of a work of art) and *provenience* (information about the spot where an antiquity came out of the ground). I could credibly hold forth on the differences between the Colt revolver Texas Ranger Sam Walker carried into his final battle and the one Roosevelt carried up San Juan Hill. Along the East Coast, I knew most of the big players, which shows to attend and whom to trust.

My ad-hoc education was complete.

I was ready to go undercover, in pursuit of the priceless.

In the summer of 1997, I got my first chance.

BODY OF WORK

CHAPTER 8

THE GOLD MAN

New Jersey Turnpike, 1997.

T HE SMUGGLERS ARRIVED TWENTY MINUTES EARLY.
Our surveillance teams were already in place and watched
them pull into the bustling Turnpike rest stop near exit 7A, halfway
between Philadelphia and New York. Undercover agents filled the
parking lot—two workmen eating Blimpie hoagies in a utility
pickup, a woman gripping a Styrofoam coffee cup and speaking
into a pay phone, a couple with lunch from Burger King lounging at
a picnic table. Inside a dark van with tinted windows, a team of two
agents aimed a video camera at the arranged meeting point—a set
of picnic tables in the shade, just two hundred feet from the Turnpike. When the smugglers parked their gray Pontiac and found a
table, I got the word by cell phone. I was parked a few miles away
in a rented tan Plymouth Voyager van with a Spanish-speaking agent,
Anibal Molina. We adjusted our body wires, stashed our weapons
under the seat, and pulled out onto the Turnpike.

On this bright and gusty September afternoon, the FBI was hunting for treasure—a seventeen-hundred-year-old South American antiquity called a "backflap," the backside of an ancient Moche king's
body armor, an exquisite piece hammered from gold. For seventeen
centuries, the backflap had remained buried in a honeycombed royal

tomb along the coastal desert of northern Peru—until 1987, when grave robbers stumbled upon the site. Since then, the pilfered back-flap remained elusive, the most valuable missing artifact in all of Peru, frustrating law enforcement officials and archaeologists throughout the Americas. Now two swarthy Miami men, the smugglers we'd arranged to meet on the Turnpike, were offering to sell it to me for $1.6 million. I didn't *really* believe these two could pull it off. I figured this was some sort of fraud or rip-off. After all, they were claiming they held the largest golden artifact ever excavated from a tomb in the Americas.

At the picnic table, the smugglers greeted us with mirrored sunglasses and crocodile smiles. We shook hands, sat down. The older one took the lead, and this was good because we had a thick FBI file on him: Denis Garcia, Hispanic male, fifty-eight years old, 225 pounds, five foot nine, brown eyes, white hair, full-time South Florida agricultural salesman, part-time antiquities smuggler. Garcia did not have a criminal record, but the FBI suspected that he had been smuggling illicit artifacts from South America since the late 1960s, when he lived in Peru and learned the pre-Columbian antiquities trade.

Garcia introduced his partner. He was twenty-five years younger and half a head shorter, a muscular man of Puerto Rican heritage. "My son-in-law," Garcia said. "Orlando Mendez."

We shook hands again, and I introduced myself using my under-cover name, Bob Clay. Mendez fidgeted nervously. Garcia was a pro, all business. He got right to it.

"You have the money?"

"No problem—so long as you've got the backflap."

"We'll be bringing it up, making final arrangements." Garcia shifted back to the money. "The price is one-point-six."

I didn't flinch. "As agreed. But I have to have it authenticated. My expert has to see it, look it over. When can we do that?"

"A couple weeks. We have a friend at the Panamanian consulate. He'll go down and get it."

"Customs?"

Garcia waved his hand. "Not a problem."

"Tell me more," I said. "How did your friend get the piece?"

Garcia launched into a cock-and-bull story about the prove-nance, a story designed to somehow lend an air of legitimacy to the illegal sale of a Peruvian national treasure in the parking lot of a Turnpike rest stop. I nodded and acted impressed. I let him finish his story—then switched gears, eager to get him on tape admitting that he knew he was breaking the law, an important distinction we would need if the case ever went to trial.

I began gently. "These things are touchy."

Garcia nodded knowingly. "They are."

"We have to be very careful when we resell it," I said. "Obvi-ously, it can't go to a museum."

Garcia opened his palms as if to say, "Of course."

Mendez, still squirming, broke in and spoke for the first time. His words came rapid fire, his tone overly accusatory. "Are you sure about this? How do you know it's illegal to bring the backflap into the U.S.?" Before I could answer, he fired again. "How do you know? How do you know?"

I acted like I had done this a hundred times. "Trust me, I looked it up." I should have left it there, but Mendez didn't look convinced, so I added an unnecessary comment. "I'm an attorney," I said.

Mendez couldn't argue with that, but I regretted the lie the mo-ment it passed my lips. A lie like that trips you up. Claiming to be a lawyer was especially dumb—it was too easy for the criminals to check, and might cause trouble if the case ever went to trial.

Mendez shifted in his seat and moved to his next question. "Bob, look—I'm sure you understand, I've got to ask you." He looked me in the eye, but I could tell he was nervous. I could guess what was coming. Mendez subscribed to an old wives' tale—the mistaken belief that the law requires an undercover officer to tell the truth if directly confronted.

"Bob, are you a cop?"

I pivoted to put him on the defensive. "No, are you?"

"Of course not," Mendez snapped. He moved to his next dumb question, the kind a veteran smuggler would never ask a fellow criminal. "Tell me more about your buyer."

I moved to retake control of the conversation and caught his gaze. "The buyer is anonymous," I said sternly. "That's all you need to know."

I turned to Garcia, the brains, and softened my tone. "Look, my buyer's a collector. He likes gold. He buys anything made of gold. Let's just call him the Gold Man."

Garcia liked that. "Perhaps I can meet the Gold Man one day?"

"Maybe," I said as we shook hands to leave. "Someday."

I got to the van and dialed the Gold Man's number.

A secretary came on the line. "U.S. Attorney's Office. How can I help you?"

"Bob Goldman, please."

ASSISTANT U.S. ATTORNEY Robert E. Goldman was unlike any other federal prosecutor I'd met.

He lived on a large working farm in Bucks County, north of Philadelphia, where he kept peacocks, horses, sheep, ducks, and dogs. Though Goldman came from a family of lawyers—and became one because it was expected of him—he liked to call himself a frustrated history professor. He wore a handlebar mustache in the style of his hero, Teddy Roosevelt, and at his home library, he stuffed his bookshelves with more than 150 Roosevelt titles. With his appreciation of history and culture, Goldman was precisely the kind of prosecutor I knew I needed if I wanted to pursue art crime. Without a kindred spirit at the U.S. Attorney's Office to prosecute art crime cases, I knew I wouldn't get very far. As an FBI agent, I could investigate almost any federal crime. But if I wanted to harness the full power of the U.S. Department of Justice—from subpoena to grand jury indictment to criminal prosecution—I'd need a like-minded Assistant U.S. Attorney as a partner, someone willing to take on tough, esoteric cases, even if the unstated goal of an investigation was not an arrest, but the rescue of a stolen piece of art. Goldman understood the value of pursuing stolen pieces of history and really didn't care if his bureaucratic supervisors shared his vision.

As important, Goldman treated FBI agents as partners, something that some of his prosecutor colleagues did not. Many young federal prosecutors are arrogant and insecure—paradoxically full of confidence and fear that they'll screw up. These prosecutors often take it out on the agents, barking orders and making menial and abusive demands. Goldman was cool. He'd already worked as a county prosecutor for nearly a decade, following detectives to crime scenes, and he had earned a healthy respect for investigators, whether local cops or federal agents. I'd learned this when we worked our first case together back in 1989, a high-profile armored-car investigation, when I'd been a rookie. Since then, I'd kept returning to him with property theft cases, steadily creating a specialty. First came the jewelry store robberies, then an antique-show heist, and now, the Moche backflap.

THE JERSEY TURNPIKE meeting had gone well, but I didn't get too excited. Start daydreaming about indictments and press conferences, you might get yourself killed.

Was I on the cusp of rescuing a South American treasure? And if so, would anyone notice? In the late 1990s, the FBI's focus was squarely on another South American commodity, cocaine. While my supervisors and the public had certainly applauded when I arrested the thugs for robbing jewelry stores, I didn't know how they'd react if we rescued a piece of stolen history, an antiquity that wasn't even American. Would anyone care?

If I recovered the backflap and received a tepid reaction, it wouldn't bode well for my fledgling career as an art crime sleuth.

I also had another worry—that Garcia might be trying to sell me a fake. And I had good reason to be suspicious.

Three years earlier, I knew, Garcia had offered to sell the back-flap for $1 million to a New York art broker named Bob Smith. I also knew that Smith believed he was close to closing the deal. As a sign of good faith, Smith even made a preliminary deal, paying Garcia $175,000 cash for an ancient Peruvian headdress. But as the months passed, Garcia kept backing out of the backflap deal, com-ing up with lame excuses, irritating the already crusty dealer. Garcia tried to buy time, offering Smith a series of paintings and antiquities that the dealer rejected as insulting fakes. Smith shrugged it off for a while, but when Garcia tried to peddle a bogus Monet, Smith ex-ploded, saying he'd run out of patience: *Get the backflap or get lost.* Garcia stopped calling.

I knew all of this because "Bob Smith" was really Bob Bazin. Smith was the name my mentor used when he worked undercover.

Bazin's gruff art-broker shtick wasn't my style, but it worked for him. When he retired with the backflap case still unresolved in early 1997, the FBI made two fortuitous decisions. First, supervisors de-cided not to charge Garcia with the illegal headdress sale; they thought it might spoil a related case, so they let him get away with it (along with the $175,000 the smuggler pocketed). As far as Gar-cia knew, Smith/Bazin was still looking to buy the backflap. Second, the bureau kept Bazin's undercover phone number active, just in case.

Then, late in the summer of 1997, out of the blue, Garcia called Smith's undercover number. An FBI operator passed the message to me; I found Bazin at his condo on the Jersey Shore and asked him to call Garcia back. The retired FBI agent fell back into his ornery covert role and lit into Garcia. He called him a joker, a poseur, a liar—a guy who made outlandish promises, then vanished for years. Bazin screamed that he didn't have time to deal with Garcia, that he was sick and about to undergo triple bypass surgery. Still, he added . . .

"I don't know why I should do this for you, but I'll give your name to my associate, Bob Clay. Maybe he'll call you."

Grateful and profusely apologetic, Garcia thanked Smith/Bazin.

Within a week, Garcia and I were negotiating a sale by phone. He demanded $1.6 million, and though the price wasn't too important—I never intended to pay—I needed to draw him out and collect as much evidence as possible. I asked for more information and he said he would mail me a package. Perfect, I thought. Use of the mails to commit a fraud is mail fraud, a serious federal crime. So even if the deal fell through, I'd have him on that charge.

Garcia's package arrived a few days later.

August 14, 1997

Dear Mr. Clay,

Enclosed please find the information you requested on the backflap. The culture of the piece is Moche. The antiquity is approximately 2,000 years old. The weight is approximately 1300 grams, length 68 centimeters and width 50 centimeters. For your review, I also enclosed pictures and two National Geographic *magazines that further explain the piece. Please do not hesitate if you need any further information.*

Sincerely,

Denis Garcia

I was grateful for the dog-eared magazines from 1988 and 1990. I'd been on the case only a week, and what little I knew about the backflap I'd learned in a brief conversation with Bazin, who'd warned me to be careful about approaching expert brokers and academics for more background information. The South American antiquities field was riddled with crooks, Bazin said. It was hard to know whom to trust. I put the *National Geographic*s in my briefcase and headed home.

After dinner with Donna and the kids, I put my feet up and settled into our comfortable old couch. Gently, I opened the first *National*

Geographic and flipped to the page Garcia had thoughtfully marked with a yellow Post-it note. The story, written by one of Peru's most prominent archaeologists, began with a call in the middle of the night.

DISCOVERING THE NEW WORLD'S RICHEST UNLOOTED TOMB

By Walter Alva

Like many a drama, this one starts violently, with the death of a tomb robber in the first act.

 The chief of police rang me near midnight; his voice was urgent. "We have something you must see—right now." Hurrying from where I live and work—the Brüning Archeological Museum in Lambayeque, Peru—I wondered which of the many ancient pyramids and ceremonial platforms that dot my country's arid north coast had been sacked of its treasures this time!

Alva wrote that he'd risen grudgingly, assuming that, as usual, the grave robbers would have already removed and sold the best artifacts, leaving only castoffs behind. But when the archaeologist arrived in the small village where they'd arrested the grave diggers, he was stunned to see what the police had seized from the looters' homes. These were no cast-off antiquities, Alva wrote, but intricately carved pre-Columbian golden masterpieces—a broad-faced human head and a pair of feline monsters with fangs flaring. *Huaqueros,* or grave robbers, had picked over the Moche tombs for centuries, but such finds were rare. The police told Alva they were hearing whispers of *huaqueros* selling similar loot for ten times the standard amount.

 Intrigued, Alva returned to the looted site at daylight to poke around. His team began to dig, and soon they found a second, sealed chamber, one that held "perhaps the finest example of pre-Columbian jewelry ever found." Alva's team kept digging and discovered chamber after chamber of priceless and long-lost Moche artifacts, five levels all, each layered on top of the other. After centuries of excavations, the looters had inadvertently stumbled upon the most important archaeological discovery in the New World. It was a royal mausoleum, the final resting place of the Moche king, the Lord of Sipan.

The find was supremely significant, Alva wrote, because so little is known about the Moche civilization, which apparently flourished from roughly A.D. 200 to A.D. 700, then mysteriously vanished. The tribe did not use a written language (leaders communicated by secret code painted on lima beans), and other Peruvian tribes from that era recorded few interactions. Much of what we know about Moche history and culture is derived from the local iconography—the sophisticated drawings, intricate jewelry, and dynamic ceramics.

I became entranced by the history of this lost civilization. The Moche lived chiefly along the narrow river valleys of a two-hundred-mile stretch of Peru's coastal desert. This tribe of weavers, metalsmiths, potters, farmers, and fishermen was perhaps fifty thousand strong. They fished in the Pacific, developed sophisticated irrigation systems linking mountain aqueducts to canals and ditches, and grew great fields of corn, melons, and peanuts. To appease the rain gods, they practiced ritual human sacrifices, elaborate ceremonies that climaxed with a quick slice to the throat. The Moche built giant, flat-topped pyramids of mud brick, man-made mountains that broke the desert horizon. The grandest, known as the Temple of the Sun, still stands, more than fifty million mud bricks piled over a twelve-acre foundation. No one knows why the Moche tribe disappeared between A.D. 600 and A.D. 700. Some blame invasions by the Huari mountain tribe; others point to a seventh-century El Niño–style weather system, believed to have triggered a three-decade drought in Peru, followed by a rebellion that shattered the sophisticated bureaucratic systems on which the giant desert civilization had come to rely. Perhaps the rebellion triggered chaos, civil war, and, ultimately, extinction.

Ten pages into the magazine article, I saw that Garcia had inserted another yellow Post-it note, just below a photograph of two backflaps. The caption explained that the Moche backflap was designed to protect the royal behind—the warrior king would have hung it from the small of his back down to his thighs. Archaeologists are divided over whether the armor, made mostly of gold but also of copper, would have been worn in combat or merely used during ceremonies, including the human sacrifices. The upper portion of the backflap, the most intricate piece of the armor, is called a rattle, and is surrounded by a spider web of gold. In the center of the web glares a winged Moche warrior known as the Decapitator. In one hand, the Decapitator wields a tumi knife. In the other, he grasps a severed head.

According to *National Geographic,* the backflaps displayed in the magazine were two of a handful known to exist. They looked a lot like the photo of the backflap Garcia wanted to sell.

I marveled at Garcia's cojones. To entice me to buy a looted relic, he'd sent me magazine articles describing the rape of the most significant tomb in North or South America, stories that made it crystal clear the sale would be illegal. Still, if Garcia's intention was to impress and excite me, to ignite a passion and lust for the backflap, it worked.

BY ANY NAME—*tombaroli* in Italian, *huaquero* in Spanish, grave robber in English—those who loot and illegally sell antiquities rob us all.

This was my first antiquity case, but as I would learn, looters are especially insidious art thieves. They not only invade the sanctuaries of our ancestors, plundering burial grounds and lost cities in a reckless dash for buried treasure, they also destroy our ability to learn about our past in ways other art thieves do not. When a painting is stolen from a museum, we usually know its provenance. We know where it came from, who painted it, when and perhaps even why. But once an antiquity is looted, the archaeologist loses the chance to study a piece in context, the chance to document history.

Where, precisely, was it buried? What condition was it in? What was lying next to it? Can two objects be compared? Without such critical information, archaeologists are left to make educated guesses about a long-ago people and how they lived.

Most pilfered antiquities follow the same path—discovered and dug up by poor, indigenous grave robbers from the Third World, smuggled to unscrupulous dealers in the First World.

Except in rare cases, namely antiquity-rich Italy and Greece, the flow of stolen artifacts largely moves from poor to rich nations. Artifacts looted from Northern Africa and the Middle East are usually smuggled to Dubai and Abu Dhabi, from there to London, and ultimately to shops in Paris, Zurich, New York, and Tokyo, the cities where consumer demand is greatest. Artifacts pilfered from sites in Cambodia, Vietnam, and China are smuggled through Hong Kong to Australia, Western Europe, and the United States.

This slippery, largely unregulated world is considered a "gray" market because the legal market is largely supplied by an illegal one. Unlike smuggled drugs or weapons, an antiquity's legal status may change as it crosses international borders—and once "legalized," a looted antiquity can be sold openly by the likes of Sotheby's and Christie's to the likes of the Getty and the Met. While the United Nations has designed international protocols to discourage looting, every nation has its own priorities, cultural interests, and laws. What's forbidden in one country is perfectly legal in another. It is illegal in the United States, for example, to sell bald and golden eagle feathers; and I spent a chunk of my career trying to stem this illegal trade. Yet whenever I visit Paris and wander through its finest antique shops along the Seine, I marvel at the American Indian treasures displayed openly for sale. I've seen full headdresses with eagle feathers selling for $30,000 or more.

The most visible criminals in the antiquity theft trade—the grave robbers doing the digging and the thieves swiping objects from religious shrines—fare poorly compared with the brokers at the other end of the smuggling chain. On average, looters earn only 1 or 2 percent of the ultimate sale price. The Sicilian men who illegally excavated a collection of Morgantina silver illegally sold it for $1,000; a collector subsequently bought it for $1 million, and resold it to the Metropolitan Museum of Art for $2.7 million. Chinese grave robbers who came across a significant Song Dynasty sculpture sold it for $900; an American dealer later resold it for $125,000.

The world's finest museums have not escaped this distasteful cycle. The J. Paul Getty Museum in Los Angeles became ensnared in such a scandal after it purchased scores of looted antiquities from renowned Italian art dealer Giacomo Medici, including a statue of Aphrodite, purchased for $18 million in 1988. Senior curators at the Getty met with top officers from Italy's Carabinieri and denied that they knew or should have known that the antiquities they'd purchased were looted. (Years after the backflap case, the Getty-Medici dispute would widen further and Italian officials would file criminal charges against an American curator and an art dealer.)

Illicit antiquity trading is said to be on the rise, and there's little doubt the technology revolution that sparked the global economy made it easier to loot, smuggle, and sell antiquities. Looters employ global tracking devices, smugglers bribe low-paid customs officials, and sellers post items on eBay and clandestine chat rooms. If a piece is valuable enough, an antiquity can be smuggled out of a country on a passenger plane in a matter of hours, arriving in London, New York, or Tokyo less than twenty-four hours after it was unearthed by looters.

How big is the problem? It's hard to say. Only a handful of countries collect reliable statistics on looting. The Greeks report 475 unauthorized digs in the past decade and say they've recovered 57,475 looted pieces, primarily in Peloponnese, Thessaly, and Macedonia. But Greece is an exception—the nation declared looting illegal as early as 1835, and its constitution specifically directs the government to protect cultural property. In most countries, looting is largely documented in unofficial ways, through anecdotes and extrapolation. Claims are made but unverified. Turkey says illegal looting is the fourth most lucrative (legal or illegal) job in the nation. Niger reports that 90 percent of its most significant archaeological sites have been stripped bare. A few criminologists have mingled these statistics and news accounts and drawn wild conclusions—for example, that organized crime figures and terrorists are major players in the illicit antiquities trade. I'm skeptical of such claims. Certainly mobsters have looted artifacts, and yes, there were reports that 9/11 ringleader Mohammed Atta tried to peddle Afghan antiquities in Germany. But a few isolated anecdotes do not a conspiracy make.

One thing is clear. As with cocaine and heroin, the buyer's market in developed nations drives supply. When demand soared for Southeast Asian artifacts after the Vietnam War, looters decapitated almost every statue at Angkor Wat. When pre-Columbian antiques became all the rage in American collecting circles in the 1980s, grave robbers targeted virgin sites in Peru.

Generally, looters prefer small, relatively anonymous pieces. Coins are best—easy to smuggle, nearly impossible to trace. Antiquities, if smuggled in small quantities, can be disguised or mixed with souvenirs. Slap a cheap price tag on centuries-old flatware or jewelry and the average customs officer isn't likely to catch on.

To disguise larger, higher-profile pieces, black market brokers sometimes engage in antiquity laundering. It's a scheme similar to money laundering—a broker uses the good name of an unwitting museum to help wash an illicit piece by creating misleading paperwork. In one scam, the shady broker uses a simple query letter to prey on the professionalism and politeness of reputable museum curators. The broker offers to loan artifacts that he expects a prestigious curator will not accept. What the broker really wants is a rejection letter on the stationery of the prestigious museum, with boilerplate language that appears to acknowledge the importance of the pieces offered, but regrets that for space, budgetary, or other reasons, the museum is not currently accessing new works. The rejection

letter becomes part of the illicit piece's provenance, one more document for the disreputable broker or dealer to display. For the buyer—
dimwitted or not—such a letter adds an air of legitimacy. If a famous
museum considered a piece, but rejected it for space reasons, it must
be clean, no?

But when an antiquity is as well known as the backflap, the
black market is the only choice.

MENDEZ CALLED ME a few days after we met on the Turnpike.

He seemed suspicious and spoke slowly. "Bob, I checked and
you're not a lawyer."

He had me.

I shouldn't have blurted out the lawyer bit without arranging for
a proper cover. I'd screwed up. All I could do was bluster, rely on
the old adage that the best defense is a good offense.

I jumped in strong, nearly shouting into the phone. "*You're*
checking up on *me*? You didn't call the state bar, did you? Now
they're going to call me, ask me what I'm doing practicing law in
Jersey. Shit. You're screwing it all up—drawing attention to me!"

"Bob, I—"

"Jesus, you really, really—you wanna know why I'm not freakin'
listed? *I'm disbarred,* Orlando. *Disbarred.*" Before he could ask how
or why, I said, "I got into a thing with my wife. Let's just say there
was violence. And boom! They took my license."

There was silence on the other end of the line. The new lie worked.
It shut him down, backed him off. Mendez was like most guys: He
was reluctant to press for personal details about another man's marriage, especially anything related to domestic violence.

There was nothing left to discuss. Mendez even apologized.

Garcia called back two weeks later. His voice betrayed his excitement. "Bob, I'm in New York. We've got it." The backflap was
stored safely at the Panamanian consulate in Manhattan, he said,

and Garcia wanted to make the exchange there. "It's perfect. It's
good," he said, because the consulate offered the same protections
as an embassy. The building and grounds were the sovereign territory of Panama, outside U.S. jurisdiction and American laws. What's
more, Garcia revealed, the top man at the consulate was in on the
deal. In fact, Garcia bragged, the consul was the mule. He'd used
his diplomatic status to smuggle the backflap from Panama to New
York.

"It's good, then," Garcia reassured me. "When can you come
up?"

I stalled for time. "That's great, great. Good news."

But it wasn't. I couldn't arrest anyone inside a foreign consulate,
much less have backup agents tail me. I needed to draw Garcia out,
and I knew I still held an ace: Garcia and his crew were already
committed. They'd invested a great deal of time and money, made a
down payment in Peru, and arranged to sneak the backflap into the
United States. They might be cautious, but I knew they were also
hungry.

"Look, I understand you want to do it up there, at the consulate," I said. "But here's the deal: My authenticator, he's an old
guy. Not in such good heath. Doesn't like to travel. So I think
you're going to have to bring the backflap down here."

Garcia didn't say anything for a few seconds. Then he said, "You
have the money?"

Bingo. He was hooked. I said, "We've got the money, we got the
money. One point six mil. What's your fax number? I'll send you a
bank statement."

Garcia gave me the number, and I asked him how he wanted the
$1.6 million. I wanted him thinking about the money, not about
where he could meet me or whether he could trust me. He asked for
$665,000 cash and $935,000 in wire transfers to bank accounts in
Miami, Peru, Panama, and Venezuela.

I jotted down names and numbers.

"Got it—see you tomorrow." With the sale closed, I got off the line as quickly as possible, before he could think of anything else.

I called Goldman and filled him in: I would meet Garcia and Mendez at the same Turnpike rest stop at noon, then we'd drive to Philadelphia to meet the Gold Man.

THIS TIME, GARCIA and Mendez arrived even earlier—11:24 a.m., according to the surveillance team—and in style, inside a dark green Lincoln Continental with diplomatic tags, a third man behind the wheel. They backed into a spot, positioning the trunk only a few yards from the picnic tables. Mendez and the third man, a strapping, gray-haired gentleman in a dark suit, grabbed a table and scanned the crisp October sky. Garcia walked over to the Burger King and returned with two coffees.

At 11:54 a.m., I pulled into a nearby parking space with my undercover partner, Anibal Molina.

Garcia greeted me warmly. "Bob!"

"Hey Denis, how're you doing, buddy?"

The third man stepped in front of Garcia and handed me his card. "Frank Iglesias, Consul General de Panama, New York." He was a bear of a man—six-one and at least 230 pounds—but he used the buttery voice of a seasoned diplomat. "How nice to meet you," he said.

We moved to the trunk and Mendez popped it. He opened a cheap black suitcase and pushed aside a pile of white T-shirts, revealing a large gold object ensconced in plastic bubble wrap—the backflap. Mendez reached into the suitcase, but I jumped in front of him. "Let me pull it out," I said.

I lifted the backflap from the trunk and tried to contain my excitement as I considered its long journey—a Peruvian national treasure, buried for seventeen centuries, stolen by grave robbers and missing for a decade, now glistening in the New Jersey sun, rescued in part by a pair of unwitting Miami smugglers.

I beamed. "You really did it!" I said, my enthusiasm genuine. "Congratulations!" I laid the backflap back in the suitcase and bear-hugged Garcia. "I can't believe it! You guys are pros." I pumped Mendez's hand. "This is fantastic. Fantastic!" I closed the trunk. "Let's go see the Gold Man. I'll drive slow so you can follow me."

We piled into our cars and they followed us down the Turnpike, the start of an hour-long ride to western Philadelphia.

After we arrived in the parking lot of the Adam's Mark Hotel, Iglesias popped the trunk and handed me the suitcase. "OK," I said, walking toward the lobby, "let's get this done." As I crossed into the middle of the lot, reaching a spot where the bad guys had no place to hide, I gave the go-sign—I brushed my backside with my left hand. (The go-sign should always be something you rarely do, so you don't give it by mistake.) Agents in raid jackets jumped out, guns drawn, shouting, "FBI! Let me see your hands! Down on your knees! FBI!" The agents pinned Mendez, Garcia, and Iglesias on the rough asphalt and cuffed their hands behind their backs. They led the Miamians away, but once they searched the diplomat, they uncuffed him. Because of his diplomatic status, we had to let him go—for the time being. To prove Iglesias had been there, we shot a picture of him standing next to me. Ever the politician, the consul general managed an awkward smile.

At the FBI offices, we put Garcia and Mendez in separate interview rooms, each with one ankle shackled to a chain bolted to the floor. I brought in the prosecutor to see Garcia.

Goldman flashed his Justice Department ID, smiled, and said, "They call me the Gold Man."

Garcia closed his eyes and shook his head.

THE AFTERMATH OF every art crime case has two parts: the routine judicial process in which the defendants hopefully go to prison—here Garcia and Mendez pleaded guilty and got nine months—and the public relations bonanza in which the press goes gaga over the rescue of the stolen art.

This always seemed to baffle supervisors who didn't appreciate the public's (and the media's) love of art, history, and antiquities. To these supervisors, art crime seemed very distant from the FBI's primary missions of catching bank robbers, kidnappers, and terrorists. Once, years earlier, after Bazin and I had recovered a painting stolen from the Philadelphia Museum of Art, we met with the brass to discuss our ideas for a big press conference. A supervisor laughed at our enthusiasm. "For this little painting?" he said. "You'll never get anyone to come!" Oh, no, we explained, the painting is a replica of a five-dollar bill by the famous artist William Michael Harnett. It's an important piece, we said; people will care. The supervisor just laughed louder. Thankfully, we had an ace in the room—Special Agent Linda Vizi, the spokeswoman for the Philadelphia division of the FBI and a friend who shared my interests in history and art. Vizi was tough and intellectual—she'd majored in classics in college, studying Latin, Greek, Russian, Spanish, Sanskrit, and hieroglyphics. She also understood the press in ways her supervisors did not. "I guarantee you," Vizi told the supervisor, "the five-dollar-bill story will make the front page." The next day, when journalists jammed the press conference, she ribbed the supervisor. An hour later, he stuck his head in Vizi's office and announced with an odd sense of satisfaction, "Well, it looks like it won't be on the front page after all. Waco is burning." Indeed, the next day's *Inquirer* front page was dominated by stories about arguably the worst moment in FBI history, the April 19, 1993, assault and subsequent inferno at the Branch Davidian compound that left eighty people dead. But at the bottom of page one, there also was a little story about a long-lost painting, rescued by the FBI.

From that day forward, Vizi and I worked together to make sure she had as much historical background as possible before we announced one of my cases. (As an undercover agent, I couldn't appear in front of cameras. I always stood in the back of the room, well out of camera shot.) She kept the press conferences lively. Hardened journalists, weary of the FBI's routine fare of violence, corruption, and bank robbery, seemed to perk up at the art crime press conferences. They were always on the prowl for something different, a legitimate good-news story, and art crime gave it to them.

The media reaction to the backflap case surpassed our expectations. Reporters fell in love with a story that offered easy comparison to *Raiders of the Lost Ark*—a case with an exotic location, grave robbers, a smuggled national treasure secreted into the United States in a diplomatic bag, the rescue of the seventeen-hundred-year-old relic at gunpoint. The story in the *Inquirer* was stripped across the front page. It began, "In a tale out of an Indiana Jones movie, the FBI has recovered an exquisite Peruvian antiquity." The headline in the tabloid *Philadelphia Daily News*, stealing a line from the second Indy movie, blared, "That piece belongs in a museum!" The Associated Press version of the story was published in papers across North and South America. The president of Peru soon announced that Goldman and I would be awarded the Peruvian Order of Merit for Distinguished Service, a gold medallion with a blue ribbon, the country's top honor for distinguished service to the arts. Goldman enjoyed the spotlight and I was glad to let him and others bask in it, deservedly so.

A few months later, we held a ceremony at the Penn archaeological museum, formally returning the piece to the Peruvian ambassador and Walter Alva, the Sipan tombs' chief archaeologist and the author of the *National Geographic* stories. As I stood to the side, out of camera range, Alva convened his own press conference, explaining the significance of the day, straining in broken English to make a comparison the reporters could understand. Finally, he said, "It is a national treasure. For you, it would be as if someone had stolen the Liberty Bell." The press fawned once more, again invoking the Indiana Jones theme.

Vizi and I were thrilled because our supervisors were thrilled.

We were making the FBI look good all over the world. At the end of a lousy decade—Waco, Ruby Ridge, the crime lab scandal, the Boston mafia fiasco—the FBI was eager for any positive publicity. The FBI brass seemed to be beginning to realize that art recovery was good for the bureau, and not just in Philadelphia.

CHAPTER 9

HISTORY OUT THE
BACK DOOR

Philadelphia, 1997.

THE SLEEPY, SOMEWHAT MUSTY HISTORICAL SOCIETY
of Pennsylvania is largely unknown outside of Philadelphia.

But the Federal-style building on Locust Street houses the nation's second-largest repository of early Americana. Founded in
1824, the HSP holds thousands of important military and cultural
pieces. The research library is stocked with more than 500,000
books, 300,000 graphic works, and 15 million manuscripts. Like
most museums, the HSP displays only a fraction of its collection at
any one time; the bulk of the collection remains in storage, where
most artifacts sit for decades, untouched and largely ignored. The
HSP had not conducted an inventory in a generation or more. It
was simply too expensive and time-consuming.

In late October 1997, the HSP embarked on its first full inventory
in decades.

Almost immediately, collections manager Kristen Froehlich found
problems. Alarmed, she called me.

So far, her inventory had revealed that four items were missing—a
Lancaster County long rifle and three Civil War presentation swords.

The rifle dated to the 1780s and probably had seen combat in
the latter stages of the Revolutionary War. The rifle's gold-tipped

barrel extended forty-eight inches, longer than most sabers, and was handcrafted by the legendary Pennsylvania gunsmith Isaac Haines. The ceremonial presentation swords, made of gold, steel, silver, enamel, diamonds, rhinestones, and amethyst, were part of a military tradition that dated to Roman times. The missing swords and scabbards, Froelich said, were presented to the Union generals George Meade, David Birney, and Andrew Humphreys following great victories. The swords would be easy to identify because each included a unique, engraved inscription and was crammed with lavish, if not gaudy, decoration. Luckily, the curator said, she had pictures and a good written description of each one. For instance, the counter guard of the hilt on Meade's sword, presented at Gettysburg, included thirty diamonds that formed two stars and the letter *M* across a blue enamel shield. I knew such swords could command $200,000 or more on the open market.

"Anything else?" I asked.

"Well, there could be more—I don't know," she said. "We think we've got twelve thousand pieces to inventory. And like I said, we're just starting."

I told Froehlich I'd come right over, and asked her to prepare a list of all HSP employees. I said I would need to interview everyone.

I didn't mention that every museum employee, including Froehlich, would be a suspect.

In art crime, 90 percent of museum thefts are inside jobs.

ARMED DAYLIGHT MUSEUM robberies, like my Rodin case, are anomalies. Most museum thefts are committed or aided by insiders, people with access who know how to exploit a building's vulnerabilities. An insider could be a ticket taker, a docent, a guide, an executive, a security guard, a custodian, an academic, even a trustee or wealthy patron—anyone tempted to use his or her access to walk away with a piece of art or history worth millions. The insider might be a temporary employee, perhaps part of a construction crew hired to perform a renovation, even a summer intern. This thief steals for any number of reasons, though greed, love, and revenge top the list of motives.

Cultural institutions are loath to suspect one of their own; they like to think of themselves as families, colleagues engaged in a noble profession. Many museums don't bother to run criminal background checks on employees or contractors. But they should. As terrible as it sounds, a museum's biggest vulnerability is its employees.

Insider thieves are everywhere: In Illinois, a shipping clerk arranged the theft of three Cézanne paintings from the Art Institute of Chicago, then threatened to kill the museum president's child if his demands were not met. In Baltimore, a night watchman stole 145 pieces from the Walters Art Museum, taking the pieces one by one over eight months—each night, while making his rounds, he pried open a display case, pinched an Asian artifact or two, then rearranged the rest of the pieces so the display wouldn't look suspicious. In Russia, a veteran curator in Saint Petersburg systematically looted the world-renowned Hermitage, removing more than $5 million worth of czarist treasures over fifteen years, a crime not discovered until long after she'd died, when the museum conducted its first inventory in decades. A legendary Ohio professor of medieval literature embarked on an audacious serial crime wave, secreting pages from rare book manuscripts at libraries across the world, from the Library of Congress to the Vatican.

The biggest art crime in history was an inside job.

On a sultry midsummer morning in 1911, *Mona Lisa* vanished from her vaunted perch in the Louvre, between a Correggio and a Titian. The theft occurred on a Monday, the only day of the week the museum was closed to the public, but it was not confirmed until late that afternoon because listless guards dickered over whether the most famous painting in the world had been stolen, or merely temporarily moved as part of a Louvre cataloging project. French detectives immediately interviewed more than a hundred members of the museum staff and contractors, including a simple-minded Italian glazer named Vincenzo Peruggia. The Parisian authorities botched a chance to catch Peruggia in the early days of the investigation when they mistakenly compared a left-thumb fingerprint found on *Mona Lisa*'s abandoned protective box to Peruggia's right thumb.

The heist garnered page-one news across the globe, and for a few weeks it became a bigger story than the looming world war. As the investigation foundered, the stories even briefly merged and sensational allegations appeared in the French media. Anti-German newspapers implied that the kaiser had played a role in the theft; opposition papers accused the struggling French government of stealing *Mona Lisa* as part of a wild *Wag the Dog* conspiracy to distract, outrage, and unite the French people against foreign aggressors. The *Mona Lisa* investigation took an awkward turn early on, when two radical modernists were wrongly detained under the theory that they'd stolen an icon of Old World art as some sort of artistic/political protest. One of the arrested radicals was a young artist named Pablo Picasso.

The real thief, Peruggia, should have been a suspect from the outset. He had the means, motive, and opportunity. A craftsman who helped build the wood and glass box that protected *Mona Lisa,* he was privy to a fateful museum secret—Leonardo da Vinci's masterpiece was secured to the wall by little more than four metal hooks and guarded only by a lone and drowsy military pensioner. The Louvre was so cavernous and in such a state of constant renovation that Peruggia, with his white workman's blouse and smock, drew little attention when he waltzed into the Salon Carré shortly after sunrise that Monday morning.

"The room was deserted," Peruggia recalled years later. "There hung the painting that is one of our great works. *Mona Lisa* smiled down on me. In a moment, I had snatched her from the wall. I carried her to the staircase, took off the frame, slipped the painting under my blouse, and left with the greatest nonchalance. It was all done in a few seconds."

Peruggia hid *Mona Lisa* in his tiny Paris apartment for two years. He was careful, of course, but like most art thieves, he became frustrated when he could not sell the painting to a legitimate dealer. In 1913, he smuggled the painting to Italy, and offered to sell it to a dealer who was close to the director of Uffizi Gallery, the most famous museum in Florence. The dealer and museum director met Peruggia in a hotel room and promised to pay 500,000 Italian lire on the condition that he bring *Mona Lisa* to the Uffizi for a final examination. They tipped the police, and officers arrested Peruggia when he arrived with the painting. Afterward, Peruggia claimed to be a patriot, insisting that he stole the *Mona Lisa* to return her to her native Italy. The story appealed to many Italians, but it fell flat in court. As prosecutors noted, da Vinci himself brought *Mona Lisa* to France during the sixteenth century, and they presented a letter Peruggia wrote to his family after the theft in which he boasted, "I have finally obtained my fortune!" At trial, Peruggia's own testimony proved his motives were not pure. He expected to claim a reward for "rescuing" *Mona Lisa*.

"I heard talk of millions," he testified.

Convicted in 1914, Peruggia spent less than a year in prison, an appalling sentence for so serious a crime, yet a trend that would haunt art crime cases throughout the century. By the time he was released, a world war raged across Europe and he was largely forgotten.

IT TOOK ME the better part of a week to interview the HSP staff. I met with thirty-seven of the thirty-eight employees—a custodian named Earnest Medford called in sick. The supervisors insisted that talking to Medford would be a waste of time. "Ernie's been here seventeen years," Froehlich said. "When we have a problem, he's our go-to guy."

We turned next to the public, and helped the museum publicize a $50,000 reward, blasting faxes to a long list of media outlets, from National Public Radio to *The Inquirer* to *Antiques and The*

Arts Weekly. This generated a quick splash of publicity, but the reward tactic that had worked so well in the Rodin case brought dubious results this time, clogging our confidential tip line with useless crap. "Caller reports suspicious man eyeing a display case. No further information," an operator scribbled in her notes. "Caller saw a sword in the backseat of a car at a parking lot on Essington Avenue near Seventy-fourth Street in a Chevrolet. Two weeks ago." And my favorite: "Caller is psychic, will volunteer time, notes a Capricorn moon day of robbery."

I turned the hunt to a more familiar and likely venue.

As it happened, one of the nation's largest Civil War shows, the Great Southern Weapons Fair in Richmond, Virginia, was scheduled for the week after we began our investigation. As a collector, I'd attended the sprawling show three or four times over the years and knew nearly every serious dealer on the East Coast would be there. I drove down with Special Agent Michael Thompson, and sure enough, we ran into prominent Pennsylvania historian and dealer Bruce Bazelon, author of a book on presentation swords. I told him about the HSP swords. Funny you should mention it, Bazelon said, and he related a story he'd heard from a Poconos dealer. According to the dealer, a customer came into his shop and showed him a picture of a presentation sword that he had for sale. The dealer had called Bazelon because he believed the sword was supposed to be in the HSP collection.

When I called the dealer, he confirmed the story. He dug into an old address book and came up with a name for the Philadelphia history buff peddling the sword—George Csizmazia.

We showed up unannounced at Csizmazia's office on a chilly morning two days before Christmas. He was an electrical contractor, fifty-six years old, with weathered white skin, thick jowls, and narrow brown eyes. He parted his silver hair on the left and wore a neatly trimmed salt-and-pepper mustache. His boss retrieved him from a job and he met us brightly.

"What can I do for you, fellas?"

"We need help with an investigation related to Civil War arti-facts," I said. "George, we want to talk to you about some swords."

Csizmazia turned ashen. "Ernie told you, didn't he?"

Ernie was the janitor, the only museum employee we hadn't in-terviewed.

I shot Thompson a look. "Of course," I bluffed. "That's why we're here."

"So where are the swords, George?" Thompson asked.

"At my house. I'll take you to them."

Csizmazia lived with his wife in a modest two-story home in a working-class suburb called Rutledge, a few miles southwest of Philadelphia International Airport. He led us upstairs, and we fol-lowed. He took us to a bedroom door; the door had more locks and alarm systems than any room at HSP. As he opened the door, he said, "I call this my museum."

The moment we entered, I knew our pudgy little electrician was a thief on a grand scale, responsible for the theft of more than three swords and a rifle.

Two hundred museum-worthy pieces from the eighteenth and nineteenth centuries lined the walls and crowded display tables. As I circled the room, I silently counted twenty-five presentation swords and fifty firearms, assorted rifles, muskets, pistols, and revolvers. Valuable relics from early Americana filled the room—an ivory tea caddy; a brass carriage clock; a Victorian silver whistle; a teetering stack of U.S. Mint Indian ten-dollar gold coins; a tortoiseshell cigar holder; a pair of Revolutionary-era oval cuff links; a Georgian sil-ver watch with a glass face; a pear-shaped silver sugar bowl; mother-of-pearl opera glasses in a leather case; a mahogany toy chest of drawers. It was all quality stuff.

Csizmazia played coy, rambling on about the vagaries of prove-nance in the military collectibles market. My partner and I didn't say much. We just stood in the room, surrounded by so much his-tory, so much evidence. We stared at the pieces and then we stared at Csizmazia. We let the silence hang, knowing he couldn't help but try to fill it. He fidgeted and fidgeted and finally pointed to a Mayflower-era sword. "I use that to trim my hedges!" I gave him a look that said we were not amused. My partner crossed his arms sternly.

"George," I said. "Come on. Don't insult us, huh?"

Csizmazia dropped his eyes. "OK."

He led us to the garage and opened a large cardboard garment box. Inside, we found $1 million worth of presentation swords, including the three missing from HSP.

There was so much stuff to seize we called for backup. Everywhere I looked I saw history. I picked up an early-nineteenth-century silver presentation wine cooler and marveled at the stylized swan-head handles, the chased rim, and an etched relief of Philadelphia's famous Fairmount Water Works. I put it down and eyed a gold presentation watch with a double woven chain as long as my arm. I flipped it over to read the tiny inscription. "Presented to Maj. Gen. George G. Meade, USA as a token of esteem and regard from his friend E.P. Dorrl, Gettysburg July 1st, 2nd, 3rd. VICTORY." I laid the watch on the table. The case was growing bigger every minute. What else was here?

Eager to learn more before Csizmazia wised up and stopped talking, I played to his vanity. "George, while we're waiting, why don't you give us the grand tour?"

He quickly agreed, moving through the room with pride, displaying one eclectic piece of American history after another: The flint-rock rifle abolitionist John Brown carried during his raid at Harpers Ferry. The telescope Elisha Kent Kane used to locate the Polar Sea. The burlwood coffer Revolutionary War financier Roger Morris used to store handwritten notes. A ring with a lock of hair from George Washington. A locket with a piece of the first transatlantic telegraph cable. The wedding band Patrick Henry gave to his wife.

Before the other agents arrived, Csizmazia stood before the two most valuable pieces of his private collection—a silver teapot with a gooseneck spout, circa 1755 and worth about $250,000, and a gold snuffbox worth $750,000 or more. The snuffbox, he explained, was the most historic because it was presented as payment to Andrew Hamilton in 1735 for his successful defense of New York printer John Peter Zenger, charged with libeling the colonial governor of New York. This landmark libel case was arguably the most important moment in American journalism history—the forerunner of the freedom of the press clause in the First Amendment, as adopted a half-century later in the Bill of Rights.

In all, Csizmazia's private collection looked to be worth millions. I recognized many pieces from HSP records.

I called Froehlich. "Kristen, do you believe in Santa Claus?"

"Uh, maybe."

"He's left you a lot of gifts."

Csizmazia wasn't repentant in the least. "Whaddya want from me?" he begged. He lamely justified that he did what he did out of love and respect for history, not for money. "The stuff had been sitting in storage boxes for decades. At least, by looking at it in my house, someone got some joy from it."

Only one question remained. "How did you steal it?"

"Ernie," he said.

Csizmazia explained: As a trusted HSP employee for nearly two decades, Earnest Medford enjoyed unfettered and unmonitored access to the museum's basement storage areas. The heavyset custodian with sunken brown eyes had first met Csizmazia when the contractor supervised an electrical job at the museum in the late 1980s. Over the next eight years, Medford smuggled more than two hundred artifacts out the back door, a few pieces at a time. The slimy collector paid the corrupt custodian roughly $8,000, for artifacts worth a total of $2 million to $3 million.

As Csizmazia laid out their scheme, the color rose on my face and I felt like a bumbling rookie, chagrined that I hadn't persisted in interviewing the one guy who'd called in sick. Lesson learned. Interview all employees—no exceptions.

Still, Csizmazia's word wasn't good enough to arrest Medford.

We needed real evidence. "George," I said, "if what you say is true, we need you to call Ernie and tape it for us. I want you to tell him you think he sent us to you."

Csizmazia didn't protest—he knew we had him. Glumly, he dialed the number. "Ernie? George. The FBI's visited me, man. Did you set the heat on me? How did they know?"

"I don't know. I didn't say anything."

"Yeah, but you know, you sold me everything. So, you know, we gotta stick together."

"Don't worry about it."

That was enough.

When I confronted Medford with the evidence and tape, he confessed. I asked him why he'd done it, why he'd systematically assaulted an institution where he'd spent nearly twenty years of his life. Medford shrugged. "I figured no one would miss it. I really needed the money."

It was fortuitous that we pressed Csizmazia at his home, because by the time he arrived at the FBI office and I took his fingerprints, reality had set in. When I handed him a copy of the initial paperwork used to charge him, he recoiled, revealing his true feelings. "Three million? The stuff was worth three million dollars? I was a fool not to be selling more of this stuff." A few minutes later, as we walked him to the U.S. Marshal's office for processing, Csizmazia began mumbling, quietly cursing himself. Like many collectors, he'd seen the notice for the reward and knew the FBI and police were searching for the HSP pieces. "I should have just dumped all that stuff in the river. You guys never would have found it. Like in a murder case. No body, no evidence, no case."

CSIZMAZIA'S REMARK ABOUT destroying the evidence triggered memories of my last face-to-face conversation with my father, who'd died about a year earlier.

Dad and I had just left Good Samaritan Hospital in Baltimore, having received a dire prognosis. He'd developed diabetes in his late forties and hadn't really changed his habits or taken better care of himself. Now, he was sixty-eight and in bad shape. The doctor had given him weeks to live.

Dad hadn't wanted to talk about it. He asked about my work, and I obliged, telling him about a burglary at Pennsbury Manor, the historical home of the founder of Pennsylvania, William Penn. I said we had a few suspects in our sights, and that we planned to interview their girlfriends the next day.

"No, no," he interrupted. "Don't tell me about the suspects. What about the antiques they took? Are you going to be able to get them back?"

That was Dad. He understood what was important—retrieving stolen pieces of history and culture, not arresting a couple of knuckleheads trying to pawn a few pieces of silver.

Another memory the HSP case triggered came later, as I kneeled in the FBI evidence vault with a museum curator, shortly after the arrests. We were cataloging each of the nearly two hundred stolen antiques, one by one, and carefully wrapping them for storage—precisely as I had done at my father's Baltimore antique shop after his death.

My dad had opened Wittman's Oriental Gallery in 1986, two years before I left the *Farmer* newspapers to become an FBI agent. He'd sold the papers and returned to his true passion, collecting Oriental antiques, renting a place with my brother Bill down on Howard Street along Jewelers' Row in Baltimore. He'd stocked it with pieces from his personal collection and with works he'd purchased by taking out a second mortgage on his home, the redbrick house where I'd grown up. He filled it with hundreds of pieces—exquisitely carved jade powder boxes, Kutani vases, ukiyo-e woodblocks, and dozens of works by the bigger names in Japanese art: Hiroshige, Kunisada, Hokusai, and Utamaro.

Dad had spent his final years among the antiques, and I think he took as much pleasure giving customers tours of the gallery, stopping to explain the significance of a Burmese textile or a Japanese figurine, as he did actually selling anything, probably more so. His collection had filled the floors and walls of the narrow shop and it nearly rivaled the holdings at Baltimore's best public galleries. Whenever I'd visit the shop with Donna and the kids, he'd dig out a piece from his collection and delight Kevin, Jeff, and Kristin with a quick lesson about Japanese culture. I always listened in and learned something new. Already, I missed that.

Now in the FBI evidence room, my eyes lingered on a stolen antique watch and I thought about how Dad might describe the piece, what history lesson it might reveal.

WE CHARGED CSIZMAZIA and Medford under a new law that made it a federal crime to steal anything worth more than $5,000 from a museum. Previously, thieves who had never crossed state lines, as was the case here, could only be charged in state court. But Congress had recently created a new federal art-crime law, largely in response to the 1990 Gardner heist in Boston, and in 1995 Goldman and I had been the first to use the law, employing it during the case of the theft from William Penn's home.

In the HSP case, Csizmazia and Medford entered plea agreements, presuming this would lead to light sentences. But the case did not end neatly.

The judge assigned to the case was a World War II veteran who did not look kindly on the theft of military artifacts. United States District Judge Clarence C. Newcomer, seventy-five years old, had a reputation for toughness at sentencing. He had presided over several celebrated mob and police corruption cases, and issued several rulings that belied his conservative bent, including one close to my heart—he was the judge who broke up the Topps baseball card monopoly, paving the way for competitors. If the judge needed a reminder of American history, his wide-windowed chambers office overlooked Independence Hall, the nation's birthplace.

A few minutes before the HSP sentencing hearing began on July 16, 1998, I settled into a seat at the prosecution table, next to Goldman. Following routine preliminaries, the judge read aloud the recommendation of the probation office—a sentence in the range of twenty to thirty months for each man. The prosecution, citing the plea agreement, asked for a twenty-month term; the defense lawyers didn't suggest a specific sentence, just something considerably less than twenty months.

Before he imposed the sentence, the judge held aloft a stack of fifteen letters from museum directors across the nation, each imploring him to impose a stiff sentence. What made art theft different from most financial and property crimes, many museum directors told the judge, is the harm to society. Such artifacts not only fill museums, they serve as the raw material for historians and scholars. Most are irreplaceable. "Any theft from any museum goes beyond the crime itself—such a destructive act robs the entire community of its history, its cultural heritage," wrote Anne Hawley, the Gardner Museum director. The president of the American Association of Museums, Edward Able, called "theft by insiders the most serious of all, involving as it does a betrayal by those charged with guarding property held in the public trust." He cited a Latin phrase whispered by wise security professionals, *"Quis custodiet ipsos custodes?"* Who shall guard the guards?

To my delight, the judge shared the museum directors' outrage. The thefts were not, as the defense claimed, some relatively minor and isolated indiscretion, an anomaly committed by two men who led otherwise productive lives. The defendants carried out their scheme in a systematic way, pilfering more than two hundred times, month after month for eight years. Worse, these thieves were not common thugs; by virtue of their positions in society as museum employee and serious collector, Medford and Csizmazia, more than most, understood the value and significance of what they took. And the harm they caused.

"The conduct you engaged in is an assault and affront to our culture, to our society, and must be dealt with accordingly," the judge said. "Therefore, it is the judgment of this court that you be sentenced to forty months. . . ."

Forty months! Double the sentence we sought!

I wanted to smile but kept FBI cool, stoic. I stole a glance at the defense table. The lead lawyer stood, mouth agape, fingers squeezing an empty legal pad. Medford dropped into his chair and slumped. Csizmazia turned to the gallery, searching for a sympathetic face, blinking back tears.

I turned to Goldman and pumped his hand. Forty months! Maybe this marked the start of a trend for art crime cases.

CHAPTER 10

A BLOOD CLOTH

Philadelphia, 1998.

WHEN YOU WORK UNDERCOVER, IT'S ALWAYS A GOOD idea to greet an out-of-town target at the airport. A guy just getting off a plane is less likely to be carrying a weapon.

I met Civil War artifact collector Charlie Wilhite a few minutes after his flight landed from Kansas City. We ducked into a shuttle bus headed to the Embassy Suites near the Philadelphia airport. It was a brisk January afternoon in the mid-twenties, and in the bus Wilhite stayed bundled in a ski jacket and gloves, gripping a large black gym bag. He carried no other luggage. I knew he was booked on a return flight that evening, so I figured he had the merchandise in the satchel. Wilhite was a middle-aged, gangly man with a pale face and a bad blond comb-over. He wore cowboy boots and spoke with a Southern drawl.

When we got to the hotel room, I tried to make Wilhite comfortable. I poured a pair of Cokes and set them on a table with two chairs, in full view of the hidden surveillance camera. "Welcome to Philadelphia," I said.

"Well thank you, bud." He peeled off the jacket and gloves. "Thank you very much."

"First visit?"

"Yeah," he said.

"Hopefully it'll be a memorable one."

"I hope so."

We both laughed.

Wilhite unzipped his carry-on and I stiffened slightly. Though I'd picked him up at the airport, you never knew what a guy might be carrying. Working undercover, rip-offs are always a real threat. Years earlier, I'd nearly been attacked by a man during a hotel sting. He'd claimed to be working for the CIA and wanted to buy $15 million worth of loose diamonds to fund covert operations in Europe. Diamond merchants in Philadelphia alerted the FBI and I had gone undercover as a diamond courier to meet the man. On the phone I played along with his crazy story and agreed to meet at a nearby hotel, telling him I would be carrying the diamonds inside a briefcase attached to my arm with a handcuff. When I met the guy in the warm hotel lobby, he approached wearing dark sunglasses and a heavy overcoat. We turned toward the elevators, but the coat and the man gave me an odd feeling, and I gave the takedown signal right there in the lobby. It turned out he was carrying a gun and a hatchet—no money for diamonds. He planned to kill me, cut off my arm, and make off with the jewels.

So I breathed a sigh of relief when Wilhite pulled from his bag a neatly folded red, white, and blue cloth—a nineteenth-century American flag in fine condition.

He unfolded the flag roughly and draped it over a small round table, the edges spilling over the side, the frayed fringes dangling inches from the ground. My eyes fixed smartly on the thirty-five gold stars in the blue corner square, and I shuddered inwardly as Wilhite manhandled this antiquity, knocking flecks of gold leaf from the stars to the hotel carpet. The stars were unusual, aligned like the night sky, haphazardly in loosely defined circles, set at different angles. At first glance, they seemed to be dancing.

In the middle of one of the seven red stripes, in capital shadow-box letters, were the words 12th REG. INFANTRY CO' A.

It was precisely as my tipster at the U.S. Army Center of Military History had described. This was the battle flag of the Twelfth Regiment Infantry, Corps d'Afrique, a near-sacred artifact in African American history, one of only five such flags to survive the Civil War. The Army museum's historical property tag—"HP 108.62"—was still affixed to the lower left edge of the banner.

Wilhite caught my eye and smiled. "Beautiful, ain't she?"

"Looks good to me, Charlie."

A BATTLE FLAG is unlike any other antiquity.

Flags hoisted by the soldiers at Fort McHenry, the marines at Iwo Jima, and the firefighters at the World Trade Center are symbols of American resolve. The legend of the Fort McHenry battle flag inspired our National Anthem. Today, the tattered Star-Spangled Banner is the most visited artifact displayed at the Smithsonian Institution's National Museum of American History, viewed by some six million tourists annually. That flag, hand-stitched with forty-two-foot reams of wool, is the most valuable artifact in the entire Smithsonian collection—worth more than the Hope Diamond, Charles Lindbergh's *Spirit of Saint Louis,* or the Apollo 11 lunar module.

As an amateur Civil War artifacts collector, I knew that regimental flags played a key role in battle—that they were not merely ceremonial. The soldiers who carried the flags served as beacons for troops to follow in the chaos and cacophony of battle. The regimental flags literally marked the battle lines, where soldiers from the North and South died by the tens of thousands. Each side tried to knock off the other's flag-bearers, eager to cut off a unit's chief means of communication. To carry a regiment's colors into battle was considered a great honor, but also a great personal burden and incredible risk.

The battle flag Wilhite brought to the hotel room was freighted with additional meaning. Missing from the Army archives for more than a decade, the Twelfth Regiment flag proudly stood for bravery, sacrifice, and racial history. After hanging for years in a place of honor at West Point, the flag was transferred to an Army museum in Washington. In the mid-1970s, the old records showed, it was loaned out as part of an exhibition in South Carolina, but never arrived at its destination.

I first learned of its theft a month before I met Wilhite. Leslie Jensen, an Army historian in Washington, called to say that Army investigators were tracking a tip that someone was shopping the Twelfth Regiment flag on the black market.

Could the FBI help? Jensen asked.

Tell me more about the flag, I said.

"At least five men died carrying it, " Jensen said. "That's why they call it a blood cloth."

This Louisiana-based regiment, the expert explained, held a particularly significant place in the history of the War Between the States—and the U.S. military, generally. The Twelfth was among the first African American regiments to see major battle. Free blacks served in the Revolutionary War and the War of 1812 in limited numbers, and they also served in the Navy in the decades leading to the Civil War, but the notion of arming full regiment-sized units of black soldiers remained controversial. At the outset of war, the South used slaves in support roles for the Confederate Army, but President Lincoln initially declined to enlist black soldiers. After the Union lost several early battles, Lincoln ordered that tens of thousands of black men be used in support positions, but barred them from carrying weapons. His Union commanders fretted that these untested soldiers might cut and run in the heat of battle. Yet faced with the realities and horrors of war, Union generals gradually changed their minds. By the fall of 1862, when Lincoln declared that all slaves would be emancipated on January 1, 1863, self-formed black units were beginning to fight alongside Union whites in Massachusetts, South Carolina, and Louisiana. One of them was the Twelfth near New Orleans.

In May of 1863, when Union troops attacked Port Hudson, the final Southern stronghold on the Mississippi River, black regiments like the Twelfth won the chance to prove their mettle in battle. In his 1887 book *The Black Phalanx,* Joseph T. Wilson, one of the African American soldiers who fought at Port Hudson, memorialized the battle in patriotic prose:

> Louder than the thunder of Heaven was the artillery rending the air shaking the earth itself; cannons, mortars and musketry alike opened in a fiery storm upon the advancing regiments, an iron shower of grape and round shot, shells and rockets with a perfect tempest of rifle bullets fell upon them. On they went and down, scores falling on right and left.

When a Confederate mortar felled the sergeant carrying the Twelfth Regiment's flag, Wilson wrote, another scooped it up.

> "The flag, the flag!" shouted the black soldiers as the standard-bearer's body was scattered by a shell. They fell faster and faster; shrieks, prayers and curses came up from the fallen and ascended to Heaven. "Steady men, steady," cried bold Captain Cailloux, his sword uplifted, his face the color of sulphurous smoke that enveloped him and his followers, as they felt the deadly hail which came apparently from all sides.
>
> Captain Cailloux was killed with the colors in his hands; the column seemed to melt away like snow in sunshine, before the enemy's murderous fire; the pride, the flower of the Phalanx had fallen. Then, with a daring that veterans only can exhibit, the blacks rushed forward and up to the brink with a shout. The defenders emptied their rifles, cannons and mortars.

The battle won, white and black Union soldiers, having fought side by side for the first time, found themselves openly bonding, a remarkable sight during that time:

> Nature seems to have selected the place and appointed time for the negro to prove his manhood and to disarm prejudice. . . . It

was all forgotten and they mingled together on terms of perfect equality. The whites were only too glad to take a drink from a negro soldier's canteen.

A white Union officer wrote to his family: "You have no idea how my prejudices with regard to Negro troops have been dispelled by the battle." Even some Southerners were impressed. The Confederate general Henry McCulloch, describing one of his troops' failed forays, wrote, "This charge was resisted by the Negro portion with considerable obstinance (while) the white or pure Yankee portion ran like whipped [dogs] almost as soon as the charge was made."

In strictly strategic military terms, the forty-eight-day battle at Port Hudson was critical. It cleared the final Confederate garrison along the Mississippi, a milestone in the Civil War. But perhaps more important, Port Hudson marked a watershed for the U.S. military and race relations. Black enlistment mushroomed following this early engagement. By the war's end, more than 150,000 African Americans had served in the Union army and at least 27,000 died in battle. They mustered in 160 regiments and participated in thirty-nine major campaigns. Yet only five battle flags from black regiments survive.

ALL OF THIS history reeled through my head as Wilhite and I held the blood cloth by its four corners in the hotel room.

I could have arrested the bastard right then and there, signaled the SWAT team and hoped Wilhite resisted. But I wanted more. I wanted to crawl inside his mind. I wanted to know more about a man who could sell such a blood cloth, especially someone like Wilhite, who professed to be a Civil War buff. How could he be so callous, so eager to seek to profit from a piece of stolen history?

Of course, I also wanted him to incriminate himself with the video surveillance tape running. To do that, I needed to prove intent— get him to admit on tape that he knew he was selling a stolen historical artifact. After the takedown, I didn't want his lawyer to claim that this was all some sort of misunderstanding, that Wilhite had obtained the flag in good faith, not knowing it was stolen.

Moving in for the kill, I eased back in my chair and sipped my Coke. "Did you ever find out where it came from?"

From a museum in Colorado, he said, making it clear it was stolen. "I'm telling you this upfront. I don't want to mislead you. Because if I could take this to a show, I know what it could bring. I didn't want to take that chance."

This was going to be easy. Wilhite liked to hear himself talk and seemed eager for me to like him. I said, "You're afraid someone will see it?" In other words, you know this is stolen property?

"Yeah," he said. "I was told—I don't know if this is correct— that it came from the West Point museum and was on its way to Colorado."

I told him that I needed to know who else knew about the flag and our deal. This was important, I explained, because I needed to protect myself and my buyer. The fewer people who knew about the deal the better. This was a trick question, of course. Almost any answer would be incriminating. He might say "no one knows" because he didn't trust anyone enough to join this illegal conspiracy. Or he might start naming names, vouching for them, not realizing he'd just outed them. He might even give up the name of a big fish, a dealer or broker not yet on the FBI's radar. Either way, the question would get him talking.

Wilhite unfolded a long tale about buying the flag from some guy on the side at a Civil War show in Chicago, a cash deal consummated in his car in a city parking garage. When he finished, I changed tactics, trying to get him to admit he knew he was peddling a piece of African American history, that men died carrying this flag in battle. "Charlie," I said, "you know much about the flag?"

"I've been told there are only five of these in existence, for colored troops."

"Colored troops? Is that the same as Corps d'Afrique?"

"Yeah, they mustered in Louisiana and saw distinguished service in Tennessee. You can look it up."

I had. "Did they have a lot of losses?"

"They had a lot of losses, yeah. They saw combat. They wasn't just scrubbing pots, whatever, like the colored troop they made a movie on, the Massachusetts group. That's what makes the piece for me."

Incredible. *A lot of losses. That's what makes the piece for me.* I masked my anger with a laugh and a swig of Coke. How far would this guy go? Wilhite seemed content, one of those people soothed by the sound of his own voice. He was tipping back in the chair now, one boot on the table, hands clasped behind his head. I said, "When you heard the history, you didn't have any problem keeping it, as far as that's concerned?"

"Me? No. I paid a lot of money for it. My buddy suggested maybe donating it to a museum and taking a tax write-off. I didn't want to do that and thought about it for a while. This friend of mine said he had connections." Wilhite pointed a bony finger at me. "Now, how you handle and market it is your business. But you want to be discreet. I don't advise you to take it to a show. You may never have a problem, but I want to level with you."

"Right, because we could get in a lot of trouble."

"Right, we could."

I had more than enough on him now. "Twenty-eight thousand. Cash, OK?"

"Yeah, if I had a cashier's check, I've got to show that to Uncle Sam and I'd like to see if I can get around that." I started to get up, thinking, I'll be sure to let the IRS boys know.

Wilhite said, "Isn't it a great piece? I told you it was."

"It is," I said, twisting my nose with my thumb and forefinger—the go-sign. "It could only come from a museum."

"Yes, sir—" Wilhite's head snapped to the right as three agents in FBI raid gear opened the adjoining door and told him to put his hands on his head. Stupidly, he jumped up, ignoring the agents, and began yelling at me. "Who *are* you? Who *are* you?"

He took an awkward step toward me, and the agents pinned him to the floor.

I'VE FOUND THAT I can read up on a stolen artifact, talk to experts about it, even hold it in my hands as the bad guys explain its black market value. But I know I won't truly appreciate an object's deeper meaning until I'm finally able to return it to its rightful owner.

And, as it was with Alva and the backflap, so it was with a group of black Civil War re-enactors and the Army's chief historian.

A few weeks after the Wilhite arrest and battle flag seizure, we convened in Washington for a remarkable ceremony in which the FBI formally returned the flag to the Army. It was February and so the return was hastily inserted into the bureau's annual Black History Month program at headquarters.

I rode to Washington with Vizi, the agent who handled the press, and the agent-in-charge of the Philadelphia office, Bob Conforti. Once inside the auditorium, they took seats of honor near the stage. Mindful of the cameras, I lingered in the back.

The long-ago-invited keynote speaker, an African American space shuttle astronaut, wowed everyone with tales from outer space, but the flag, a last-minute addition, stole the show. Flanked by an honor guard of African American re-enactors from Philadelphia, the flag loomed over the seated dignitaries, the astronaut, FBI Director Louis Freeh, and a pair of Army generals.

Joseph Lee, who leads the Philadelphia-based re-enactors group, took the podium in the Union blue full replica regalia of the United States Colored Troops, Third Regiment. He opened by describing his experience the previous month, when I had invited him to see the rescued battle flag in our Philadelphia office. "I was admonished not to touch it," Lee recalled. "And having served in the United States

Marines and Air Force, and being the sergeant major of our group, I knew how to follow an order." He paused, wiping his lower lip with a white dress glove. "But that was one order I could not follow. Touching that flag sent chills through my body. Even thinking about it now, tears well in my eyes. They cause my heart to palpitate. Because this was true, living African American history. I had heard about it, read about it, dreamt about it, but now I was part of it." Lee saluted the flag. "The dead still lie in shallow graves along the field of battle, where they fought and died. This flag honors them all." Lee removed his hat and held it to his breast. "God have mercy for the deeds committed there, and the souls of those poor victims, sent to thee without a prayer. All hail, all honor, the gallant soldiers who fought for Uncle Sam."

Even the stone-faced Freeh seemed moved. I now realized our case had handed Freeh and the FBI a remarkable public relations coup—not only the rescue of a significant historical artifact, but an opportunity to help improve the bureau's poor record on race relations. It certainly didn't hurt my quiet aspirations to expand my art crime horizons beyond Philadelphia to the national and international stage.

Before I got too carried away with such grandiose thoughts, the Army's chief of military history, General John Brown, took to the microphone.

Think of the stress of combat that was on the soldiers of the Twelfth. They could not see the faces of their loved ones; they couldn't see the monuments that made this city great. They couldn't see purple mountain majesties or fruited plain. But what they could see above the smoke and din of battle was the flag. And for soldiers always, the flag has captured the essence of everything that they are fighting for. It is all that is on the battlefield with them when they face death. I think it's particularly fitting that this flag represents men who rose to fight against slavery for themselves and their families and in the course of contributing to the Union Army did in fact secure their freedom and all their descendants' for all the generations to come. It was the first in many steps of trying to affirm the American dream that all people are equal.

As he spoke, I couldn't help thinking about my parents, the soldier and the Japanese bride.

CHAPTER 11

BEFRIEND AND
BETRAY

Santa Fe, 1999.

THE PALACE OF THE GOVERNORS ON THE SANTA FE
Plaza is said to be the oldest continuously used public building
in the United States, and it is a must-see stop for any visitor. Built by
the Spaniards in 1610 as the northern seat of power for New Spain,
the low-slung, block-long adobe and timber structure remains the
gravitational center of Santa Fe culture. The Palace houses the popular Museum of New Mexico and, outside, along the balustrade
that overlooks the Plaza, Native American craftsmen peddle hand-
made jewelry to tourists.

Joshua Baer positioned his Indian art and antiquities gallery
half a block away from the Palace, at 116 East Palace Avenue. A
discreet wooden shingle read, GALLERY UPSTAIRS—OPEN. A poster
at the entrance read, WHY TAKE RISKS? BUY AUTHENTIC ART.

On an unseasonably cool summer afternoon in 1999, my undercover partner and I headed upstairs, fake identification and tape
recorders stuffed in our pockets.

The sale of counterfeit Indian art is a $1-billion-a-year problem,
but it's still dwarfed by the illegal trade of Native American religious objects, particularly those featuring eagle feathers. The crime
had vexed law enforcement and tribal leaders for years, and it

didn't help that many in New Mexico, including some judges, Indian leaders, and state officials, openly criticized the federal law protecting eagle feathers. It was easy for law enforcement to target the low-level "pickers," the scavengers who scoured reservations, acquired religious objects from dirt-poor Indians, and sold them to Santa Fe dealers. But it was a lot tougher to target the dealers. Dogged federal agents from the U.S. Fish and Wildlife Service had launched a major investigation six months earlier, and now suspected that Baer and four other dealers were illegally selling Indian religious objects, including eagle feathers. But they couldn't prove it. They knew the only way to snare the dealers was to set up a sting, yet the tight-knit and suspicious nature of the Santa Fe arts community made it almost impossible to use local agents undercover.

So Fish and Wildlife had enlisted two outsiders, an FBI agent from Philadelphia and a Norwegian police detective, to try to make a bust big enough to frighten nefarious dealers and put them on notice. They chose me because of my background in art crime and the Norwegian because Native American religious artifacts—eagle-feather headdress, Zuni corn mothers, Hopi ceremonial masks—are popular in Europe, where their sale is perfectly legal. Wealthy Europeans often travel to Santa Fe to buy Native American artifacts, and they often bring expert American brokers along for advice. Here, I'd play broker to my undercover rich Norwegian friend Ivar Husby, with his Nordic good looks, borrowed Rolex, and Hugo Boss suits.

Husby and I bounded up the brown-carpeted steps to the second-floor gallery. An affable-looking man, six foot three, 220 pounds, stood in the center of the gallery, beside a bureau filled with a collection of Hopi kachina dolls. High-end Navajo rugs covered two walls opposite windows looking out onto Palace Avenue. The man gave us a minute to take it all in. Then he stuck out his right hand.

"Josh Baer. Welcome."

"Hey Josh. Bob Clay, from Philadelphia." I nodded at the rugs. "These are amazing."

The Norwegian stepped forward. "Ivar Husby," he said, shaking Baer's hand. "I am living in Oslo in Norway."

"Ivar's a collector," I said, slapping the Norwegian on the back. "I'm helping him out a bit because his English isn't very good. He's a good client of mine."

Baer turned to Husby. "What business are you in?"

Husby was fluent in four languages, but he spoke to Baer in broken English. "Family business is oil. I own Internet company."

Baer's brown eyes widened. "Let me know if I can help you." He showed us a few Navajo rugs, but I soon let him know that we were more interested in ceremonial pieces. "Ivar collects religious artifacts of the Laplander tribes in Scandinavia," I said. "They're similar to the Native American. That's why we're here."

I handed him my card: ROBERT CLAY, ACQUISITIONS CONSULTANT.

Baer dipped into a back room. He brought out a Mimbres ceremonial bowl that dated to A.D. 900 (price: $6,000), a four-inch-high Acoma wooden kachina doll ($5,500), and a Kiowa Ghost Dance shield ($24,000). We spent about forty minutes with him but didn't buy anything. As we began to leave, Baer invited us to an antique postcard show at his gallery that evening. We dropped by the reception later that night for a few minutes and spoke with him briefly. "Swing by tomorrow," he said, with a tantalizing hint of promise. "I've got a few things to show you."

"I look forward to it, Josh," I said.

UNDERCOVER WORK IS like chess.

You need to master your subject and stay one or two moves ahead of your opponent.

I've taught hundreds of federal agents. Forget what you've seen on television, I always tell them. That's not real life. The FBI's training is fine, but the best undercover operative relies on his own instincts. I learned more from my years selling advertising for the *Farmer* newspapers than from any FBI manual.

These aren't skills that can be learned in a class—an agent who doesn't possess the natural instincts and traits to work undercover probably shouldn't. You either have the innate sales and social skills to do the job—to befriend and betray—or you don't.

You start with a name. Every undercover agent needs a false identity. Unless your first name is unusual—say Ulrich or Paris—it's best to use your real first name. This adheres to my cardinal rule of working undercover: Tell as few lies as possible, because the more you tell, the more you have to remember. The less you have to remember, the more comfortable, natural you'll be. Using your first name can also protect you if you happen to run into a friend or colleague who doesn't know you're working undercover. In the opening minutes of the battle flag case—when I met Wilhite at the airport—I unexpectedly ran into a neighbor. "Hi, Bob," he said. I nodded, quickly said hello, and kept moving with Wilhite. If that neighbor had called me by any other name, it might have blown the case.

The last name you use should be bland and fairly common, something hard to pin down with a simple Internet search.

Once you've picked a name, you'll need a paper trail. The FBI calls this backstopping—the false-identity paperwork you need to do your job. To help an undercover agent create a second identity and backstop his persona, the FBI employs teams of agents, analysts, and support staff in Washington.

Because the FBI's undercover rules tend to be tedious and bureaucratic, I did a lot of my own backstopping. I filled my undercover wallet with secondary identification—a Philadelphia library card, a U.S. Airways frequent-flyer card, discount cards from Barnes & Noble and Borders, a family membership card for the Philadelphia Museum of Art, a random gallery receipt with my false name. I also created a few undercover Hotmail e-mail accounts. I suppose I should have filled out paperwork for those, too.

But if I'd followed every FBI undercover rule to the letter, I'd never have gotten anything done. Most supervisors understood this. Usually, they looked the other way.

The next step is to create your bona fides—professional but understated business cards, phone numbers, and, if possible, a public-records history. For my small one-man operation, I didn't need much. Mostly I simply used my cell phone and e-mail. That's all it took. If necessary, I knew I could always rely on the bureau. In special situations, I might even approach a private corporation or university. Sometimes, real companies help undercover FBI agents establish false identities, loaning a company's good name, stationery, and identification badges.

Backstopping is relatively easy. It's largely a game of paperwork and patience. Almost anyone can do it. The next steps take guts and a special set of personal skills.

What follows is my *personal* approach to working undercover.

Going undercover is a lot like sales. It's all about understanding human nature—winning a person's trust and then taking advantage of it. You befriend, then betray.

Every undercover case is different. But I think most can be boiled down to five steps: You assess your target. You introduce yourself. You build rapport with the target. You betray. You go home.

Step One: Assess the Target. Who's your target? What's he peddling? A sure-thing investment? A tax scheme? Bribes to a city councilman? Drugs? Whatever it is, you've got to master that realm.

Let's say your target is selling cocaine. You've got to master the drug as it's used today, forgetting what you've seen on television or witnessed in college. You need to know how to handle cocaine, how to cut it, how much the average person might snort. You'd better know the current street prices in your hometown—from a kilo to a gram. You need to master the lingo: With cocaine, you should know that an *eight-ball* equals three and a half grams; *soft* means cocaine powder; *hard* means crack; a *hammer* is a gun. And while you can still call cocaine *blow, yeyo,* or *powder,* you'd better not use dated terms like *nose candy* or *snow*—or worse yet, use law-enforcement-only terms like *user*—as in, "He's a user" or "She uses cocaine."

This translates to any genre. When I began selling the ads for the *Farmer,* I quickly learned that this city boy had better know the difference between a Holstein and an Angus cow. One is a dairy cow, the other a beef cow. One you milk, one you eat. One is a valued member of a farmer's family, the other dinner.

In most situations, once you master a realm, you can use this knowledge in case after case, targeting the same kind of criminal. Skills learned for a Ponzi-scheme sting can be transferred to the next undercover financial crimes case. Drug and corruption cases tend to follow a predictable pattern—and there are a limited number of drugs or bribery schemes to master. Art crimes are different, some would say harder, because there are so many genres. For virtually each case you need to shift gears and research the market, learn the lingo.

Step Two: The Introduction. There are two ways to meet a target. I call them the bump and the vouch.

The *bump* is tough to pull off. It takes a lot of preparation and a little bit of luck. The bump is exactly what it sounds like: You find a way to bump into the target in a way that appears perfectly natural. You bump into him at a bar or a club or a gallery. Sometimes, you've got to spend weeks, perhaps months, creating your bona fides in your target's world. If he's an outlaw biker, you'll have to find a way to hang out with biker gangs, waiting for the right chance to bump into him.

Much faster is the *vouch,* in which someone verifies that you're the real deal. The vouch is usually made by a confidential informant or cooperating witness. In the backflap case, Bazin was my vouch, and one of his informants was his vouch. The vouch doesn't always have to come from a person. It can be anything that convinces the target that you are who you say you are—in my case, an expert in a particular area of art. You can create the virtual vouch by demonstrating your expertise. In the battle flag case, I lured the Kansas City man to Philadelphia after multiple phone conversations in which I made it clear I was well traveled on the Civil War collectors' circuit.

Step Three: Build Rapport. You need to win a target's trust, and the best way to do that is to infatuate and ingratiate. You can do this with drinks and dinner, chauffeuring him in your shiny car, but subtler techniques are more effective. Psychological tricks work best.

First impressions are critical. From the outset, you want to create a friendly aura. Facial expressions are the most important, because that's how we most visibly communicate as social creatures. When I meet someone who smiles, makes soft eye contact, and shakes my hand reasonably, I'm apt to think he's a nice guy. When I meet someone who grimaces, glares, and bear-grips my hand, I'm immediately on guard, thinking, this guy's either an enemy or a competitor. It's far more nuanced than the fight-or-flight reflex—I work the margins of a target's personality. (If I encounter a competitor, I let him excel at his thing, but insist he let me excel at mine. If he's a thief, I let him call the shots when it's time to steal, so long as he lets me call the shots when it's time to deal.)

Don't underestimate the importance of a friendly smile. If you smile, odds are good the target will smile too. It's human nature for people to mirror what they see. It's a primal psychological reaction, a trait learned during infancy. When you smile at a baby and she smiles back, it's not because she likes you. It's because the baby is mirroring you. Scowl and the baby will cry. It's a survival technique every infant learns in her first few months. We retain it our whole lives.

The mirroring technique works in other ways. It's gratifying when you make a point and someone says, "Hey, that's a good idea." People let their guard down when they're hanging out with people just like them. A good undercover operative uses this to his advantage. If a target sits close to the table, you sit close. If he puts on his sunglasses, you do too. If he smiles, you smile. Whatever he says, find a way to validate it. If he says it's hot out, you agree. If he criticizes a politician's position or character, agree that the politician is vulnerable on many issues. If he orders iced tea, you do the same.

Once the two of you start talking, share. Tell the target about yourself; ask him about himself. Exchanging personal information is a great way to develop a rapport, build that critical trust.

But tread carefully. Make sure that whatever you say can be verified, or is so personal that it can't be verified. Stay as close to the truth as possible—don't say you have six kids if you only have two, because somewhere along the line you're likely to screw up.

How do you befriend someone who repels you? You try harder. You look for the good inside that person and focus on that. No one is completely evil. Does the target care about his family? Does he care about injustice? Do you share the same taste in music? Women? Food? Football? Politics? Cars? Art? If you focus on a person's criminal and immoral traits, you'll never find genuine common ground.

A critical point: To keep yourself out of tricky situations down the road, drop hints early about your views on marriage and drinking. If you are married, be married and say you are deeply in love with your wife. If you are "deeply in love with your wife," that means you don't mess around. If you don't want to drink, tell the target that you don't drink because you're an alcoholic prone to bizarre blackouts. Never say you don't drink or fool around because it's morally wrong. It will sound like bullshit (you're supposed to be a criminal, for God's sake!). If you drop these early hints, it makes it a lot easier when a target tries to test you later. You can say, Look, I'm not a player. I'm a businessman. I'm here to do a deal, not to party.

It's important to get into a role, but be careful, stay sharp. When you work undercover, it's easy to lose touch with reality and let the lies and deception take over.

Step Four: Betray. Get the target to bring the contraband to you in a controlled situation—a hotel room adjacent to a SWAT team, if possible. Get him to incriminate himself on tape.

Step Five: Go home. Finish safely, and return home to your wife and family. Never let your undercover life subsume your real life. It's not—repeat, not—more important. If something comes up during a case that makes you feel uncomfortable, don't do it. If a bad guy asks you to get in his car, and this makes you nervous, come up with an excuse. If a supervisor or the FBI agent handling your undercover work asks you to bluff expertise you don't have, don't do it. Above all, you've got to be comfortable in your role. It's got to come from within. Remember, I tell the agents I teach: You've got to be yourself. Don't try to be an actor. You can't do it. No one can. Actors have scripts and get multiple takes. You only get one. They flub their lines and they get another chance. You make a mistake and you can end up dead—or worse, get others killed too.

IN THE BAER case, we used the bump—a direct frontal assault—because there was no quick, easy way to work a vouch. We didn't know anyone on the inside.

But that didn't mean we didn't have decent intelligence. Our friends from the Fish and Wildlife Service had busted enough low-level players—so-called traders and pickers who scour reservations for religious artifacts and sell them to the shady gallery dealers—that we knew how the illegal sales worked. To circumvent the eagle feather law, dealers like Baer would speak in code. They always referred to eagle plumes as "turkey" feathers. And they never actually *sold* artifacts with eagle feathers—they *gifted* them to customers who also bought legal Native American artifacts at obscenely inflated prices. Such a customer might knowingly pay $21,000 for a legal artifact worth $1,000 and receive an illegal artifact worth $20,000 as a gift.

The afternoon after our brief exchange at the wine-and-cheese reception, we returned to Baer's gallery and he greeted us warmly.

"C'mon in the back," Baer said as he opened a door off the gallery floor to a private room. He brought out a set of wooden parrots, and explained that they were used as part of a Jemez Pueblo corn dance. He showed us a Navajo singer's brush, a sacred artifact used by a medicine man to wipe away evil spirits; and a pair of Jemez hair ornaments, consisting of four foot-long feathers tied to an inch-wide wood shaft. The hair sticks were perhaps one hundred years old, constructed of cotton string, two red-tailed hawk feathers, a golden eagle feather, and a macaw feather.

"It would be hard to imagine something more ceremonial," Baer said.

Or, I thought, something more illegal. I offered the code phrase. "These are what, turkey?"

"Yep," Baer said, smiling. "Turkey feathers."

He quickly made clear he'd received them as a gift from a broker with whom he did a great deal of business. "You know," he said, "it was a thing like where I purchased something from him and he gave me these."

"Just like if you had something you could give to Ivar as a gift?"

"Right," he said. "It's not the kind of thing that should be sold to somebody. Somebody's in your life and they're helping you."

I smiled. "That's very commendable."

Baer laughed.

I turned to Husby. "You're interested?"

He nodded. "May I take a photograph of this?"

Baer shook his head. "Sorry, can't allow it."

"Oh, OK."

"After I give them to you, then you can take a photograph." We all laughed again. We were all friends now, conspirators, and Baer began to open up. "I have to be frank with you. It's really no fun dealing with the federal government in terms of the legality of these things."

"What's the problem?" I said.

"They are interested in harassing people who buy and sell American Indian material," he said. Baer launched into a long justification about how illegally trading sacred Native American artifacts is a victimless crime, one encouraged and manipulated by tribal leaders to reward friends and punish enemies. "It's a political thing."

"I had no idea," Husby said.

"So I'm not going to sit here and ask for identification or be a jerk about this," Baer said. "I mean, obviously, you guys are serious people. But my concern is that this is not the kind of thing that should be discussed."

"No, right, right," I said. I turned to Husby. "I've got to find a way to get this to you."

Baer said, "I understand what he's looking for. If we have some kind of working relationship, everything will be fine."

"So, between you and I," I whispered, acting if such words ought to be said just out of Husby's earshot, "we'll just tack on the price?"

"Yes," Baer said.

I beamed. "I'd like to start up a working relationship."

Husby and Baer discussed customs hassles for a few minutes. When they finished, I said, "One of the things Ivar was interested in was a war bonnet."

Baer perked up but didn't say anything.

"Can you get that?" I asked.

"It would take some time," Baer said carefully. "It is possible but it's very, very difficult. It's not the kind of thing that we can call up and order."

"No, I understand," I said.

Husby jumped in. "We have looked on many days and have seen none."

"I'll find you one," Baer said. "But it will take some time."

I needed time too. I had to get back to Philadelphia.

On the day after Baer promised to find me a headdress, Hurricane Floyd, which had already caused so much flooding and misery in North Carolina, arrived in southeastern Pennsylvania, bringing a foot of water and seventy-mile-an-hour gusts to my neighborhood. Our new home was particularly vulnerable because the builder was still struggling to fix punch-list problems, even two years after we'd moved in. When the storm reached Pennsylvania, Donna called me in Santa Fe to gave me a damage report. The carpets were soaked. Water was flowing down the walls on the *inside* of the house. The ceilings were bulging with water, leaking everywhere. I imagined the looming bills, new construction headaches—new drywall, stucco, landscaping, gutters, and windows. The Baer case would have to wait. I hustled back to my room and arranged for a flight home.

GOING UNDERCOVER CAN be tough on the family.

You're gone for long stretches of time. You leave your spouse home alone with the kids, with all their activities, homework assignments, trips to the doctor, housekeeping, and car problems. You can't say precisely when you'll leave or when you'll be back—it might be a few days or it might be weeks. Your spouse knows where you're going and has a general idea of what you're doing—and that it might be dangerous—but for your own safety, you tell her she can't discuss it with anyone.

I certainly leaned on Donna for support. She came from a line of strong women. Her upbringing—especially what she learned from her mother, Jerry—guided us through our toughest times. Jerry would frequently remind us to "slow down and smell the roses." Whenever Donna's parents visited, they would bring the boys a bushel of enormous Maryland steamed crabs. Jerry would bring for Kristin her sewing machine and quilting fabric. For Donna, she'd bring hand-sewn drapes to hang in our new home. Jerry lived by example, offering her unconditional love and support, beginning with my car accident and continuing through her long, valiant battle against breast cancer. Donna had the same focus and strength imparted to her by her mother. As a result my family thrived.

Which made it easier for me to go undercover with a clear mind.

* * *

UNDER THE FBI's strict undercover rules, you're only supposed to work one case at a time. I never followed that rule. It made no sense: Most opportunities in life don't come along so conveniently, one neatly after the other. It seemed silly to ignore a chance to solve one case simply because another was still evolving. Besides, my supervisors certainly couldn't complain when I worked multiple cases. They didn't have an alternative. I was the FBI's only undercover agent working the art crime beat.

When I returned home to inspect the hurricane damage, I received an e-mail from a Penn museum curator, a woman I'd met during the backflap case. Her tip was unrelated to the Baer investigation, but by coincidence involved the illegal sale of eagle feathers. Someone was offering a war bonnet once worn by the Apache warrior and medicine man Geronimo.

"Not sure if this is a prank, nor if it would interest the FBI," the tipster e-mailed, "but thought it might be of interest regardless. Please see the forwarded post below."

> Subject: Authentic Geronimo autograph $22,000
>
> Serious inquiries only. His original headdress is for sale for one million dollars but it is not allowed in this country because of the feathers. Serious international inquiries only. Contact Steve at the e-mail address Gourmetcook@aol.com

I e-mailed "Steve." The next day, a fast-talking Marietta, Georgia, car salesman named Thomas Marciano called my undercover cell phone. Indeed, he said, Geronimo's eagle-feather war bonnet was still for sale. Excellent condition, he said. I asked about provenance and Marciano explained that Geronimo had worn the headdress in October 1907 to mark the Last Pow-Wow, a carnival celebrating Oklahoma's transition from territory to state. By then, he said, Geronimo was no longer a legendary military and spiritual leader but a seventy-eight-year-old prisoner of war, a tragic over-the-hill celebrity granted regular leave to appear at fairs and parades. The Last

Pow-Wow was one such gig, but more significant than most because the great chief had dressed in full regalia and took center stage during a ceremony in which he performed spiritual dances. Afterward, Geronimo presented the headdress he wore to his military escort, a half-Cherokee named Jack Moore. Later, Moore gave the war bonnet to a good friend, C. W. Deming. The man's grandson, Leighton Deming, inherited the headdress and kept it mothballed in a trunk for decades. Deming had recently fallen on hard financial times, Marciano explained, and was looking to sell the headdress.

Wow, great story, I told Marciano. I've got an interested buyer in Europe. Mail me some pictures and background, and I'll take a look, I said. OK, he said, but be careful. It's illegal, he warned me, to sell eagle feathers in the United States. With the tape recorder rolling, I acted surprised. Are you sure? Yes, yes, he insisted, I'm quite sure. Hmm, I said, I dunno.

There are plenty of dumb criminals out there—the prisons are full of them. But Marciano tops my list. Eager to prove he was correct, that our deal was indeed illegal, he mailed me a copy of the law— 16 United States Code 668, The Bald and Golden Eagle Protection Act of 1940, which explicitly prohibits the sale of eagle feathers.

"You were right," I said when we spoke again, acting amazed. I tried to lure him north so I could work the case on my home turf with Goldman, who was restricted to prosecuting cases in the Eastern District of Pennsylvania. "Tell you what," I said. "I wanna do this, but I'm kind of busy. Can you make it up here? How about we meet at the Embassy Suites in Philadelphia, the one right at the airport?"

Marciano and Deming arrived at the hotel room on an early October afternoon, carrying a turn-of-the-century trunk. They set it beside the couch, right below the hidden surveillance camera. I'd brought along a friend from New Mexico—the expert Fish and Wildlife Service agent in my Santa Fe case, Lucinda Schroeder. She would know immediately whether the headdress was made of eagle feathers, or the common fake material, turkey feathers.

Deming and Marciano couldn't have been more different. Deming was a laid-back Southerner, fifty-five years old with a bulging nose, tired blue eyes, bushy black eyebrows, thin lips. Back in Sewanee, Georgia, he was a lawyer and president of the Gwinnett County Optimists Club. Deming liked to talk and slowly unspool family yarns in a silky voice—"My grandfather was friends with Jack Moore. Grandfather was in the oil business out there and Jack Moore used to come to his home, break down the door in the middle of the night, and sleep off the whiskey. And then two weeks later, Jack would be all sobered up by now, he'd come back and bring him a cow or something. My grandfather liked Jack Moore, so he never said anything. That was just Jack Moore." One day, instead of a cow, Jack Moore showed up and handed the grandfather Geronimo's headdress and a few other souvenirs, including an autographed photo.

Marciano, by contrast, couldn't sit still. Forty-two and beefy, with thick brown hair that receded to the top of his crown, he bounced about the room, throwing out factoids about Geronimo in a hard Boston accent—how he was a prisoner of war, how he spent his final decade peddling souvenirs. "It's how he earned his living. He kept a valise of hats. He would put one on and sell it and then get another and put it on. He would cut a button off from his jacket and sell it and then have his wife sew on another one. It's kind of sad, really."

As the men held forth, Schroeder studied the headdress a few feet away. After a few minutes, she pronounced the war bonnet likely authentic. We moved to the guts of the deal, and Deming proposed a way around the Bald and Golden Eagle Protection Act: He would sell me the Geronimo autographs for $1 million and loan my buyer the headdress indefinitely. OK, I agreed, but I insisted that he sign a bill of sale agreement. This was Goldman's idea—he wanted Deming to admit that he was selling the eagle feather war bonnet. I told Deming that my buyer insisted on a contract to protect him from Deming's heirs. Without a signed contract, I said, Deming's children might someday make a claim for the headdress. Deming hesitated.

He eyed the undercover Fish and Wildlife agent suspiciously. "I'm sure you're a nice lady, but I don't know you."

I turned to her. "Why don't you step outside for a minute?"

After she left, I braced for an argument from Deming, but he instead leaned close and spoke in a whisper. "All bullshit aside, Bob, I'll sign this and then do another one when she comes back in." He was offering to sign two contracts, a secret one admitting that he was selling the headdress and another in front of my expert with no mention of the headdress. That way, he figured, if she turned out to be a cop, he'd be OK.

"Absolutely," I said, pushing the incriminating document in front of him. We signed the contract mentioning the headdress and Deming watched me stuff it in my pocket.

I said, "Before she comes back, between us, how many other people are involved in this? . . . Because I don't want to get in any trouble."

Deming: "Shit no."

"One other thing," I said, slowly, almost in a drawl. "Once overseas, this thing ain't never coming back. We understand that, right?"

They nodded. I let Schroeder back in, Deming signed the second contract and the two men were so pleased with themselves that they dug the artifact out of the trunk to pose for one last series of pictures wearing Geronimo's headdress.

"You did the right thing bringing it to me," I told them.

"Well, it's a piece of history," Deming said.

I gave the code phrase for the SWAT team: "You guys hungry?"

After the arrests, FBI Philadelphia spokeswoman Linda Vizi received a call from the chief of the Lenape tribe in Delaware. He told her that the headdress, dormant in a trunk for three quarters of a century, needed a spiritual cleaning, to wipe away the bad spirits and influences. He offered to perform a smudging ceremony. The chief repeated what I'd heard in New Mexico: A headdress must be respected and kept pure, because the eagle feather is considered a telephone to God. Vizi and I felt we should honor the request. What was the point of rescuing a piece of antiquity if you couldn't respect its raison d'etre?

The next day, the Lenape leader brought a batch of herbs to a sterile FBI conference room in Philadelphia. He lit the herbs like incense, filling the room with a pungent smell of sage. Vizi watched nervously as a trail of smoke drifted toward ceiling fire detectors. The Lenape chief rubbed his hands through the smoke, softly chanting prayers, and began blessing and massaging the wilted feathers. The sage cleansed, he explained, driving away evil influences. Next, he burned sweetgrass, an herb designed to draw positive spirits. He stepped aside when the ritual was over. The feathers had perked up, and the headdress looked like new.

When the FBI announced the Geronimo arrests at a press conference that week, I took my regular spot in the back of the room, out of camera shot, careful to preserve my undercover identity. This time, Vizi took an extra precautionary step, one that probably saved us from inadvertently ruining my case in Santa Fe.

She spoke to the journalists off the record and asked them not to report my name or the fact that an undercover agent from Philadelphia was involved. The information about my name and my role was publicly available—as required by law, it was filed in the court affidavit I'd signed laying out the facts of the case, and it was the kind of document reporters routinely used to write their stories. Thankfully, all of the journalists honored her request.

WHEN I CALLED Baer in Santa Fe the day after the Geronimo press conference, it was the first thing he mentioned.

"Bob! You OK? Man, I thought maybe you got swept up in that thing in Philly. You know, some guys got busted trying to sell a headdress. It was Geronimo's!"

I played dumb. "No kidding? For real?"

"Yeah, I got the paper right here. Big story in the *New Mexican*." Baer began reading the story aloud: " 'An FBI affidavit filed yesterday said an undercover agent received an electronic message early last month in an Internet chat room.' " I recognized the wording. It was the story from the *Philadelphia Inquirer*, reprinted word for word in the Santa Fe paper. Damn, I thought, good thing Vizi got to the reporters. Baer, still fired up, read through the whole article.

I said, "That's incredible, Josh, just incredible."

"Yeah, well, you have to be careful, because of who is running these things and is behind these stings. It's nuts. Hey, you know what, Bob? That Geronimo war bonnet was way overpriced. I wouldn't have paid more than a hundred grand."

I flew out to see Baer in November. I enjoyed his company, despite his crimes, and he taught me a great deal about Native Americans and their fascinating rituals. Between mid-August and January, I met with him more than a dozen times in Santa Fe and spoke with him on the phone at least ten times. I ate at his home and treated him to dinner at his favorite restaurants. We talked about our families, but mostly about art deals. Baer was an intellectual, a connoisseur of fine Indian art and good wine, but he was no snob—he didn't sniff when I told him I didn't drink alcohol or roll his eyes when I asked an ignorant question about Native American traditions. He'd begun his career in New Mexico in the mid-1970s, spending years on the pueblos building relationships with the Navajo, and brokering their rugs, their art, and their sacred artifacts. Baer was a San Francisco liberal who fit in easily in hoity-toity Santa Fe, but many in Indian country found him off-putting, the epitome of a patronizing White Man. He lived in a fine home and drove a Mercedes, but he lived precariously. His bank balance varied widely month to month and he always seemed on the cusp of the big deal. Baer had a ready justification for selling illegal Indian religious and eagle-feathered artifacts: "It's all about karma," he would say. "I've given so much stuff back, repatriated it to the tribes—they give me stuff, I give them stuff. It's all good karma. You gotta be careful, do things right, or it will come back to haunt you."

Early on, Baer aired suspicions that I might be a Fed. He never directly confronted me; he would say that others suspected it. Once, he began asking me so many questions, I tossed him my wallet and told him he was free to rifle through it. "I don't have anything to hide," I said. I think the thing that ingratiated me with him the most was my offer to rip off my own client. I proposed that we inflate Husby's price, then split the profits fifty-fifty. In Baer's eyes, my crime—fraud against the Norwegian—was far worse than breaking some silly law about eagle feathers. That's when I knew I had connected, that I had him.

I flew to Santa Fe a week after we spoke on the phone, and Baer offered good news: He'd found an eagle-feather bonnet in Colorado. We could buy it for $75,000, he said, and charge the Norwegian $125,000. I brought Husby to the gallery.

Baer beckoned us to the back room. "This is your lucky day," he said. He lifted a shopping bag and pulled out an eagle-feather headdress, laying it across a table. "I'm proud to show you this," he said, then left us alone to appreciate it. The headdress was intoxicating: seventy golden eagle feathers stitched together in a five-foot-long tail, with domed brass buttons, rawhide, and strips of braided human hair. Husby noticed a tiny label that said "RI66Y," clearly an inventory mark from a museum. When Baer returned, Husby acted thrilled. Baer explained that the headdress, of course, would be a gift and that Husby would buy a quiver and a few other legal artifacts at sharply inflated prices. The total sale price would be $125,000. We shook hands and celebrated that night with a dinner at Baer's home with his wife. After dinner, Baer took out the headdress and placed it on Husby's head, a crowning end to a fun evening.

It would have been perfect, too, if not for an incredibly frustrating discovery late that night—the batteries on my hidden tape recorder had died. I'd have to find a way to get Baer to repeat his incriminating statements.

I called Baer the next morning and steered him toward reliving the moment when Husby first saw the headdress. Together, we mocked the gullible Norwegian.

Baer laughed. "The look on your guy's face was just—"

"Shocking."

"Priceless," Baer said.

I told him Husby ought to have the $125,000 available in a few days. Baer reminded me that our take would then be $25,000 each. We were talking like partners now, working together, watching out for each other.

"We just have to proceed in a sensible fashion," Baer said. "I mean, we got the quiver as a bona fide transaction."

"Yeah," I said. "Exactly."

IF YOU LISTEN to the undercover tapes I made during the Santa Fe sting, you'll hear me whistling quite a bit—whistling as I stroll to Baer's gallery, whistling as I walk away.

I'm whistling because it reduces my stress.

The physical and mental demands of going undercover can be overwhelming. It's stressful to stay focused, to toggle between personas, even simultaneous cases, especially when there's downtime between acts, waiting for deals. I whistle as I ramp up and whistle as I ramp down.

That doesn't mean I don't enjoy the thrill of going undercover. I do enjoy it, especially the challenge of outthinking a criminal, feeding him enough rope to hang himself with his own words.

It's kind of weird. Sometimes, when I've slipped into a role, I really don't want it to end. Which is why, when a case does end, I always feel a little deflated.

Almost everyone who goes undercover experiences this letdown. It's normal to feel a sense of loss. After working so hard to ingratiate yourself with a target, thinking about a case day and night for weeks and months, it's only natural to miss that high, to even feel a bit depressed. You invest a great deal—turn it on, turn it off, call your target, call your wife—and then suddenly, the case is over.

Sometimes, I feel slightly guilty about the betrayal. If I've done my job correctly—built rapport with the target, befriended him—I'll feel a gnawing in my stomach. It's normal, I guess, but that doesn't make it any less mind-bending. FBI agents are trained to uphold our motto—"Fidelity, Bravery, Integrity." Working undercover, we violate every tenet of that creed: We are disloyal. We act cowardly. We lie.

Undercover FBI agents are trained to compartmentalize, to be careful not to get too close to their targets. In theory, it's a nice thought, but you can't work well undercover if you suppress your emotions or follow a rulebook. You have to follow your instincts. You have to be human. It's hard, and it can eat you up at times. I don't worry about the true criminals, but sometimes basically good people get into desperate situations and do dumb things. Sometimes, it can almost seem unfair.

Baer liked to talk about the influence of karma and mysticism, and in the world of stolen art and antiquities, I think there's something to that. The Missouri man who sold me the Civil War battle flag died of cancer less than a year after we arrested him. The backflap seemed to haunt all who touched it. The grave robber who discovered the Moche tomb was later killed by police; the first wealthy Peruvian to obtain the backflap died mysteriously; the second went bankrupt; the son of the Miami smuggler Mendez was born prematurely and lived less than two months. As the infant lay dying in his arms, Mendez swore his son's shriveled face resembled the Decapitator god engraved on the backflap.

I thought about all that as we moved to snap the trap shut on Baer with one final, orchestrated maneuver. His karma was about to take a turn for the worse.

MY JOB ON January 19, 2000—the day Baer was arrested—was simply to do a little friendly hand-holding, ahead of the afternoon raid on his gallery and home.

In the hours before the bust, we wanted to keep in close contact with Baer to make sure nothing unexpected popped up. And I wanted to cement the case. We met in his shop around noon and discussed final arrangements for the purchase of the headdress, a Corn Mother, and a few other items. He reminded me that we now each stood to earn about $32,000 on the $200,000 deal. I promised to meet him for dinner.

I did not join the team of federal agents on the raid.

Baer was charged with illegally selling or trying to sell seventeen artifacts, including the Navajo singer's brush, the Jemez hair tie, a pair of Hopi wooden birds, the Cheyenne headdress, and a rare and most sacred Santo Domingo Corn Mother, a deity represented by a corncob with sixteen golden eagle feathers wrapped by cotton, buffalo hide, and string. The indictment set the total value of the illicit artifacts at $385,300.

I never expected to hear from Baer again. But two days after the bust, he e-mailed me. The subject line read, "Here's to the Good Times." I didn't know what to make of that as I clicked open the message.

> Dear Bob: I don't know what to say. Well done? Nice work? You sure had me fooled?
>
> We're devastated, and I guess that's the idea. But, even though we're devastated, we enjoyed the times we spent with you. Thanks for being a gentleman, and for letting us have a pleasant Christmas and New Year's. If you hadn't done what you did, they would have brought in someone else to do it, and I don't think we would have found him as personable as we found you. So there's no blame involved. We just have a lot of facts to face.
>
> This letter is neither a joke, a scam, an appeal nor a message containing anything other than what it says. Best wishes, Joshua Baer.

It was a classy note from a thoughtful guy, and it triggered a momentary pang of guilt. But his graceful e-mail couldn't change the fact that he had consciously and repeatedly violated the law and violated the trust of the Native American people he so professed to love.

I thought about it for a while and then wrote back the next day. "This was the hardest case I had because I really like you and your family. Call me anytime."

I meant it.

CHAPTER 12

THE CON ARTIST

Bryn Mawr, Pennsylvania, 2000.

IF THE CARDINAL RULE OF WORKING UNDERCOVER IS *Keep the lies to a minimum,* a close second is *Avoid working in your hometown.*

For me, "hometown" didn't just mean Philadelphia. It meant the art and antique circles throughout the Northeast where I'd spent years learning, lecturing, and developing sources. Eleven years into the job, this began to pose a bit of a catch-22: The more people I met in the art world, the more people knew my face, and the more dangerous it became to work undercover.

Sure enough, in 2000 I found myself investigating three prominent Pennsylvania appraisers who specialized in eighteenth- and nineteenth-century arms and militaria, and visited the same Civil War shows I frequented. All three suspects knew me. The eldest was the respected former director of the Civil War Museum of Philadelphia, and we'd chatted several times. The two younger suspects knew me from the Historical Society of Pennsylvania museum case—following the arrests, they'd helped the FBI make a formal appraisal of the value of the works the janitor had stolen for George Csizmazia.

This investigation was also particularly sensitive because it involved a sensational allegation, the kind of accusation against quasi-public figures that made my FBI supervisors nervous. The two younger suspects were star appraisers on the highest-rated program on PBS, *Antiques Roadshow*.

The integrity of the reality show hinged on the honesty of the on-the-spot appraisals of the items people brought—an heirloom Civil War sword, an Oriental vase discovered at a flea market, an old tea set gathering dust in Grandma's attic. We'd heard rumors that the fix was in—that the two young suspects were faking the *Antiques Roadshow* appraisals to market their business.

Because I could not go undercover, and because the case involved a slog through tens of thousands of pages of bank, business, and court records, the *Antiques Roadshow* investigation became one of the longest of my career. The scandal singed the reputation of a PBS program beloved by million of viewers, disgraced the retired museum director, and left swindled victims, descendants of genuine war heroes, steaming that someone could act so cruelly.

THE CHIEF VILLAIN was a classic con artist. Russell Albert Pritchard III, tanned face, blue BMW, George Will haircut, Brooks Brothers ties, presented himself to all the world as a man who had it made.

Thirty-five years old, the appraiser lived with his comely wife and four children in a five-bedroom stone house at the epicenter of Philadelphia's rarefied Main Line, half a block from the leafy campus of Bryn Mawr College. The family home, which he'd purchased from his father for $1 a decade before, was worth at least $1 million. Pritchard had trained to be an insurance salesman, but soon joined his father, Russ Pritchard Jr., in the family business, selling eighteenth- and nineteenth-century military artifacts. The father was an established and respected authority in the field—the former director of the Civil War Museum in Philadelphia and author of several books on Civil War weapons, equipment, and tactics. Together, father and son owned two-thirds of a military antiquities and memorabilia brokerage, which they gave the grand and somewhat misleading name American Ordnance Preservation Association, a moniker that suggested it was some sort of charity or nonprofit organization. The third partner was a gregarious thirty-seven-year-old appraiser from Allentown named George Juno.

Pritchard III and Juno scored their big break in 1996 when they won jobs as television appraisers for *Antiques Roadshow.* They traveled the country with the show for its first three seasons, performing instant, on-camera appraisals of guns, swords, uniforms, and other military artifacts. Pritchard and Juno were not paid for the work. But for such relatively young appraisers, the value of such national exposure—ten million households a week—was incalculable. Business for their brokerage boomed.

MY INVESTIGATION BEGAN years later. In 2000, a subpoenaed VHS tape arrived in the mail from WGBH, the Boston PBS affiliate that produces *Antiques Roadshow.* I found a player and cued it up.

It was a raw tape from the first season and it began with a familiar scene: two people sitting before what looked like a TV anchor's desk, a silver sword lying between them, and dozens of casually dressed bargain hunters shopping for antiques in the background. The video opened with a sound check. A man with a well-groomed brown mustache, a three-piece suit, and his hair held snug with hair spray looked into the camera and spoke his name: "George Juno, American Ordnance Preservation Association." Juno nodded at his guest, a nerdy-looking man in a need of a haircut, perhaps forty years old with a rumpled blue oxford shirt and gold wide-rimmed glasses. The man said his name, "Steve Sadtler."

The segment began as typically as any on *Antiques Roadshow,* with an understated, somewhat stilted conversation.

"Steve, thank you for coming in today."

"My pleasure."

"This is an interesting sword you brought in. What can you tell me about the background?"

"Well, it's a sword that I found twenty-three years ago. My folks bought a house down in Virginia and my folks decided they were going to rebuild the house. My brothers and I got stuck with the job of taking down the chimney. That required going up into the attic, and I found this thing"—he paused to point to the sword—"hanging on a post. Pretty much for me, it became a plaything. For the last ten or fifteen years, it's been stored away."

"Well, Steve, it's quite a sword." As Juno began to describe the object, his name and the name of his company appeared at the bottom of the screen. "If we look on the back of the blade we see the maker's mark. It says Thomas Griswold, New Orleans. They imported items from England. The blade is etched in the middle, *CS*, on both sides, for Confederate States. The castle you see etched in the guard is actually a fort, Fort Sumner. . . . This would have used a solid brass scabbard. They used this for their artillery sabers and their cavalry sabers. It would have been a very flashy sword, gold plated all over the hilt. This is definitely the highest-quality pattern."

Juno handed Steve a set of white gloves. "It's always good practice to use the white gloves," the expert explained, "because your hands have salts in them and after you put the sword away, the salts will continue to rust the blade and cause problems with the brass." He turned the blade over. "Notice the crossed cannons? And on this side, floral, finely etched."

When Juno finished his brief lesson, he laid the sword on the table and he paused before the big *Antiques Roadshow* moment, the one where the appraiser teases, "Do you have any idea what it might be worth?"

Sadtler said, "I was going to tag it for a garage sale between fifty and two hundred dollars."

"Well," Juno said, "this sword could have bought you a new garage."

The camera zoomed in on Sadtler as his eyebrows narrowed with anticipation.

"That's right," Juno said. "This sword is worth thirty-five thousand dollars. This happens to be one of the great rarities in Confederate swords."

"Did you say"—he gulped—"thirty-five thousand dollars?"

"Thirty-five thousand. You've made a great find here."

"Whoa!" Sadtler's mouth dropped open, and he seemed to struggle to restrain his joy, as if to remind himself that while this was a reality show, it was buttoned-down PBS, not *The Price Is Right*. He shook his head several times and said, "Man, I was going to get rid of it."

Juno said, "You made a smart move taking it to us to have a look at it."

"As a kid, I used this to cut watermelon."

Juno gave an aw-shucks grin. "You're lucky you didn't get too much moisture on it."

"Wow, thank you very much."

The segment was so good—an instant *Antiques Roadshow* classic—that PBS aired it over and over, and used it in a fund-raising video. Some viewers suspected it was too good. Rumors began to circulate in the collecting community about the "watermelon sword."

I tracked Steve Sadtler through the phone number he provided to WGBH on the standard *Antiques Roadshow* release form. I reached him in Seattle.

I told him I was investigating Pritchard and Juno for fraud. Look, I said, just tell me the truth and you won't get into trouble. But don't lie, I warned. It's a federal crime to lie to an FBI agent.

Sadtler confessed immediately. The segment was indeed a setup, he said. Pritchard and Sadtler were close; Sadtler was a groomsman at Pritchard's wedding. The night before the PBS taping, the two met up with Juno in a hotel room, where Pritchard concocted the story about finding it in Sadtler's Virginia home, and paid him $10,000 for his help.

And that sword?

It belonged to Pritchard and Juno.

"THIS IS THE case we've been waiting for," Assistant U.S. Attorney Bob Goldman said over lunch one summer afternoon, after I finished telling him about my conversation with Sadtler. "I'm telling you, this is it."

I nodded, and as Goldman spoke I scooped a spoonful of kung pao chicken onto my plate. We sat in the back of Szechuan China Royal, a popular Philadelphia law-enforcement haunt—reliable, reasonably priced specials with well-spaced tables in a discreet basement dining room, a joint generally ignored by the white-collar mob that swarms Walnut Street at lunchtime.

"This is the case where we'll make a difference," he said. "This is great."

Goldman, historian, collector, federal prosecutor, was a huge *Antiques Roadshow* fan. He watched it nearly every week. But like others, he'd long suspected some segments might be staged. It was too smooth. People offered things they inherited or discovered— a chair, a sword, a watch, an armoire, whatever—and voilà, an expert offered an off-the-cuff appraisal. How could the so-called experts make such quick appraisals? Didn't they ever have to look anything up? Didn't they ever make a mistake? Or simply get stumped?

"Bob," I'd always tell him, "relax. It's just TV, just entertainment."

"Yeah," the prosecutor would say, "but they're passing themselves off as experts. Television has this way of deifying people. Viewers believe what these guys say."

Faking a segment on a TV show isn't, by itself, a federal crime. But faking a segment on TV to further a scheme to defraud collectors *is* a crime. And now that I was beginning to confirm that

Pritchard and Juno had used some PBS segments to help trick viewers into selling other pieces at absurdly low prices, I shared Goldman's outrage.

We also knew that Pritchard and Juno were busy helping the mayor of Harrisburg, Pennsylvania, acquire a collection for a new Civil War museum, not far from Gettysburg. The mayor expected to spend $14 million on acquisitions—enough money, as my prosecutor friend liked to say, "to blind the conscience and steal the soul." We'd already confirmed at least one case in which Pritchard and Juno used *Antiques Roadshow* and the Harrisburg museum deal to scam a collector. If there was one, there were probably many more.

Goldman was right: This just might be the case we'd been waiting for.

He and I often lamented over the unregulated, buyer-beware antiques and collectibles market, which operated largely on an honor system, where everyone was a salesman, provenance was sketchy, and dealers lived by their reputations. Hustlers sold fakes and reproductions, and unscrupulous dealers ripped off the naive. Honest brokers complained from time to time, but law enforcement agencies rarely showed interest. The cons were usually too small to attract the FBI's attention, and too complicated for local police departments with little or no art crime experience and limited resources. Most such sales were poorly documented; often, evidence consisted of little more than a handshake and a promise. Besides, proving fraud in the antiques trade isn't easy: Who's to say what's a fair deal? Where do you draw the line between a sucker deal and a scam?

To be sure, there's always been a reasonable amount of salesmanship in the collectibles and antiques industry. The law even allows a bit of puffery. Say, for example, an antiques dealer offers an opinion—"This is the best Chinese vase in the shop"—that's puffery, and perfectly legal. But if the dealer offers a lie—"This is the best authentic Ming vase in the shop," and he knows the vase is not authentic Ming—that's fraud. Dealers understand this difference and exploit it. Lately, the number of unscrupulous dealers seemed to be growing. And no one in the federal government seemed interested in doing anything about it.

Goldman and I longed to send a message to the antiques and collectibles community, something that would make a big splash, enough to frighten shady brokers and alert unsuspecting collectors. But we needed a high-profile case, one with overwhelming evidence of widespread fraud, featuring white-collar collectors or appraisers, the antiques world equivalent of a Ken Lay or Bernie Madoff.

Pritchard and Juno presented such an opportunity. Here were a pair of local but nationally known appraisers, public television stars no less. If we could prove that they were dirty—that they fixed *Antiques Roadshow* segments and ripped off viewers in other sales—we wouldn't just be sending them to prison, we'd be putting the collecting community on notice.

"I know it sounds like a cliché," Goldman said as the waiter brought our fortune cookies and the check. "But we've got to let people know there's a new sheriff in town, that somebody out there is watching."

I agreed with Goldman, thrilled with his assessment and support. Still, I couldn't help tweaking my friend. "OK, excellent, excellent. I'm in. But one thing: If there's a new sheriff in town, I'm Wyatt Earp and you're Deputy Dawg."

MOST FBI AGENTS love to dive into piles of documents, combing through bills, credit card receipts, phone bills, letters, e-mail messages, bank statements, E-ZPass logs, court depositions, and other paper records, emerging from these fishing expeditions with smoking-gun evidence of a crime.

Not me.

I certainly subpoenaed records and used them as leads. But my skill was getting out and talking to people.

Thankfully, in the Pritchard and Juno case, my FBI partner, Jay Heine, and I had a head start on the dreaded paper trail. The assist came courtesy of the great-great grandson of the Confederate general George E. Pickett. His lawyer had already collected a mountain of paper evidence against the appraisers.

Months before we formally opened our investigation, the lawyer for George E. Pickett V sued Pritchard and Juno for fraud in federal court in Philadelphia. He alleged that Pritchard tricked him into selling significant Civil War artifacts his ancestor had carried during his calamitous charge at Gettysburg on July 3, 1863, the skirmish that is considered the high-water mark of the Confederacy because that is as far north as the rebels reached. The sale included the blue kepi hat and sword Pickett wore as he rode into the war's bloodiest battle, as well as a map he sketched of Gettysburg hours before the famous charge. The Pickett family also sold the remnants of the general's war souvenirs—his officer's commissioning papers, a blood-stained sleeve ripped from his jacket after a bullet struck his arm, and a stack of letters. Pritchard appraised the artifacts for $87,000 and told Pickett's descendants that they would have a better home in the new Harrisburg museum. This would be a great way to honor their ancestor's legacy, Pritchard argued. The Picketts agreed to the sale at the appraised price, $87,000.

Later, George E. Pickett V was stunned to learn that Pritchard had sold the collection to the Harrisburg museum for nearly ten times as much, $850,000. In his lawsuit, Pickett cried foul. More incriminating evidence emerged during the civil trial, and Pickett prevailed with an $800,000 judgment.

Heine and I cherry-picked the best of the Pickett lawsuit records, but it was just the beginning. We pursued our own leads, subpoenaed our own documents, and interviewed our witnesses—not only in the Pickett case, but also in dozens of others that looked suspect. For each transaction, we tried to answer a simple set of questions: What pieces did Pritchard and Juno obtain? Was the price they paid fair? What promises did they make to the victims? Where did the pieces end up?

What we found made me nauseous.

LIKE A LOT of other *Antiques Roadshow* viewers, George K. Wilson of New York City became intrigued watching Juno and Pritchard appraise weapons.

His family owned a Civil War dress sword presented to his great-great-grandfather, Union Army Major Samuel J. Wilson. George Wilson wondered if the sword held historical value. Was it worth selling?

He went to the *Antiques Roadshow* website and found contact information for Pritchard and Juno. What happened next—according to the account Wilson gave me when I interviewed him—offers a window into Pritchard's confidence game.

After some quick preliminaries on the phone, Pritchard asked if the sword had ever been appraised.

No, Wilson said.

Well, I'll have to see it in person to give you an appraisal, Pritchard said. I'll do it free of charge, just like I would on *Antiques Roadshow,* if you FedEx it to me. I'll even send you the packaging. We do this all the time.

How can you afford to do this all the time at no charge?

The museums and collectors pay us for the appraisals if we sell them. Are you interested in selling the sword?

No, Wilson said. But I'll be in touch.

Wilson called his mother, explained the offer of a free appraisal, and they agreed to send it to Pritchard. What did they have to lose? When Pritchard received the sword via FedEx, he called Wilson.

The sword is in pretty good shape, Pritchard said, but it needs some professional conservation. There may be some oxidation damage to the steel blade.

OK, Wilson said, how much is it worth?

Well, this sword is not uncommon, Pritchard said. It's probably worth $7,000 to $8,000.

Hmm, how much will it cost to get it professionally conserved?

About $1,500. Maybe more. But there's another option. I'm working with the City of Harrisburg, which is about to open a new Civil War Museum. This piece might make a nice addition. If you sell the sword to the museum, their conservators will restore it. They could feature the sword in the museum with a photograph of Major Wilson and a map showing the battles he fought in.

Wilson called back the next day and the two men struck a deal. The museum would buy the sword and include it in its collection. A month later, Pritchard sent Wilson a check for $7,950 drawn from the Pritchard/Juno business account, not from the museum or City of Harrisburg. Confused, Wilson called Pritchard.

Don't worry, the broker said. We're just the agent. You'll be contacted by the museum soon enough.

Wilson cashed the check. It bounced.

Sorry about that, Pritchard said. Must have been an accounting error. I'll send you a new check. By the way, the museum examined the sword and it's in worse shape than I thought. You're lucky the blade didn't break off. They'll have to do some heavy repairs before it can be displayed in the museum. But you know what? Good news! I'll be touring with *Antiques Roadshow* at the Meadowlands in a few weeks. You should come!

The second check cleared and Wilson showed up at the TV taping to ask Pritchard about the progress of the sword conservation. Soon, Pritchard promised, soon. Over the next two years, every month or so, Wilson continued to call with the same question. Each time, he got the same answer.

When Wilson learned of Pickett's lawsuit, he angrily confronted Juno and Pritchard. He demanded to know why the sword wasn't displayed in the museum, as promised. Now Pritchard had a new answer: The museum ran out of money, so we sold it to a collector who's thinking about starting a museum in the Poconos.

Wilson was apoplectic. He demanded to see records proving this, and he offered a ruse of his own to get them, saying that he needed the document for tax purposes.

OK, Pritchard said, but please understand. We have a lot going on and this was a small piece. I'm a good guy, really. Ask around. This Pickett lawsuit hassle is all a misunderstanding. After all, the *Antiques Roadshow* producers are sticking with us. That should tell you something. You know, it's too bad we haven't had time to become better friends.

Just send the documents, Wilson said.

As I later discovered, Pritchard never offered the sword to the Harrisburg museum. He let Juno use it as collateral for a $20,000 loan.

Pritchard and Juno pulled similar scams. Pritchard approached the descendants of Union general George Meade and offered to appraise a presentation firearm Meade received after the Battle of Gettysburg. This was an astonishing weapon—a mahogany-cased, .44-caliber Remington pistol with engraved ivory grips, silver-plated frame, and gold-washed cylinder and hammer. Pritchard told the family it was worth $180,000 and promised to place it in the Harrisburg museum. Three months after the Meades sold him the firearm, Pritchard sold it to a private collector for twice the price.

Once, while working with his father, Pritchard received from a Tennessee family an old Confederate uniform, one worn by their ancestor, Lieutenant Colonel William Hunt. The Pritchards falsely informed the family that the uniform was counterfeit and said that because it was worthless they'd donated it to a local charity. In reality, the Pritchards had sold it to a collector for $45,000.

The market for Civil War uniforms was so dirty that even Pritchard himself was once burned. He bought what he thought was a rare Union Zouave jacket, worn by a soldier in a New York regiment. With its ornate chevrons and puffed shoulder pads and a design based on the classic French Legion dress uniform, the

Zouave would have been worth $25,000, if it had been authentic. It was not. It was a Belgian infantry jacket, worth only a few hundred dollars. Furious, Pritchard pulled a scam of his own to fix the problem. Using contacts at the Harrisburg museum, he slipped inside, removed the museum's authentic Zouave jacket, and put the cheap Belgian jacket in its place.

The man was merciless. Pritchard once appeared unannounced at a nursing home to target a ninety-year-old woman said to possess great Confederate treasures. When he realized the lady was too infirm to talk, he slipped a nurse $100 to get a look at her file, and a phone number for her next of kin.

IT'S HARD TO quantify Pritchard's individual acts of cruelty. But it would be difficult to top the emotional damage he inflicted on the Patterson family of Salisbury, Maryland.

Donald Patterson, a local businessman and active re-enactor, spent a lifetime collecting Civil War memorabilia with his middle-class family—his wife, Elaine; stepson, Robert; and two daughters, Robynn and Lorena. The family helped maintain Don Patterson's wide-ranging collection of swords, rifles, pistols, uniforms, and knickknacks in a bedroom everyone affectionately called "the Museum." The holdings included a rare Confederate overcoat, worth at least $50,000 to $100,000.

In a series of FBI interviews and letters to the government, family members described the role Don Patterson and the Museum played in their lives. "My whole life, since I was able to walk, I was with my father picking things out from old antique stores, things from the Civil War," daughter Robynn wrote. "The Museum was just down the hall from my bedroom from fourth grade through high school," stepson Robert recalled. "It was always there, always part of us. We didn't fish, we didn't play catch, we didn't go camping— we collected irreplaceable pieces of history. In truth, almost my entire childhood was represented in the collection. My dreams, aspirations, my values came to be in large part because of my involvement with the collection." The stepson made a career in the Army, rising to the rank of lieutenant colonel.

The Patterson family's halcyon life shattered in late 1995, when Mr. Patterson killed himself, as well as his secret mistress. "As you can imagine, our whole family was absolutely devastated," his widow said.

Like a vulture, Pritchard visited Salisbury just months after the murder-suicide. The nice man charmed the widow, driving her to pick up her disabled daughters from school, eating meals at the Patterson kitchen table, and assuring them that the artifacts from the Museum would be in better hands in a real Civil War museum. He told her about the new one rising near Gettysburg and presented letters and brochures from the City of Harrisburg, including one that promised a "Donald Patterson Memorial Collection" room. In 1996, one year after Don Patterson's death, the family agreed to Pritchard's plan. The nice man gave them $5,000, packed away the best of the collection, and drove it north. Shortly after he left, the widow noticed, it became harder to get him to return her calls. The betrayal was under way.

By the time I spoke with Mrs. Patterson in 1999, and after three years of Pritchard's deceptions, she just wanted the truth. I've always found it's just best to deliver bad news directly. So I told her what I'd learned from Pritchard's records: Her husband's collection wasn't in any museum. Pritchard had sold it to two private Civil War dealers for $65,000. It was gone.

"My whole being has been violated and I have been emotionally raped," the widow recalled.

Pritchard had to be stopped. He wasn't just conning people out of money. He was stealing their heritage.

IN MARCH 2001, based on the evidence we presented to the grand jury, Pritchard and Juno were indicted on various federal charges, including defrauding the Wilson family and the Pickett family. The men faced as much as ten years in prison.

We were not finished. We had brought the initial indictment that March because the five-year statute of limitations was about to expire in the Wilson and Pickett cases. But we still had more time to bring a superseding indictment on charges related to the Zouave uniform, the Meade presentation pistol, and the Patterson family collection. We also weighed whether to charge Pritchard's father for his role in the Hunt Confederate uniform scam. So far, I hadn't interviewed the elder Pritchard.

I dreaded the confrontation. I'd known the elder Pritchard for more than a decade and had long respected him as a top man in the museum field. I'd visited him a dozen times at the Civil War Museum in Philadelphia to research cases and learn more about collecting. A well-thumbed copy of his three-volume treatise on Civil War weapons and uniforms sat on my desk at home.

Fortunately, I didn't have to meet him face to face. The elder Pritchard was living in Memphis at the time, so I called him there. I made it clear that although he and I knew each other, this was an official FBI interview. I told him that we were going to charge his son with the Hunt uniform scam. I gave the father a choice: Cooperate on this one facet of the case or face a felony charge.

"Look, Russ," I said. "Just tell me the truth and everything will go away." In other words, you won't be indicted. If he told us the truth, Goldman planned to exercise his prosecutorial discretion and leave him out of the next indictment. If he lied, Goldman planned to charge him.

"I'm sorry, Bob," the elder Pritchard said. "I can't help you."

He couldn't admit to me that he'd conspired with his son to swindle the Hunt family. I doubt this was because he wanted to protect his son. He knew it was too late for that. I think he couldn't admit what he did because he knew it would ruin his reputation in the field.

I gave him one more chance. "Tell me what happened, Russ."

"Bob, I can't."

"OK, but you're going to go down."

"I know. But I just can't do it."

Juno, on the other hand, played it smart. He knew we had a solid case against him, and he knew he could shave years off a prison term by pleading guilty and cooperating.

Two days after my conversation with the father, we filed the superseding indictment against both Pritchards.

Within a month, the Pritchard son and his attorney came to the FBI office in Philadelphia. He met with me, Goldman, and Heine to give a proffer statement, a private off-the-record confession, the prelude to a plea agreement.

Over two hours, Pritchard confessed to everything, and even dimed out his dad. Proffer sessions and confessions are incredibly stressful for defendants. They have to look their accusers in the eye— the very prosecutor and agents who've been hounding them for years, dragging their name into the newspaper, embarrassing their families, scandalizing their friends—and admit that yes, indeed, they did it. They did it all. Proffers are rarely pleasant and sometimes contentious. I've seen defendants leave a proffer session looking as if they've aged a couple of years. Pritchard? He didn't look mussed at all.

When it was over, he walked over to shake Goldman's hand, gripping the prosecutor's elbow with his left hand, an old politician's trick to keep the other man from pulling away.

"Mr. Goldman," he said, "I want to thank you for bringing my act to an end. This is good for me. I'm glad you're bringing these charges against me."

Goldman raised his left eyebrow, broke away, and gave Pritchard a hard stare that said, "Don't bullshit me."

In 2001, the year Pritchard and Juno pleaded guilty, Harrisburg's redbrick $50 million, sixty-five-thousand-square-foot National Civil

War Museum celebrated its grand opening. It featured state-of-the-art displays and dioramas with genuine artifacts of war, including the kepi hat that Pickett wore at Gettysburg.

Like the Picketts, most families didn't get their treasures back. The courts concluded that despite the frauds, the descendants no longer enjoyed legal title to the artifacts Pritchard had sold. The mayor of Harrisburg successfully argued that the city, too, was a victim of Pritchard and Juno, and that it was not required to return the items it acquired for its museum.

The Pritchard father would go to trial on the single charge related to the uniform scam, lose, and be sentenced to six months in a halfway house. Juno also got a few months in a halfway house. The Pritchard son would get a year and a day in prison and be ordered to pay $830,000 in restitution.

Despite the relatively light sentences, Goldman and I were thrilled with the outcome. The *Antiques Roadshow* investigation sent several important messages, and I couldn't help but think of my father and all the other honest antiques dealers down on Howard Street in Baltimore, working to make a living on small margins. To them, the case demonstrated that someone cared, that someone was watching this unregulated industry—and that unscrupulous dealers faced public shame and possible imprisonment.

The public response was even greater than we'd hoped. In the collecting community, the *Antiques Roadshow* investigation represented such a watershed that one of the major trade publications printed the Pritchard indictment word for word. Surfing the wave of publicity the case brought, I received a torrent of tips that led to more important recoveries, including a Confederate regiment's battle flag and a priceless sword presented to a Union hero of the great *Monitor–Merrimack* battle, missing since its theft from the U.S. Naval Academy in 1931. Goldman and I followed up the *Antiques Roadshow* prosecution with another indictment that shook the collectible world, charging two prominent Midwestern dealers with using fake appraisal documents to con a wealthy businessman into grossly overpaying for four antique firearms. One of the weapons in evidence was the world's first Magnum revolver, a six-shot, .44-caliber Colt, the very handgun that Samuel Walker, the famed Texas Ranger, carried into his final, fatal battle against Mexican guerrillas.

But long before the *Antiques Roadshow* scandal wound toward its conclusion and Pritchard reported to prison, I was already turning my attention to my next case, my first international art crime investigation. Within months, I hoped, I'd be stalking stolen art in South America.

CHAPTER 13

A HOT HAND

Rio de Janeiro, 2001.

IN A CABANA ON IPANEMA, ASSISTANT U.S. ATTORNEY David Hall and I sipped milk from coconut shells.

Before us, Brazil's trendiest beach buzzed under brilliant sunlight. Barefoot kids kicked up sand, playing volleyball with their feet. Rollerbladers in short shorts cruised the sidewalk. Bronzed hunks in Speedos preened, chatting up young ladies in thongs. The Latin pulse from a boom box dueled with the reggae beat from café speakers. At the opposite end of Guanabara Bay, a scarlet sun hovered over Sugar Loaf Mountain.

It was a Monday afternoon in early December, the heart of summer in South America. Blue skies, a pleasant breeze, seventy-five degrees. Back in Philadelphia, temperatures were falling and my FBI colleagues were bracing for a formal inspection by bureaucrats from Headquarters.

I swirled the straw in my coconut and dug my toes in the soft, yielding sand. After landing in Rio that morning following a ten-hour flight jammed shoulder to shoulder in coach, the stress was flowing out of me, down through my toes into that luxuriant sand. I felt well rested and invigorated by the beach scene. A deeply tanned, nearly nude couple pedaled by on a bike. I shook my head and raised the coconut in toast to my traveling partner.

The federal prosecutor hid behind his shades and Penn baseball cap, silent.

I said, "I can't believe your bosses thought this was some sort of boondoggle."

That drew a wry smile. And then a frown. "You know we've got a weak hand."

I nodded. Hall was right. We held few cards.

We were in Rio to try to solve a cold case, one that had frustrated the FBI for more than two decades—the theft of $1.2 million worth of Norman Rockwell paintings stolen from a gallery in Minneapolis in 1978. It wasn't a well-known art theft, but it was one that resonated with me. How could we fail to go after thieves who stole the works of an iconic American artist?

The U.S. government and the FBI routinely helped other nations retrieve stolen art and artifacts smuggled *into* our country. But the Rockwell case, if we pulled it off, would mark the rare repatriation of American artwork *from* a foreign country. We were only three months removed from the September 11 attacks, and we felt a special duty to recover these classic pieces of Americana. The most valuable of the stolen paintings, *The Spirit of '76,* depicted a fife-and-drum corps of multiracial Boy Scouts from northern New Jersey, marching with the Stars and Stripes, the faint image of Manhattan and the twin towers in the background.

Our target was a wealthy Brazilian art dealer who claimed that he'd purchased the paintings in Rio in the 1990s and therefore legally owned them under Brazilian law. The dealer was said to be politically connected and shrewd. Hall and I had spent two years working through diplomatic and legal channels to arrange a meeting with him, and that meeting was now set for Wednesday, in two days' time.

We weren't sure what to expect, largely because the United States and Brazil had recently ratified their first mutual legal-assistance

treaty and our case would mark the inaugural joint criminal investigation between the two nations. There were a lot of uncertainties.
We still didn't know, for instance, if we would be allowed to directly question the Brazilian art dealer, and if so, whether he would
be compelled to answer. In many countries, American prosecutors
and FBI agents must put questions in writing or submit them to
local magistrates for approval. I had also heard that it was not uncommon for witnesses in foreign countries to invoke the local
equivalent of the Fifth Amendment and refuse to cooperate with
American inquiries. If that happened here, we'd be screwed, and
probably would be met with scorn by colleagues when we returned
to Philadelphia tan but empty-handed.

I didn't know how the week would play out, but I was quickly
settling in for a good challenge, an away game with mysterious
rules. I enjoyed the uncertainty of it all.

Hall was a seasoned advocate and a fun traveling companion, a
friend. He and Goldman were the two prosecutors in Philadelphia
who shared art crime cases—the three of us met at least once a
week for lunch to strategize. Goldman had been busy with a drug
trial and so Hall had drawn the Rockwell case. A bald, soft-spoken
Yale grad of subtle intellect, Hall was also a commander in the
Navy Reserves and held a black belt in karate. By nature and military and legal training, Hall needed rules of engagement and a clear
strategy. He liked to enter a mission well armed, with a plan.

I turned to him as he fiddled with his coconut. "Stop worrying,"
I said. "This is going to be fun." I surveyed the beach scene again,
my confidence building. "What we'll have to do is treat this like a
UC case, except we won't be working undercover. We find out what
the guy wants and see if we can give it to him. React to whatever he
throws at us. Whatever we need to get it done, we'll do. It'll be
great."

*　*　*

THE ROCKWELL PAINTINGS were stolen on February 16, 1978, only hours after they were feted as the new star attractions at a Minneapolis gallery.

The party, at a gallery called Elayne's in an affluent Twin Cities suburb, was well attended, despite the single-digit temperatures and a half foot of frozen snow on the ground. The owners, Elyane and Russell Lindberg and their daughter Bonnie, mingled with more than a hundred guests, sipping champagne and munching white sheet cake. Dozens of paintings for sale lined the walls, but the star attractions were a Renoir seascape and seven Norman Rockwell originals. The Lindbergs owned two of the Rockwells, a matching pair called *Before the Date/Cowboy* and *Before the Date/Cowgirl*. The two pieces were among the last of the artist's works to grace the cover of the *Saturday Evening Post*. The five other Rockwell paintings were on loan, four of them from Brown & Bigelow, the Minnesota calendar company that had printed the Boy Scout calendars illustrated by the artist for more than a half a century.

The police report on the crime was sketchy: The party wound down around 10 p.m. The Lindbergs cleaned up, carefully activating the alarm and locking up. Then, at 12:50 a.m., a Pinkerton security guard making rounds discovered the back door to the gallery open, the deadbolt punched out, the phone and electrical lines severed. The distraught Lindbergs and police hustled to the crime scene to find the seven Rockwells and the Renoir gone. The invisible thieves left behind two clues: a pair of garbage bags and a size-ten footprint in the snow. Not much to go on.

The early days of the investigation were rich with mostly useless tips, with the public flooding Minneapolis police and FBI agents with leads. The primary focus fell on three unidentified white men said to have been acting oddly during a visit to the gallery on the day of the crime. The scruffy-looking trio hadn't looked like art aficionados—at least, not your typical Norman Rockwell fans—and Russ Lindberg said he'd heard them argue in whispers over the value of the Renoir and Rockwell paintings. As the men left in a dirty white 1972 Chevy Impala hours before the reception, the suspicious gallery owner jotted down their license plate number. The FBI and police put out an all-points bulletin on the car. In a Teletype to headquarters a week later, an FBI agent reported little progress. "Whereabouts of current owner of vehicle negative to date, as it has been sold three times in the past month. . . . Investigation negative for any possible information."

The FBI kept at it. Special agents from FBI divisions in Minneapolis, Los Angeles, Las Vegas, Chicago, Miami, New York, Philadelphia, and Detroit worked dozens of leads. They scoured prison phone records at Folsom State Prison in California, tracked a gang of burglars from New York City making their way west through northern states, and interrogated a Chicago area burglar with a passion for stealing valuable postage stamps.

Over the next twenty years, the Rockwell heist drew intrigue, excitement, and dead ends. The Lindberg family fielded repeated calls from people who claimed to have the paintings. In the late 1970s, an undercover FBI agent and Elayne Lindberg flew to Miami to meet a Cuban art dealer who falsely claimed to know a Japanese diplomat willing to sell a few of the stolen paintings. In the 1980s, a Detroit man engaged in months of negotiations with prosecutors and FBI agents, then suddenly vanished. At one point, a Minneapolis man caused a few hours of hysteria and hope when he called Russell Lindberg, claiming he'd found one of the paintings. But when Lindberg showed up, he realized the man was a fool. What the man believed to be a Rockwell original was nothing more than a $10 canvas print.

By the late 1980s, agents in the FBI office in Minneapolis wanted to forget the case and move on. Insurance companies compensated the three owners for their losses—the Lindbergs, for *Cowboy* and *Cowgirl,* a Minneapolis family for *Lickin' Good Bath,* and Brown & Bigelow for *The Spirit of '76, She's My Baby, Hasty Retreat,* and *So Much Concern.*

Although ownership of the stolen paintings officially passed to the insurance companies at settlement, Bonnie Lindberg continued to pursue all of the Rockwells, conducting her own investigation. She publicly criticized the FBI for dropping the case, and the bureau remained stoically silent. Lindberg spent a decade chasing leads that probably came from con men. Her efforts cost tens of thousands of dollars and earned her nothing but frustration.

But in late 1994, curators at the Norman Rockwell Museum in Stockbridge, Massachusetts, received a curious letter from a man who identified himself as Jose Maria Carneiro, a Brazilian art dealer based in Rio. Carneiro offered to sell *The Spirit of '76* and *So Much Concern,* for "a fair price." The curators declined, but they passed the letter to Lindberg.

The FBI in Minneapolis also received a copy of the letter, but the Rockwell case had long been closed.

THE CASE WAS so old that I didn't even know it had existed when I got a call in January 1999 about suspicious Rockwells for sale in Philadelphia.

George Turak, an honest broker and a longtime source, told me that a Brazilian man had hired him to sell two Rockwell paintings on consignment, *She's My Baby* and *Lickin' Good Bath*. Turak said his research showed the paintings were stolen from Minneapolis in 1978. I confirmed this with a simple Internet search followed by a call to the Minneapolis FBI office, and an agent there briefed me on the heist. He also told me about the five remaining missing paintings. Intrigued, I went to Turak's gallery and seized the two paintings.

Within days, the agent in Minneapolis called back with important news.

It turned out that Bonnie Lindberg had followed up on the 1994 letter from Brazil and that she'd partnered with a local television station, KARE 11, to document her dealings with Carneiro. The two-part exclusive would be running in a few weeks—the station was holding it to air during February sweeps. A few weeks later, after the series aired, I received a tape. For the FBI, it was a public relations disaster.

"Tonight," the anchor intoned, introducing the story, "new information on a case long ago abandoned by the FBI. It's a case where no arrests have been made and no paintings ever found—until now."

Part One of the series recapped the 1978 theft and retraced the family's detective work. "Bonnie Lindberg runs the gallery today," the reporter said, "and she's been the lead investigator in this case after the others walked away, after the FBI gave up, when literally no one seemed to care." The reporter continued, "It's amazing what Bonnie did on her own, following leads on four continents, crisscrossing the U.S. as well, a wild ride of faxes and phone calls. . . . In the last three years, all leads began to lead to Rio, leads the gallery says were rejected by the FBI."

Part Two of the series began with Lindberg unwrapping a large package she'd just received in the mail from Brazil. Inside, she found *Before the Date/Cowgirl,* and she grew emotional as she held it. Next, the cameras followed Lindberg to Rio to negotiate the purchase of the companion painting, *Before the Date/Cowboy,* from Carneiro. During the visit, Carneiro also showed off *The Spirit of '76,* which hung prominently in his home, as well as *So Much Concern* and *Hasty Retreat.* The reporter said of Carneiro, "He says he's done everything properly to purchase the paintings, and that appears to be true. There are certificates from the Art Loss Register in New York and London, verifying that the paintings are not stolen. . . . And while he's willing to let the paintings go, he wants his money back first, three hundred thousand dollars."

The TV report presented a somewhat misleading picture, omitting several relevant facts, including that Lindberg had agreed to pay Carneiro $80,000 for the *Before the Date* pair. Also, because my recovery of the two Rockwells in Philadelphia did not fit the reporter's neat narrative, he mentioned the FBI's role only as a brief afterthought, as if it were nothing. What's more, KARE 11 failed to report that Bonnie Lindberg, so tearful on camera, had already visited New York auction houses, where she'd been told the *Before the Date* pair would fetch her $180,000. (Apparently, Lindberg was unaware that the Elayne Gallery had received an insurance settlement and therefore no longer owned the paintings; in purchasing the paintings from Carneiro, she believed that she was recovering what was rightfully her family's property.)

The February 1999 news series concluded with a flourish— flashing images of *The Spirit of '76, So Much Concern,* and *Hasty Retreat,* juxtaposed with a grinning Brazilian art dealer, the beach at Ipanema, and a reporter's authoritative TV voice.

"So the question remains. What will it take to bring the Rockwells back to their rightful owners? . . . Carneiro knows that possession is nine-tenths of ownership, and he has that pretty much locked away in Brazil—Rockwell, our Boy Scouts and our flag."

ON THE MORNING of September 11, 2001, I was at my desk by eight thirty, flipping through a file of Rockwell correspondence from the FBI agent at the U.S. embassy in Brazil.

It was eighteen months after the KARE 11 broadcast. By then, we had endured more than a year of the kind of diplomatic and bureaucratic delays that threaten every international case, and our Rockwell investigation was entering a new phase. With a new U.S.-Brazil mutual legal assistance treaty in place, the Brazilians had finally approved our request to question Carneiro. Hall and I were making last-minute preparations for a trip to Rio in late September or early October.

A few minutes before nine o'clock, a colleague hustled into the squad room, breathless. "Anyone got a television?"

I plugged in my four-inch black-and-white portable and aimed the antenna at a window. Crowded around the tiny screen, seven of us squinted at the burning World Trade Center, and saw the second plane hit the second tower. Within the hour, a supervisor was ordering us to go home, pack enough clothes to last three days, and stand by for orders.

Donna met me at the door. "How long will you be gone?"

"They say three days, but . . ."

By the next morning, I was on my way to Ground Zero.

I CALLED HALL as I sped up the New Jersey Turnpike, red lights flashing. We knew the Rockwell case would have to wait. Each of us expected to be busy for a while performing our secondary, or "collateral," jobs. He was a commander in the Navy Reserves, assigned to an intelligence unit that specialized in terrorism, and he was guessing he'd be called up soon.

My collateral duty was working with FBI colleagues in times of the greatest mental stress. I was coordinator of the FBI Employee Assistance Program in the Philadelphia division, responsible for the psychological well-being of more than five hundred employees and their families.

It was solitary, sensitive, and confidential work, a job I had volunteered for following my acquittal at the Camden courthouse in the mid-1990s. I tried to help anyone struggling in our office—whether with drugs, alcohol, cheating spouses, difficult bosses, or serious medical problems. Colleagues came to me and unloaded horrific stories—about children or spouses killed, arrested, or dying of some dreadful disease. I did a lot of listening. I wasn't a shrink and didn't pretend to be. My primary credential was empathy. I knew what it was like to face trauma, the death of a good friend, and the stresses of a years-long fight to avoid prison. Hopefully, if nothing else, I stood as an example of perseverance. I could look a desperate person in the eye and honestly say, "Stay strong. The worst thing you can do when you go through a traumatic experience is to lose your faith that you will survive. Have no doubts: It's painful, and that's normal. You will get through this. Whatever you do, do not give up."

I didn't enjoy reliving my own trauma, and I never publicly

discussed the accident. But I volunteered to become the bureau's EAP counselor in Philadelphia because I thought it was the best way I could give back to an agency that had refused to give up on me.

Although the work was fulfilling, there was a dark side I hadn't considered—experiencing firsthand the shock that victims' families suffer. When an agent died, the FBI often sent me to notify the family. At funerals, I was tasked to discreetly escort elderly and young family members. When the Washington, D.C., sniper killed a Philadelphia man, I had to physically restrain a child who erupted in fury when I arrived at his doorstep to deliver the sad news. After jobs like those, I started to see in the victims' families the specter of Donna and our kids.

Witnessing so much death and heartbreak posed psychological risks for an undercover agent. Working undercover is a mental game and you can't let yourself become distracted by fear or emotion. For many years, I volunteered for a program called C.O.P.S. Kids, part of Concerns of Police Survivors, and its participation in National Police Week in Washington, which culminates with a wreath-laying ceremony for fallen officers. One year, as the ceremony wound down, I saw a nineteen-year-old son in a wheelchair and his mother struggling up a hill toward the Washington Monument. I strolled over to help and we began chatting. The young man was a paraplegic, an accident victim. His older brother and father, both police officers, had died in the line of duty in one year. As we moved up the hill, the son suddenly grabbed my arm and began screaming and crying. "Never get hurt! Promise me you'll never get hurt." I held it together until the drive home. By the time I crossed the Maryland-Delaware state line, I started shaking and crying. I never returned to National Police Week. I couldn't take it anymore. When I worked undercover, I couldn't afford to have scenes like that floating in my head.

I arrived at Ground Zero late on the afternoon of September 12.

The FBI had sent me to counsel firefighters, police officers, agents, paramedics, soldiers—anyone who needed it. But when I first arrived, everyone was still busy pulling at the rubble, digging for survivors. So I joined the rescue. I stood in a bucket line, one hundred people long, passing dirt and debris from corners of the World Trade Center foundation.

Eight days later, when the rescue mission officially became a recovery effort and the FBI sent me home, I returned to suburbia. Within hours, I found myself on the soccer field, coaching Kristin and her fourth-grade girls' team, the Green Hornets. I was wearing a new set of clothes, but I could still smell Ground Zero.

I remained in Philadelphia but did not leave 9/11 behind. Every few days for the next year, my FBI colleagues in New York sent me the effects of local victims found at Ground Zero—credit cards, wallets, jewelry, cell phones, driver's licenses, anything that could be identified. As EAP coordinator, it was my job to return them to the next of kin.

NORMAN ROCKWELL, DEAD for twenty-three years, already was making a comeback when the terrorists struck.

The long-held sentiment by "serious" critics—that Rockwell was a mere illustrator, who painted nostalgic caricatures of an innocent, largely bygone America—began shifting in the late 1990s. In 1999, a retrospective of his work, seventy paintings from 1916 to 1969, began a three-year tour to heavy crowds and uncharacteristically rave reviews.

"I think you can put it down to trendy revisionism and opportunism," *Newsweek* art critic Peter Plagens said at the time. "There is also a built-in hipness about liking Rockwell: It goes against the orthodoxy of Modernism. . . . The funny thing is, Rockwell wasn't the cracker-barrel philosopher straight out of *It's a Wonderful Life* we might imagine."

That stereotype was based on Rockwell's earlier work for *Boys' Life* and the *Saturday Evening Post*—saccharine paintings of kids at soda fountains, families gathered around a Thanksgiving meal, Boy

Scouts saluting the American flag, Rosie the Riveter and private Willie Gillis promoting the war effort against Germany and Japan. In the 1950s and 1960s, critics sniffed at Rockwell's precise realism, labeling it banal. "Dalí is really Norman Rockwell's twin brother kidnapped by Gypsies in babyhood," the critic Vladimir Nabokov famously sneered. The term *Rockwellesque* became a pejorative.

The revisionist view that culminated with the 1999 retrospective was that Rockwell was misunderstood, both by critics and fans who wrongly presumed he represented all values conservative. Looking deeper, it turned out that Rockwell was a sly progressive. In an essay that accompanied the 1999 national tour, art critic Dave Hickey argued that Rockwell's art in the fifties helped inspire the social revolutions that followed. He invoked one of the stolen paintings, *Hasty Retreat,* produced for a 1954 Brown & Bigelow calendar. It depicts two young bathers snagging their clothes, high-tailing it past a sign that says, "No Swimming!"

"Rockwell was one of the few creatures in American popular culture in the fifties who actually encouraged disobedience, willful disagreeableness and a tendency to break rules. I don't know if we'd have had a lot of the sixties without the sort of benign permission of Rockwell's images. There's a wonderful painting of a girl with a black eye sitting outside the principal's office, having gotten in a fight and obviously won. It's not hard to imagine her a few years later burning her bra."

After the September 11 attacks, as patriotism soared, so did Rockwell's stock. He was one of America's best-known artists, and a frightened nation found comfort in his well-known idealistic, nationalistic images. As part of a "United We Stand" campaign, advertisements of updated Rockwell images appeared in the *New York Times*. On Thanksgiving Day, the *Tampa Tribune* splashed across its front page a photo illustration based on Rockwell's famous *Freedom from Want,* showing the matriarch of a large American family laying the turkey on the dinner table.

One of the three stolen Rockwell paintings became especially symbolic during that tumultuous post-terror time.

Painted for the Boy Scouts and Brown & Bigelow, *The Spirit of '76* was timed for the U.S. Bicentennial in 1976. The work, one of Rockwell's last before dementia consumed him, is an homage to the famous nineteenth-century painting by Archibald McNeal Willard, in which a fife-and-drum corps from the Revolutionary War marches in front of the American flag. Willard's work, originally known as *Yankee Doodle,* was painted for the Centennial Exposition of 1876 in Philadelphia. In Rockwell's updated version, the fife-and-drum corps are Boy Scouts. And in the background is the unmistakable Manhattan skyline and the twin towers of the World Trade Center— a tiny detail that would later help keep our case alive.

After the September 11 attacks, many good cases, complicated investigations with years of work invested, fell by the wayside. Understandably, the recovery of stolen property, let alone stolen art, became a very low priority for the FBI in the fall of 2001. Like almost every agent on my squad and others, I was assigned to check out the hundreds of dubious and frantic calls, reports of terrorists, anthrax, the Taliban, and Middle Eastern–looking men lurking and plotting in Philadelphia neighborhoods. I did the job quietly and diligently, waiting for the right time to raise the Rockwell case.

My prosecutor partner, Hall, faced different priorities and a looming deadline. He received orders to report to his Navy unit by mid-December and to expect a yearlong deployment. Hall told me that if we didn't fly to Brazil by early December, he wouldn't get to go at all. In late October, he approached his immediate supervisors carefully. Though they'd approved the trip before 9/11, they'd never liked it. They were control freaks who thought the best ideas came from management, from the top down, not from the people doing the actual work. His supervisors also didn't see how Hall could justify a five-thousand-mile flight to solve a case that wouldn't conclude with an arrest. In their view, a prosecutor put criminals in prison; he didn't travel the globe, rescuing stolen cultural property. So when Hall broached the subject again in October, Hall's supervisors, citing new priorities since 9/11, said no. A trip to Rio was out of the question.

Hall called me in a fury. He was thinking about going over his supervisors' heads.

I was equally angry and told him to go for it. I added, "If you don't go to Brazil, Dave, I don't go." He was my partner. I had his back. Hall, Goldman, and I believed we were working together to change the long-held law-enforcement mentality that art crime isn't a priority. To accomplish this, we needed each other.

Hall set up a private meeting with the new U.S. attorney's top deputy, the true brains of the office. Hall gave a five-minute pitch, then pulled out a color print of *The Spirit of '76*. He pointed to the lower right-hand corner and the faint image of the twin towers. The second-ranking prosecutor in the U.S. attorney's office smiled. He was a former Supreme Court clerk, a Bush appointee whose political instincts were as sharp as his considerable legal skills. He immediately recognized the public relations value. If we were successful in Rio, his boss would soon be standing before television cameras with the three Rockwells as backdrop, and the image of the towers.

HALL AND I arrived in Rio early on a Monday that first week in December, and rested up on Ipanema. We unpacked, uncoiled, and enjoyed feasting on two of the best steaks of our lives.

The next day, the FBI agent who worked at the U.S. embassy in Brasília, Gary Zaugg, met us in Rio. He drove us to meet the local prosecutors. The Brazilians were pleasant but not optimistic that we would be able to charge Carneiro. We freely acknowledged that we had an ancient case, thin evidence, and that our best witness, Lindberg in Minneapolis, was uncooperative. The prosecutors made clear that extradition was next to impossible. In Brazil, they explained, flight is considered as natural a right as freedom of speech. There's no crime in Brazil for resisting arrest or fleeing prosecution.

Worse, the prosecutors said, no one seemed to know if Carneiro still held the paintings. The local police had already searched his home and business, and come up empty. Our weak hand grew even weaker.

On Wednesday, we returned to the prosecutor's office to meet the man we'd waited so long to question.

Josc Carneiro was a short, wide man of fifty, with a broad face and thinning black hair that clumped by his ears. He owned an art gallery, a private school, and was the author of books on art and poetry. He greeted us warmly in English and with a hearty baritone. He came alone, showing great confidence.

The Brazilian prosecutors went first. They reminded Carneiro he was under investigation for failure to pay the national property tax for the purchase of the Rockwells. This was a minor crime, a mere financial nuisance, and Carneiro knew it. He shrugged.

Hall tried next, opening with a prosecutor's traditional tack, threatening prison to get what he wants. "You're in a lot of trouble," he told Carneiro. "The evidence is strong. You've admitted you have stolen American property. This is a serious crime in the United States. If we charge you, we'll extradite you, fly you back in handcuffs, put you in an American prison. You'll be there a long time."

Carneiro responded with a throaty laugh. At worst, he knew, a U.S. extradition request would limit him to travel inside Brazil, a country nearly as large as the continental United States. Carneiro swept an open palm arm toward a window and its majestic vista of Rio. "I can't leave Brazil? Welcome to my beautiful prison!"

Hall sat back, done. He had firm constraints. As an assistant U.S. attorney, he needed to tread carefully. Department of Justice guidelines limited what he could say, even in a foreign country. He represented the U.S. government, and any offers or promises he made could be binding—and he was under strict orders to offer no more than a promise not to prosecute.

On the other hand, as an FBI agent I could say anything,

promise anything. My promises were worthless, but Carneiro didn't know that. I could lie, twist facts, make threats—do almost anything except beat a suspect to get the job done. I put on my salesman's hat.

I opened by trying to even the playing field, framing the issue as a geopolitical dilemma, not a potential crime. "Jose, let's see if we can fix this, maybe make it all go away. Let's try to find a way to do that. We get what we want, you don't get in any trouble, and the prosecutors here get what they want. We all look good, everybody's happy. What do you say?"

"I like it when everybody is happy," he said.

It was a start. "Why make it worse, Jose?" I said. "Why pay more taxes? What are you going to do with these paintings? What good are they to you? Are you a Norman Rockwell lover to the point that you want to have these on your walls forever and leave a problem for your children and everybody else? Because you know you can't move them outside of Brazil. And let's be honest, these paintings are far more valuable in the United States than anywhere else. You'd get twice the price for them in the U.S. than here, but that's the one place you can't sell them. What good are they to you, Jose? Why are you holding these pieces hostage against America?"

Carneiro raised a finger. "Oh, Bob. I love America! We're good friends. I love United States. I go to buy art all the time."

"Great, wonderful," I said, leaning forward but keeping my voice friendly. "But I'll tell you what, Jose. If you don't do this for us, maybe we can't do anything to you here, but I guarantee you I'll put you on a list where they'll never let you inside the United States again." It was a bluff. In December 2001, the terrorist watch lists didn't yet exist. "You say you love the United States, but you're holding our art hostage. Norman Rockwell is the quintessential American artist. In my country, everyone knows his work. You're holding one of the patron saints of American art hostage. And you think you're going to make friends doing that?"

Carneiro didn't appear moved by my appeal, but he didn't reject me either. "Let me think about it," he said. We agreed to meet again on the next day.

ON THURSDAY, CARNEIRO opened with an offer.

"Three hundred thousand," he said. "And you promise not to arrest me."

In Europe, it is not uncommon for governments to pay ransom and offer amnesty to recover kidnapped paintings. It's a game the thieves, the insurance companies, and the governments play. No one publicly advertises this, because they don't want to encourage more thefts. But the bottom line is that the museums get their paintings back, the insurance companies save millions on the true value, the thieves get their money, and the police get to close the case. The United States doesn't play this game.

The $300,000 figure set Hall off. "That's crazy," he said. "We're talking about stolen art." The U.S. government would not pay a cent for the Rockwells, he said. Carneiro needed to know he was not negotiating with the deep pockets of the U.S. treasury. "Bob and I are here to help, to be the go-between for you and Brown & Bigelow. You make an offer and we'll run it by them."

While Carneiro considered that, I stepped out to call my contact at Brown & Bigelow in Minneapolis. The call was quick. The $300,000 offer was rejected out of hand and I returned to the negotiating table. We haggled for the bulk of the afternoon—pushing Carneiro lower and lower, ducking out to make calls to Minneapolis. When the price reached $100,000, I began to try to convince both sides that this was a good deal. I told the folks in Minnesota they'd be getting $1 million worth of paintings for $100,000. I told Carneiro he'd be getting enough to wipe out his debt and tax bill and walk away. I gave them both the same advice: "You're not going to get a better deal. At $100,000, you're going to walk away a winner."

Carneiro wanted a letter from Hall promising he wouldn't be prosecuted. "Done," Hall said.

Carneiro stood. "I let you know tomorrow. I call you in the morning."

Late that evening, Hall and I wandered out to the water's edge on Ipanema. We lit Cuban cigars. The stars of the Southern constellations crowded the night sky. We puffed in silence for a few moments.

Hall turned to me. "Well?"

"He's looking for a way out," I said. "Gotta save face, get the tax man off his back, not get killed financially."

"Right, so what do you think?"

I lifted my cigar. "We're playing a hot hand."

ON FRIDAY MORNING, Carneiro called Gary Zaugg, the Brazil-based FBI agent, and accepted the deal. He invited us to pick up the paintings at his school in Teresópolis, sixty miles to the north.

On the two-hour ride out of Rio, we passed mile after mile of shantytowns—open sewers, barefoot children in ragged clothes, corrugated huts that stretched to the horizon—poverty only intensified by its proximity to the opulence of Ipanema. Beyond the city limits, the road wound up into the beauty and mountains of Serra dos Órgãos National Park, a lush land of peaks, rivers, and waterfalls three thousand feet above sea level. We arrived at Carneiro's school, a stucco storefront on the main street in Teresopólis, shortly before noon.

We confirmed Brown & Bigelow's $100,000 wire transfer and Carneiro's assistants brought out the paintings. He shook our hands vigorously, clearly pleased. He insisted that we pose with him for pictures with the paintings. In the photo, Hall and Zaugg stood in front of *The Spirit of '76* and *So Much Concern*. Hall had a smile on his face now, his frown from the beach a few days before long forgotten. I held up the much smaller painting, *Hasty Retreat*.

Carneiro urged us to examine the paintings closely before we left. "I have kept them in excellent condition, you see." We saw that he had.

To consummate the deal, we appeared before a local magistrate for a quick hearing conducted in Portuguese. Zaugg translated. Hall and I had trouble following the proceedings. We smiled and nodded a lot. Ten minutes later, we were out the door with the paintings, headed back to Rio.

"Let's make our own hasty retreat," Zaugg said as we moved to the car. "Let's grab your gear at the hotel and find the first flight out." On the ride back, he called colleagues at the embassy and made the arrangements.

At Galeão International Airport, Zaugg used his diplomatic credentials to whisk us through security and customs with our three oversized packages. At the Jetway, I discreetly approached a Delta stewardess, careful not to spook anyone. Three months after 9/11 most American passengers and crews were still jittery, especially on long-haul flights.

I showed her my FBI badge and explained the situation. "We have to carry these onboard. They can't go in the hold, and we can't stuff them in the overhead racks."

"No problem. We've got a closet between first class and the cockpit. You put them there. They'll be safe."

"Great, thanks. Really appreciate it. But, um, it's a ten-hour flight, and I've got to keep the paintings in sight at all times. Our seats are in coach."

The stewardess looked down at her folded passenger manifest. I could see from her list that first class was only half full. "Official FBI business, right?"

"Official business."

"Well, then I'll guess we'll have to find you seats in first class."

A FEW DAYS later, the new U.S. attorney in Philadelphia, the ambitious Patrick L. Meehan, convened his press conference. I watched

from the back of the room as Meehan stood in front of the paintings before a bank of television cameras and a room jammed with
reporters.

"Norman Rockwell was that most American of artists," Meehan said. "Here is a guy who has really caught the character of the
United States, especially in times of crisis. This is an important case
for the American psyche at this time."

The next morning, a photograph of the U.S. attorney pointing to
the twin towers in the background of *The Spirit of '76* ran in newspapers across the country. Hall saw it in the Washington papers.
He'd reported to duty at the Pentagon the day after we returned.

We'd proved we could take our art crime show overseas. Now it
was time to raise the stakes and try it undercover.

CHAPTER 14

THE PROPERTY OF
A LADY

Madrid, 2002.

THE BRIEFING WAS SCHEDULED FOR 7 P.M., A CONCES-
sion to the broiling June sun.

We filed into a sterile, windowless conference room inside the
American embassy—four FBI agents and four *comisarios*, or supervisors, from the national police force, the Cuerpo Nacional de
Policía. The Americans slid into seats on one side of an oblong conference table; the Spanish team sat on the other side.

On my first undercover mission overseas, I'd traveled to Spain
to try to solve the nation's greatest art crime—the theft of eighteen
paintings worth $50 million, stolen from the home of a Madrid bil-
lionaire, a construction tycoon with close ties to King Juan Carlos.
The case also carried geopolitical ramifications. It was one year after
9/11 and the FBI was aggressively courting allies against al-Qaeda.
With this in mind, FBI director Robert Mueller III had personally
reviewed and approved our op plan.

At the embassy, the *comisario* began his briefing in the clinical
tone of the cop on the beat, a just-the-facts style that masked the
political pressure he surely felt.

"On 8 August 2001, three unknown men broke a window at the

private residence of Esther Koplowitz located at Paseo de la Habana 71, Madrid. This lured the lone security guard outside and they overpowered him. The suspects used his passkey to gain entrance to the second floor. The victim was away and because the residence was being renovated, the paintings were stacked together against two walls. Eighteen paintings were stolen. They are by Goya, Foujita, Brueghel, Pissarro, and others."

The *comisario* flipped the page in his briefing book. "We determined that the guard was involved and that his role was to give information to Juan Manuel Candela Sapiehia, the mastermind. Señor Candela is well known to us. He is a member of a criminal organization run by Angel Flores. They call themselves Casper and specialize in bank robberies and high-end property theft. We have been investigating this gang for eleven years."

I already knew the details of the Casper gang and as the *comisario* droned on, my mind drifted to my son Kevin's high school graduation two weeks earlier. I couldn't believe I'd soon have a kid in college. Donna was thinking about going back to college herself, eager to finish the last credits she needed for her degree. Jeff was a sophomore, Kristin an eighth-grader. Maybe I'd bring one of them to Madrid next time. . . .

The *comisario* held aloft an ugly mug shot and I snapped back to attention. The man in the photo was bald and bug-eyed, bucktoothed with long black eyebrows. He didn't look like much of an art buff. More like a stone-cold criminal.

"This is Señor Candela. Age: thirty-eight. Señor Candela has been arrested seven times. Drug trafficking, falsifying official records, armed robbery."

The *comisario* held up a second mug shot. This man was bald too, but heavier, with a scruffy goatee and hard brown eyes. "Angel Flores. Age: forty-two. Señor Flores has been arrested five times. Drug trafficking, possession of stolen goods, and armed robbery. His last arrest was 22 June 1999 for homicide—not convicted." I did a double-take. Homicide? I knew Flores had a long rap sheet and that he'd bragged about supposed influence with Spanish judges and police, that charges against him seemed to suddenly vanish, but no one had mentioned a murder charge. I jotted this down.

"On 4 December 2001, we searched their homes and the homes of four known associates. We found"—he turned to an aide—"*commo pruebas circunstanciales?*"

"Circumstantial evidence."

"*Sí*. We found circumstantial evidence but no paintings. In February this year, we were contacted by our American friends."

The FBI agent sitting next to me took the cue and stood. Konrad Motyka was a towering figure with bulging forearms, a thin goatee, and a crew cut. He was assigned to a Eurasian organized crime squad in New York.

"OK," he said, "here's what we know: In February, an extraterritorial source"—a foreign FBI informant who lived overseas—"called me to report that Angel Flores had approached him about buying the stolen Koplowitz paintings for twenty million dollars. Flores called my source because the source has extensive organized crime contacts in the former Soviet Union. My source reported that Flores was growing desperate, was short of cash and worried about paying for chemotherapy treatments for his mother, who has cancer.

"All right," the FBI agent continued, "at our direction, my source told Flores that he's located a potential buyer, a wealthy Russian who works with a corrupt American art expert. After many phone calls and a visit here with the source, Flores has agreed to sell the paintings for $10 million, once the art expert authenticates the paintings."

Motyka pointed to me. "This is Special Agent Robert Wittman. He has an extensive background in art and has worked undercover on many occasions. He will use his undercover name, Robert Clay. Flores will expect him to bring bodyguards when he inspects the paintings. I will play one of the bodyguards. The other will be Special Agent Geraldo Mora-Flores, sitting here next to Agent Wittman. We call him G.

"Angel Flores is expecting us to deliver one million euros in cash

and transfer the rest by wire to his bank. Flores may demand rout-
ing numbers to verify that we have the funds in place. We have
placed nine million U.S. in a foreign bank account."

The FBI agent sat and the *comisario* continued. "We have one
million euros, cash, from the Banco de España. For Señor Clay, we
have reserved a suite on the eleventh floor of the Meliá Castilla
Hotel, downtown. We will position agents in the next suite, in the
lobby, and on the streets outside the hotel. One of my officers will
deliver the money to the hotel room. He will be armed. I regret that
under Spanish law, foreign police officers are not permitted to carry
weapons." We knew better than to try to argue the point.

Motyka wrapped up the briefing. "Tomorrow, they're expecting
a call by cell from a man calling himself Oleg. That'll be me."

"You speak Spanish?"

"French," Motyka said. "I don't speak Spanish and from what I
understand, they don't speak English. But we all understand French."

"Which painting will you ask to see first?"

All eyes turned to me. "The Brueghel," I said. *"The Temptation
of St. Anthony.* It's valuable, worth $4 million. It's probably the
hardest one to fake because it's very complex—large and filled with
tiny hobgoblins, wild fires, and satanic images—and because it's
painted on wood and attached to a cradle frame."

When I got back to the hotel, the jet lag hit me hard. Motyka,
fired up but also nervous because he was about to go undercover
for the first time in his career, invited me to dinner. I begged off—
"I'm an old man, I need to be well rested tomorrow"—and went to
my room. I changed, poured a Coke from the minibar, and flipped
on the TV. I found the BBC, the only channel in English. As I drifted
off, I worried how the case was shaping up.

Tomorrow, if everything went according to plan:

I'd be entering another hotel room across town.

To meet a desperate, possibly homicidal gangster eager to close
a $10 million deal.

Unarmed.

Dangling a million euros cash as bait.

Working with an FBI partner in his first undercover case.

Negotiating in French, a language I didn't understand.

Swell.

I WOKE EARLY the next morning and rang up room service.

Stabbing at a plate of eggs, I paged through a stack of seventeen colored prints, pictures of the stolen works I'd downloaded from the FBI's public art crime website: *The Swing* and *The Donkey's Fall* by the Spanish master Francisco Goya. *Girl with Hat* and *Dolls House* by the Japanese modernist Leonard Tsuguharu Foujita. An Eragny landscape by the French Impressionist Camille Pissarro. *Carnival Scene* by the Madrid intellectual José Gutiérrez Solana.

The multimillion-dollar art was as intoxicating as any I'd chased.

Yet something nagged. Something felt different about this case. It was the victim.

For the first time in my career, I wouldn't be risking my life to return works of art to a museum or public institution. I'd be trying to rescue art stolen from a private home. For a lady I'd never met.

Who was she?

I pulled a dossier from my suitcase and opened it.

Esther Koplowitz was an heiress, a tycoon, a philanthropist, and a recluse.

A raven-haired beauty with chestnut eyes, Koplowitz was connected by birth and social status to Spain's royal families. Her slightly younger sister, Alicia, was also a billionaire, and for decades they vied for the title of wealthiest woman in Spain. Together, their story was the stuff of Spanish legend. In business and charitable circles, the glamorous sisters were revered. In the tabloids that chronicled their soap-opera lives, the Koplowitzes drew comparisons to the Carringtons of the American television series *Dynasty*.

The sisters' father was Ernesto Koplowitz, a Jew who fled Eastern Europe to Franco's Spain before World War II and went on to run the cement and construction company Fomento de Construcciones y Contratas, a company he aquired in the 1950s, shortly before his daughters were born. The company was a public works behemoth. Founded in 1900, FCC had laid the tar for Madrid's first paved roads in 1910, won the first contract to collect household trash in Madrid in 1915, and rebuilt bridges and railways blown up during the Civil War in the 1930s. When Ernesto Koplowitz took over FCC in the 1950s, he expanded efforts to win government contracts, in part by hiring executives with connections to the corrupt regime, including the father-in-law of Franco's daughter. FCC laid the first kilometers of modern highway in Spain, built a U.S. Air Force base, and modernized Madrid's telephone exchange. Ernesto Koplowitz died unexpectedly in 1962, after he fell off his horse while riding at the chic Club de Campo in Madrid. He left FCC to his daughters, who were not yet teenagers. A caretaker executive ran the company until 1969, when, to great fanfare, Esther and Alicia Koplowitz married a pair of dashing banker cousins, Alberto Alcocer and Alberto Cortina, and installed them as top executives at FCC. For two decades, the husbands grew FCC dramatically, winning major public works contracts across Spain.

Scandal struck in 1989. Paparazzi photographed Alicia Koplowitz's husband dancing in the arms of the scantily clad wife of a Spanish marquis. Alicia promptly divorced her husband and fired him from FCC. When a second tabloid caught Esther Koplowitz's husband cheating with his secretary, she too filed for divorce and expelled him from the family company. The publicity-shy sisters suddenly found themselves feminist heroes in Spain and majority owners of a $3 billion company. In 1998, Esther bought out Alicia's stake in FCC for $800 million.

By the time I arrived in Madrid in the summer of 2002, Esther Koplowitz was principal shareholder of FCC and an accomplished businesswoman in her own right. The company's annual revenues were approaching $6 billion and it employed ninety-two thousand people worldwide. FCC grew so large it was now one of the thirty-five publicly traded Spanish corporations whose stock price set the Ibex index, the local equivalent of the Dow Jones Industrial Average.

Koplowitz had also become a noted philanthropist. A patron of the arts and the infirm, she started a foundation that contributed more than sixty-two million euros to Spanish charities. She gave fifteen million euros to create a national biomedical research center, and millions more to fund group homes and day-care centers for adults suffering from mental illness and cerebral palsy. Koplowitz and her three daughters enjoyed homes in the country, the city, and at the shore. The white, modern, two-floor penthouse from which the paintings had been stolen overlooked a lovely Madrid park.

UNDERCOVER WORK TAKES patience.

Criminals are rarely punctual. They may show up early to conduct countersurveillance or, more likely, arrive late to demonstrate who's in control. Or forget where or when they were supposed to show up. They're criminals, not bankers. Sometimes they just get there when they get there—whenever they feel like it, whenever they finish whatever it was they were just doing.

This drives most cops and agents nuts. They like to be in charge and are trained to try to control every situation. They take comfort in military precision and punctuality. They like to make a plan and follow it. I learned long ago to play it much looser.

On the morning of our sting, June 19, 2002, I locked my real wallet and passport in my hotel room safe, swapping them for my Robert Clay identification. I met Motyka and G in the lobby and we took a cab to the gleaming Meliá Castilla Hotel, where the Spanish police had reserved the suite in my name. The five-star Meliá rises in the heart of the city's commercial center, not far from the Santiago Bernabéu soccer stadium and Paseo de la Castellana, one of Madrid's grandest tree-lined avenues.

From my undercover suite, Motyka dialed Flores on his cell phone, at 10 a.m., right on schedule.

No one answered. Motyka tried again a half hour later and once more an hour after that. Each time, the call went straight to voice mail. At noon, Motyka dialed again.

He snapped his cell phone shut. "Negative."

The *comisario* in the room frowned. He'd positioned perhaps one hundred officers in plainclothes wandering the lobby and streets outside the hotel. A lot of them were probably working overtime, earning time and a half. I chuckled to myself. Apparently, working a major undercover case in Spain was no different from working one in the United States—sometimes you had to work just as hard to keep your own side calm and focused as you did chasing your targets.

I broke the uneasy silence. "Hey, who's hungry? Should we get some lunch? Walk around?"

"Good idea."

We killed an hour wandering through the shops near the hotel, Motyka gripping his cell phone so he wouldn't miss Flores's call. I found a lovely hand-painted fan, black with red flowers, and bought it for my daughter, Kristin. G found a few souvenirs of his own. We slipped into one of the Museo del Jamón sandwich shops, with large hunks of ham hanging in neat rows. We ordered a couple of sandwiches and bottles of Orangina, and grabbed a standing table in the back, out of the sun.

Motyka glared at his silent cell phone. "I think the Spanish police are ready to pull the plug. What do you think?"

G said, "I don't know. Doesn't look good."

I said, "I think everyone should relax. Give it time." I held up my sandwich, trying to change the subject. "This is great, huh? Wonder if I could smuggle one on the plane for the ride back?"

"Shit," Motyka said. "He's not gonna call."

"Whoa," I cautioned. "These things happen on their own timetable. We gotta give it some time. Don't worry about what the *comisarios* are saying—that this isn't going to work out." I lowered my voice. "Look, buddy, you've got to remember that the Spanish police have their own agenda here. They can't be too crazy about us being here, after working a case for six months, getting nowhere. What's it going to look like if the FBI waltzes in here and solves it in a few days? Now, they couldn't refuse our offer to help—that would look bad—but they're probably going to be pretty quick to shut us down. That way they can say they gave the FBI plan a fair shake. You can't worry about that. What you've got to do is stay positive."

"I don't know."

"Give them a couple of days," I said. "We're offering ten million. They'll call."

Motyka looked glum. "Hmmm."

"Look," I said, "we finish our sandwiches. We walk back. We call again. If Flores doesn't answer, we call back in a few hours. It's all we can do."

"I don't know." He was beginning to repeat himself.

But back at the hotel, Motyka couldn't keep his itchy finger off the redial button—3 p.m., 5 p.m., 6 p.m., and 9 p.m. I began worrying about the repeated calls. Only cops and fools pushed that hard. We had the money. They wanted it. We held the upper hand. The calls made us look desperate. Like amateurs, or worse, cops.

I let Motyka know. He shrugged off my advice.

When yet another call failed—this time around midnight—the *comisario* finally stepped forward.

"I'm sorry, but it's late," he said. "My men have been waiting a long time."

Motyka reluctantly nodded. Suddenly, everyone seemed to be giving up. Some of the FBI agents even started talking about arrangements to fly home. It seemed premature, but I kept my mouth shut. It wasn't my call. As I left for the night, Motyka was still huddling with an FBI agent from the embassy.

I went back to my hotel to call home and say good night to Donna and give my love to the kids, and then grab some sleep.

MY PHONE BUZZED in the early morning darkness.

"Bob?" It was Motyka.

"Yeah, what's up?" I groggily asked, blinking at the alarm clock. It was 6 a.m. What the hell?

He could barely contain his excitement. "I talked to Flores! I tried him one more time after everybody left. And he answered! We got cut off but we spoke three times. He says he's got the paintings. It's on!"

I sat up wide awake. "Dude!"

"Yeah, I know."

I wanted details. "So what was the deal? Why wasn't he answering his phone?"

"Some bullshit. Said he had to go out of town. He says he'll be back this afternoon, and to call at 5 p.m. But bottom line: We're on."

I asked about backup. "The *comisarios*?"

"Sanchez got 'em to agree to give us one more day."

"Great news. I love good news. Nice work, buddy."

We met again in my suite at the Meliá that afternoon. At 5 p.m., we gathered around as Motyka dialed Flores.

No answer.

Motyka tried five more times over the next four hours. At 9 p.m., the *comisario* stepped in and shut down the operation. It appeared, he said, that the Flores gang was toying with the great FBI. These were very good criminals, the *comisario* said, with very good sources. Perhaps they'd gotten wise to the sting. Perhaps they were bluffing all along. Tell you what, he said. We feel bad about this and we've arranged to take you out to dinner tonight. Our treat.

The consolation dinner at the hotel restaurant was grim. What was there to say? We'd be returning empty-handed. The FBI director would receive a full report. We'd wasted a lot of time and money. I still couldn't believe we were giving up so soon. But, keenly aware of the political realities, I didn't say a word.

By dessert, we'd run out of small talk and fell into silence. G poked at the half-eaten flan on his plate. Motyka stared blankly into a full glass of sangria. The *comisario* chiseled a thick wedge of chocolate cake with a spoon. I stole a glance at the newspaper by G's elbow, headlines from the international edition of *USA Today*. "Housing starts soar, lifting economy. Gov. Ventura drops out of the race. Fires rage in the West. Senate tells baseball: Test for steroids. . . ."

Motyka's phone rang, startling us out of our listlessness.

He spoke in French. "*Oui? . . . Oui? Bon, bon. Pas de problème.*" Motyka broke into a smile. "*Vingt minutes? Um, uh, l'entrée du Hotel Meliá Castilla? . . . Mmmm . . . OK, à bientôt.*"

He snapped the phone shut. "We're on again. The lobby. Twenty minutes."

WE WAITED FOR the targets in richly upholstered high-backed crimson chairs in the lobby. A pair of Asian blue and white vases, probably cheap knockoffs, stood behind us. A set of antique locks lined the shelves of a hutch against the far wall. Those, I could see, were real.

Motyka spotted Flores and Candela in the foyer and met them with firm handshakes. They lingered for a few minutes and the FBI agent brought Candela to meet me and G in our seats. Flores stayed about twenty feet away, standing, arms crossed.

To my surprise, Candela spoke English.

He seemed thrilled to meet an American art expert and I seized on this, turning to a technique I call "the decoy." With the decoy, you create a bond by finding a common interest, one that doesn't have anything to do with the case at hand. If I pulled it off, the target would be lulled into thinking he was teaching me something I

didn't know. It was the same technique I'd used when I got Joshua
Baer to teach me about Indian artifacts, when I got Dennis Garcia
to send me magazines about the backflap, when I got Tom Marciano to mail me a copy of the law that says selling eagle feathers is
a crime.

I offered my opening gambit to Candela. "Hey, do you like antiques?"

"*Sí.*"

"Come here, I want to show you something I really like." I led him
by the arm to the far wall and to the display case of antique locks. For
a few moments, we talked about craftsmanship and history.

"They're from Seville," he said. "These locks are famous there."

"Really?" I said, feigning interest.

"If you like, I'll take you to Seville sometime and show you."

"Sure, I'd like that. You could show me which are the best to
buy."

We moved back to the red chairs to talk about the paintings. I
nodded at Motyka and said, "My friend takes care of the money. I
take care of the paintings." Candela smiled at that.

I told him I'd want to see the Brueghel first for verification. He
agreed, but just to be sure we understood each other, I took out my
stack of pictures of the stolen paintings.

"Brueghel," I said, flipping to the page with the painting. "*The
Temptation of St. Anthony.*"

He looked at me quizzically.

"Brueghel," I said again.

Candela studied the paper printout. "That's from the FBI," he
said. "This list, from the FBI."

I caught my breath. Candela was better than I thought. The pictures were indeed from the FBI's public website. I'd cut them out
and pasted them on blank pages, figuring they were just pictures of
paintings. But Candela instantly recognized the sizes and formats
from the bureau website. Apparently, he'd been busy researching
his robbery.

Concealing my terror, I stuck close to the truth. I smiled and said, "You recognize that, huh? The FBI site, yes. Only place I could find all the pictures."

Candela let out a hearty laugh. "Ah, the Internet. Yes, the FBI has best pictures."

I laughed too, trying not to sweat. What a screwup. What a save.

Candela took the stack of images and began thumbing through them, putting a check by the paintings still for sale, an X by the ones he'd already sold.

When he finished, I said, "You've sold seven already?"

"For eight million."

I didn't know whether to believe him. "Nice," I said.

"How about I show the Foujita? It's smaller. Fits in a suitcase."

"No, no," I insisted. "The Brueghel."

"OK, let's go," he said, standing. "I take you to the painting."

We weren't prepared for a rolling surveillance, and I worried the Spanish might move in and ruin everything if we started walking toward the door.

"Whoa, I'm not going anywhere," I said, trying to look as terrified as possible. "You bring me art, I'll look at it. I'm an art professor, not in your business."

Candela smiled, knowingly. He turned to Motyka. "Ah, that's right, he's not a professional like us. He's afraid."

Candela stood. "Tomorrow afternoon, then." We shook hands.

Motyka walked with him to Flores, still standing about twenty feet away. I couldn't hear them, but I presumed they were making the arrangements.

I looked at my watch. It was nearly 1 a.m.

THE NEXT AFTERNOON, in the minutes before Candela arrived in our suite, I dozed off, slouched in a chair.

I woke to the Spanish undercover agent staring at me. "How can you sleep? Aren't you nervous?"

I could understand why *he* was nervous. He was guarding 500,000 euros with a tiny five-shot pistol, toting it to and from a bank vault each day, putting his career on the line each time he took the cash. I said, "Nah, I'm not nervous. Jet-lagged, hot." It was 6 a.m. in Philadelphia; the air-conditioning in our five-star suite was broken. It was 90 degrees, inside and outside.

I wandered over to the window and opened it, hoping to catch a breeze. I stuck my head out. I looked down and jumped back inside. "Yo, G! Check this out!" I motioned out the window with my eyebrows. G ran to look.

Ten stories below, we could see the pool, surrounded by a bevy of topless bathers. G whistled. Motyka took his turn. Our fun lasted only a moment. A supervisor came running in from the surveillance room next door. Cut it out, he said. We're getting this all on tape!

Candela arrived a few minutes later. On time!

"Bonsoir," he said brightly, bearing a rectangular package wrapped in black plastic. He shook hands with Motyka, G, me, and the Spanish undercover agent, the guy with the revolver hidden in his pants.

Candela eyed the open gym bag on the bed brimming with bank notes.

He crossed and dug his hand inside. Instantly, he said, "This looks like only half of it."

"Euros," Motyka explained. "It's easier than dollars."

Candela kneeled on the bed, closer to the money. "It's fine. I can take some bills out?"

"Of course, take your time."

He started to count the money. He pocketed a 20-, a 50-, and a 100-euro note from the bag, saying he needed to check to see if they were counterfeit. I stole a glance at the Spanish undercover officer. I could tell he was thinking he was going to end up 170 euros light.

Finally, Candela finished his tally. He stood and nodded.

Motyka spread his arms and smiled. "I showed you the money. You know we are serious."

"*Oui, mais . . . un moment, s'il vous plaît.*" He took out his cell phone, punched a number, and cupped his hand as he spoke. He moved toward the door, leaving both the money and the package on the bed. "*À bientôt,*" he said. He'd be right back.

The Spanish undercover agent looked at me, confused.

"His package was a decoy," I explained. "He'll be back."

Three minutes passed. Candela returned, huffing, as he lugged a second package in plastic through the doorway.

"Now," he announced. "We can be more relaxed."

For show, I put on a pair of gloves before unwrapping the painting. "This is beautiful, amazing design." I wasn't lying. The fine brushstrokes showcased Brueghel's special skills, the way he depicted movement in pre-surrealist form, naked demons dancing around a cauldron as St. Anthony reads his Bible. Even after four centuries, the colors—magenta, crimson, ivory—remained vibrant. It was truly a masterpiece.

Candela agreed, but for different reasons. "Yes, it's one of my favorites. You can see people fucking. *Il faut jouir de la vie*—one must enjoy life, no?"

He started rambling, talking about the sale of the first set of paintings, sold to a Colombian drug dealer. "They paid in euros, a huge amount of small bills."

I engaged him as I studied the painting in my hands. "Huge quantity, huh?"

"Phew, yeah. They filled the whole back of an SUV."

Everyone laughed.

I walked the painting to the darkest corner of the room.

Candela followed, interested in my examination. "Four hundred and fifty years old," I said, whistling. "Painted on board, not canvas."

Candela nodded. He, of course, didn't have any doubts about authenticity, and seemed to be dropping his guard. "It's good to verify the merchandise because you might imagine that we could be putting copies out there—make ten copies and sell to ten different people." As he hovered, he bragged about his exploits. "I make things happen. I've been robbing banks and taking things from museums for eighteen years and I've never been caught."

"No kidding?" I sounded impressed.

He laughed. "Everyone knows it's me. When the paintings are stolen, they arrest me but don't have proof. The papers were saying it couldn't be me! I could not pull off a job this big. This"—he pointed to the painting—"is the proof and would be the end for me. That's why I was afraid to come with a big painting." He looked around the room and then focused back on me. I was still hunched over the painting. "So," he said, "you are happy?"

"Mmmm."

Candela kept jabbering, and offered to hire me. "You work for me and I'll pay you really, really well."

I kept my eyes glued close to the painting.

He tried again. "I'm going to have four van Gogh and one Rembrandt in September."

This got my attention. "Really? Four van Gogh?"

"I haven't taken them yet." As he said it, I saw the Spanish agent pick up the phone. I inched toward the bed with the Brueghel.

I turned to the undercover Spanish cop and gave the code word. "It's real."

He spoke into the phone.

In seconds, the connecting door swung open and a team in black riot gear swinging automatic weapons roared in. Candela cried out and the men in black piled on top of him, throwing punches into his soft midsection. Shielding the Brueghel with my body, I leaped out of the way and rolled to the side of the bed, yelling, "*Bueno hombre!* Good Guy! *Bueno hombre!* Don't shoot!"

Flat on the floor, I winced as the Spaniards pummeled Candela.

Downstairs, the Spanish police converged on Flores, who was waiting with nine paintings in the back of an SUV. Later, the police would recover the rest of the paintings at the Colombian drug dealer's beach house.

MOTYKA AND G flew home, but I stayed behind to help create a cover story to protect the source.

I would be identified as an FBI agent, but the two "bodyguards" in the hotel room with me—Motyka and G—would be Russians named "Ivan" and "Oleg." In the chaos and confusion of the take-down, the cover story went, the police mistakenly arrested me, allowing Ivan and Oleg to escape. The police planned to leak this story to the local media.

When we finished with the paperwork and cover story, I wandered into the sultry Madrid evening and caught up with Donna for a few minutes from my cell phone. After a few blocks, I found a bench and sat down. I unwrapped a Partágas cigar and lit it.

I puffed and watched a couple stroll by a newsstand. I thought about what tomorrow's headlines might say. I also recalled that Koplowitz had willed the paintings to the state. Someday, these works by Goya, Foujita, Pissaro, and the others would hang in the Prado, the country's most prestigious museum. I felt a calm sense of satisfaction.

I thought about how the case might be received back home. I was sure it would make a splash, both inside the FBI and in the media. The Madrid case would mark a new chapter for me and for the FBI's art crime effort. I could feel it. I was sure that from now on, we could go anywhere, anytime in pursuit of priceless cultural treasures. We could deploy even when the stolen property wasn't American. We could lend a helping hand across oceans and nations— and be welcomed.

I kicked back on the bench, stretched my legs, and soaked up the moment. I sat there until the embers on the fine Cuban cigar singed my fingers.

CHAPTER 15

NATIONAL
TREASURE

Raleigh, North Carolina, 2003.

THE UNMARKED BUSINESS JET PIERCED THE POWDER blue Carolina sky.

The FBI director's plane is reserved for the bureau's most sensitive missions. With a top speed of 680 miles per hour and a bank of secure radios, phones, and satellite connections, the Cessna Citation X can fly the director or the attorney general coast to coast in four hours. It is the jet the FBI uses to scramble its elite hostage rescue team and fly government experts to crime scenes at a moment's notice. On occasion, the FBI deploys the Citation X for the secret rendition of terrorists.

Inside, I sprawled in one of six large leather chairs, sipping a Coke, across from my partner, Jay Heine, and our supervisor, Mike Thompson. The fragile cargo we guarded was strapped to the seat next to mine, snug inside a custom-built three-by-three-foot wooden box. Its appraised value was $30 million. We flew in silence.

A small computer screen embedded in the cherry wood bulkhead projected our arrival time in Raleigh. We were ten minutes out.

In a few hours, we would present our boxed cargo to the U.S.

marshal in Raleigh, concluding a case in which we'd used an undercover sting to recover a seminal document of American history, a parchment stolen as a spoil of war more than a century ago.

Inside the box, we carried one of the fourteen original copies of the Bill of Rights—so valuable because it was the sole surviving copy missing from government archives.

The jet banked gracefully to the left and we began our descent. I glanced out the oval window and spotted the Confederate-gray dome of the North Carolina state capitol, the scene of the crime.

NORTH CAROLINA'S COPY of the Bill of Rights was no "copy."

On September 26, 1789, a clerk of the First Session of the United States Congress took a quill pen to fourteen sheets of vellum. On each page, he crafted in large calligraphic hand identical versions of a proposed "bill of rights," a series of amendments to the Constitution adopted just days earlier by the Senate and House of Representatives. The presiding officers of the chambers, Speaker of the House F. A. Muhlenberg and Vice President John Adams, signed each of the fourteen copies. On orders from President Washington, the clerk sent one copy to each of the thirteen states for consideration. The final copy remained with the new federal government.

The proposal Washington sent to the thirteen states was a working document, one that contained twelve proposed amendments, including the ten amendments most Americans associate with the Bill of Rights—freedom of religion, the right to due process, the right to trial by jury, etcetera. The two amendments that did not make the original cut were administrative, related to congressional pay raises and apportionment.

Remarkably, the twelve proposed amendments fit on a single sheet of parchment thirty inches high.

In early October 1789, Governor Samuel Johnston received North Carolina's copy. Upon ratification of the Bill of Rights by the states, including North Carolina, the ten amendments to the Constitution took effect immediately, without additional paperwork. Thus, the fourteen original copies of the parchment with the twelve proposed amendments became the document we now recognize as the Bill of Rights—the one on display at the National Archives and commonly sold as a souvenir in tourist shops.

In North Carolina, the state's copy of the Bill of Rights and Washington's transmittal letter were immediately treated as historical documents, and a legislative clerk placed them in a strongbox. The records did not find a permanent home until 1796, when the state finished construction of the State House in Raleigh. North Carolina's new capital, like Washington, D.C., was a planned city— ten square blocks that rose from a former plantation and were modeled after the cityscape in Philadelphia. Although the State House burned in 1831, aides hustled nearly all of the records out in time to save them. When North Carolina completed construction of a new three-story, cross-shaped granite State Capitol in 1840, it filed the most important historical documents in the offices of the secretary of state, treasurer, and State Library, and in alcoves next to the State Senate. Generally, these records were folded in half, bundle-wrapped in plain paper, secured with twine, and placed in pigeonhole cabinets with doors. According to the most likely account, the file containing the Bill of Rights was stored in the first-floor offices of the secretary of state, inside a vault, inside a locked box.

There the historic parchment remained, apparently undisturbed, until the final hours of the Civil War.

ON APRIL 12, 1865, three days after Lee surrendered to Grant and two days before Booth shot Lincoln, Sherman gathered 90,000 troops on the outskirts of North Carolina's capital.

At midnight, Governor Zebulon B. Vance locked the Capitol doors and fled on horseback.

He left a letter for Sherman with the mayor: Promise not to sack and burn Raleigh, and Confederate troops will abandon the city.

"The Capitol of the State with Libraries, Museum and most of the public records is also in your power," the governor wrote to Sherman. "I can but entertain the hope that they may escape mutilation or destruction in as much as such evidence of learning and taste could advantage neither party in the prosecution of the war whether destroyed or preserved." The Union troops who received the letter on the city's outskirts made no promises, and the Confederates retreated anyway.

Sherman's soldiers not only ignored the governor's entreaties, they also violated their own rules of war. The occupying forces ran right over Army General Order 100, Articles 35, 36, and 45, as if they hadn't heard about them, which they probably hadn't. Issued by President Lincoln on April 24, 1863, these articles of war marked one of the first modern edicts protecting cultural heritage during conflict: "Classical works of art, libraries, scientific collections or precious instruments, such as astronomical telescopes, as well as hospitals, must be secured against all avoidable injury, even when they are constrained in fortified places whilst besieged or bombed . . . In no case shall they be sold or given away, if captured by the armies of the United States, nor shall they be privately appropriated or wantonly destroyed or injured. . . . All captures and booty belong, according to the modern law of war, primarily to the government of the captor."

The tens of thousands of Union troops who streamed into Raleigh that day commandeered nearly every building, private or public. The Capitol itself did not fare well. Sherman's troops ransacked the Legislative Records Room and soldiers scrawled graffiti on Capitol walls. The Union provost marshal occupied the governor's two-suite office in the building, and hundreds, perhaps thousands, of troops wandered through the finest building in Raleigh, to attend meetings or simply sightsee. "The interior of the Capitol presented a scene of utmost confusion," a soldier later recounted in an unofficial history of one Union regiment. "Bound legislative documents and maps lay strewn about the floor of the library. The museum rooms were in even worse plight."

When North Carolina officials returned months later, they found a mess—and several of the state's most cherished documents, including the Bill of Rights, were missing. A furious state treasurer complained fruitlessly to Washington: "This capture was rapacious and illegal, as I think, and consequently impolitic."

The Bill of Rights, now a spoil of war, had begun a mysterious journey.

HISTORY IS LITTERED with tales of art stolen during wartime.

The Roman Empire famously looted spoils of war, but also was among the first to implement rules to protect cultural heritage: Roman armies were ordered to loot only *spolia,* routine war booty, not *spoliatio,* cultural artifacts such as art and religious objects.

During the Thirty Years' War that engulfed Germany and much of Europe in the 1600s, Protestant and Catholic armies voraciously looted vanquished foes. Protestant troops led by the Swedish king Gustavus Adolphus raided Catholic churches and monasteries throughout Europe, cherry-picking the finest art to fill Stockholm's castles and museums. Armies backed by the Catholic Church proudly brought trophies to Pope Gregory XV, including hundreds of books from the Protestants' famed Palatine Library in Heidelberg. As Napoleon marched across Europe, and as Britain colonized portions of the Middle East and Asia, they took treasures to stock museums in Paris and London.

Adolf Hitler's ferocious war machine ran protection for history's most carefully plotted looting and destruction of Europe's cultural heritage. When German forces began to march across Europe starting with the annexation of Austria in 1938, Hitler's armies systematically confiscated the paintings and statues the Führer coveted and destroyed the art and cultural landmarks that celebrated the races he believed to be inferior. In Poland, Holland, Belgium, Italy, and Russia, Hitler's armies seized tens of thousands of works, including pieces by Rembrandt, da Vinci, Raphael, and Michelangelo. The Nazis were not as successful in France. When they reached the Louvre, they found only empty frames. The French had evacuated thousands of pieces before the invasion; Mona Lisa was wrapped in red satin and secreted away in an ambulance to a remote château in the south of France. At the end of the war, Allied soldiers found forty tons of stolen works, stored in Alpine chalets or hidden deep inside Nazi salt mines.

Art suffered greatly during all of Europe's post-colonial conflicts and civil wars. During the Khmer Rouge wars in the 1970s, thousands of Buddhist temples were destroyed and sculptures looted at Cambodia's finest cultural institution, the Dépôt de la Conservation d'Angkor.

The plundering of cultural treasures in Iraq and Afghanistan demonstrates that the phenomenon continues well into this century. During the 2003 U.S. invasion of Iraq, looters ransacked unguarded museums and hundreds of priceless treasures were lost, many dating to Babylonian times. In Afghanistan from 1979 to 2001, three hostile forces—the Russians, the mujahideen rebels, and the Taliban—pilfered most of the nation's best art and antiquities.

Art may suffer during wartime, but looted spoils are not necessarily lost forever.

One of my favorite such legends is a Philadelphia story: When the British invaded the American capital city in 1777, pushing the Continental Army back to Valley Forge, redcoat officers occupied Benjamin Franklin's vacant house for many months. When Franklin, who'd been in France, returned, he saw that the British had stolen most of his valuables, including a cherished Franklin portrait that had hung over the mantel of a fireplace.

The painting would not be rescued until the early twentieth century, and only by a stroke of luck. An American ambassador to England happened to visit the home of a descendant of a redcoat commander and noticed the Franklin portrait hanging in the library.

In 1906, after years of polite negotiation, the British presented the painting to President Teddy Roosevelt.

Today, the Franklin portrait hangs in the White House.

IN 1897, NORTH Carolina's missing copy of the Bill of Rights surfaced in the most unlikely of places.

Incredibly, an inquisitive newspaper reporter noticed it hanging on an office wall at the Indianapolis Board of Trade building.

The parchment was displayed inside a frame in the office of Charles Albert Shotwell, a handsome and well-respected business-man who ran a grain, flour, and feed service. In May 1897 he wel-comed a reporter from the *Indianapolis News* into his office for an interview. When the curious reporter asked about the Bill of Rights hanging on the wall, Shotwell told him an astounding story that began three decades earlier.

It was the year after the Civil War had ended, Shotwell ex-plained, and he'd gone home to visit relatives in Ohio. He took time to visit boyhood friends in a neighboring town to see how they'd fared in battle.

"I went into one of the stores of the town that day, where I met one of the boys that I had known before the war," Shotwell recalled. "He told me several of his experiences as a soldier, and one was of his being in Sherman's army when it marched thru Georgia to the sea. He told me of that Army going into the City of Raleigh, North Carolina . . . and he was one of a company of sol-diers that went thru the State House and helped themselves to whatever they pleased to take. They went into the Office of the Secretary of State and forcibly took . . . the parchment that is now in my possession. He told me he brought it with him as a Sol-dier out of the state, so it was contraband of war and lawfully his possession."

Shotwell told the reporter he'd bought the Bill of Rights from the solider for five dollars, and the astute reporter knew he had a helluva story on his hands.

The Raleigh newspaper reprinted the *Indianapolis News* story in its entirety, playing it huge. STOLEN HISTORICAL RELIC, TAKEN FROM THE CAPITOL HERE BY A YANKEE, the headline screamed.

Walter Clark, a justice of the North Carolina Supreme Court, became infuriated when he read the story. A Confederate veteran who fought at Antietam, Clark urged North Carolina officials to go after the purloined parchment. The state treasurer tried, approaching Indiana cabinet officers, but Shotwell refused to cooperate and he soon took the war trophy underground.

The Bill of Rights didn't surface again for twenty-eight years.

In 1925, a friend of Shotwell's son contacted North Carolina officials and proposed to sell the document back to the state. "The old gentleman who bought it off the soldier did so in the belief that it was contraband of war . . ." wrote the friend, Charles Reid of Harrisburg, Pennsylvania. "The possessor is a very old man and has treasured this manuscript for the past fifty-nine years. I believe a need of money has prompted him to offer it for sale. I believe he would be disposed to consider and accept any reasonable honorarium . . ." The secretary of the state historical commission wrote back on behalf of the state. Essentially, he told Reid that the man holding the Bill of Rights hostage was a dishonorable possessor of stolen state history. "So long as it remains away from the official custody of North Carolina," the official wrote in a high-minded tone, "it will serve as a memorial of individual theft."

When his father died, Shotwell's son inherited the framed Bill of Rights. He made no attempt to sell it; instead, he and his wife proudly but discreetly hung it in their living room in Indianapolis. When they died, their daughters, Anne Shotwell Bosworth and Sylvia Shotwell Long, secured the piece in an Indiana bank vault.

In 1995, more than a century after its long, strange exile from North Carolina's state capitol, the two Shotwell women took their first steps toward selling the Bill of Rights.

Very quietly, they enlisted an Indianapolis attorney. He is said to have unsuccessfully approached several wealthy and famous collectors, including the likes of Michael Jordan, Steven Spielberg, and Oprah Winfrey. A prominent Connecticut art broker, Wayne Pratt, known for appearances on *Antiques Roadshow,* showed interest. Pratt hired a prominent and politically connected Washington, D.C., lawyer, John L. Richardson, who was a fund-raiser for President Clinton and whose wife was commissioner of the Internal Revenue Service. Pratt and Richardson did not immediately buy the Bill of Rights, but they began to work as discreetly as possible to try to broker it.

In October 1995, Richardson contacted senior North Carolina officials and proposed a complicated deal cloaked in mystery, refusing to identify his clients. He said the price would be $3 million to $10 million, depending upon a set of independent appraisals. In a long fax to the state secretary of cultural resources, Richardson warned of dire consequences if the deal failed or became public. "Please let me emphasize again how important it is that we proceed quickly and with maximum confidentiality. I have no direct relationship with the people who have the article, and there are at least three intermediaries between me and these people. . . . The people insist on anonymity. We are warned they are nervous, and if they believe their identity may be disclosed against their will, they may act in a manner which will not be in any of our interests."

North Carolina officials debated the offer internally, and even quietly approached a private foundation about buying the document. Ultimately, they abandoned the idea, coming to the same conclusion as their predecessors had: The state would not pay ransom for stolen government property. Stymied, Richardson broke off contact with North Carolina officials.

Five years later, North Carolina's Bill of Rights made a brief surprise appearance in Washington.

In February 2000, a woman who did not identify herself called one of the nation's foremost authorities on documents from the era,

Charlene Bangs Bickford, the codirector of the First Federal Congress Project at George Washington University. The caller claimed to have a copy of the Bill of Rights and asked Bickford to take a look. The historian agreed and one afternoon a short while later the woman appeared at the university offices with three men and a large box. Bickford introduced herself and her staff, and found it odd when the four visitors refused to give their names. The visitors unveiled the package and within minutes the scholars concluded that it was likely genuine. But because the parchment was framed and behind glass—and the visitors refused to remove it—they could not view the back to scrutinize the telltale docket information that would reveal which state had received it in 1789.

Bickford asked the visitors about provenance. They remained silent.

"Well," she said, "this document is priceless and at the same time worthless. You can't legally sell it."

Without a word, or even so much as a thank-you, the mysterious visitors packed up the parchment and hustled out, taking the Bill of Rights underground again.

THREE YEARS LATER, in March 2003, I received an urgent call from my Philadelphia colleague, Special Agent Jay Heine.

It was a Thursday evening, an otherwise unremarkable day at work. I was driving home and he caught me on my cell phone.

"You're not going to believe this," Heine said.

"Believe what, buddy?"

Heine said he didn't have all the details but summarized what he did know: The FBI office in Raleigh needed our help, urgently, and it was tied to our home turf in Philly. It concerned the new National Constitution Center, the state-of-the-art museum under construction opposite the Liberty Bell and Independence Hall. The museum, dedicated to celebrating the Constitution and the Amendments, was a private, nonpartisan, and nonprofit venture, and anticipated to become one of Philadelphia's largest tourist attractions. The Constitution Center was backed by powerful politicians, including Governor Ed Rendell and U.S. Senator Arlen Specter. Supreme Court Justice Sandra Day O'Connor was scheduled to preside over the ribbon cutting in just a few months on July 4, and museum officials were still scrambling to make last-minute acquisitions. In recent weeks, Heine told me, the Constitution Center had come across an original copy of the Bill of Rights. The seller wanted $4 million.

I was confused. "Wait—how can you sell the Bill of Rights?"

"Exactly," Heine said. "Look, you need to call this agent down in Raleigh, Paul Minella. He's expecting your call."

I dialed Minella.

He brought me up to date: A month before, a Washington lawyer named Richardson and a Connecticut dealer named Pratt had quietly offered to sell the Bill of Rights to the Constitution Center. Although I didn't know it at the time, the two men were the same ones who'd tried to sell the parchment to North Carolina in 1995. The Constitution Center's president and lawyer had hired an authenticator to examine the document, and this specialist had sent pictures of the front and back of the parchment to experts at George Washington University. These were the same experts who'd examined it three years earlier. The experts there concluded that a docket entry on the back proved this was North Carolina's long-lost copy, looted during the Civil War. When the Constitution Center's president learned that the document was a spoil of war—stolen property—he called the governor of Pennsylvania for advice. The Pennsylvania governor called the governor of North Carolina, who told him that the state would not pay to have it returned. An aide to the governor of North Carolina called the U.S. attorney and got the FBI involved. Moving swiftly—just that morning, the agent in Raleigh said—federal prosecutors in North Carolina had convinced a magistrate to sign a seizure warrant for the Bill of Rights.

Things were racing at light speed in North Carolina, the agent told me, with attention at the highest levels. "The U.S. attorney and the governor here are personally involved."

"OK," I said. "So where is the Bill of Rights now?"

"We don't know." Although the FBI suspected it might be in Pratt's office or home in Connecticut, it was too risky to try a search, he said. I understood. If the agents on the raid didn't find the Bill of Rights in either spot, the people holding it might get spooked and take the document underground again.

I dialed the president of the Constitution Center, Joe Torsella, and arranged to meet him the following morning in the office of the lawyer negotiating the deal for the museum.

That night, the FBI office in Raleigh faxed me eighty pages of documents forwarded by North Carolina state archivists, a century-long paper trail that included the newspaper article quoting Shotwell in 1897, the 1925 offer from Reid, and the 1995 offer from Richardson.

At 9 a.m. the next day, Heine and I arrived at the crimson-carpeted legal offices on the thirty-third floor of a modern Philadelphia skyscraper. A receptionist ushered us into a corner office.

Torsella, forty years old, was a rising political star in Philadelphia, a former deputy mayor and confidant of the governor. He had quarterbacked the campaign that raised $185 million in private funds to build the Constitution Center. His wife was Senator Specter's chief counsel on the Senate Judiciary Committee and she aspired to be a federal judge. Torsella did not hide his own ambition to become a congressman or senator.

His lawyer, Stephen Harmelin, was an even bigger fish. He had graduated from Harvard Law School in 1963, the year Torsella was born, and was now the managing partner of Dilworth Paxson, a white-shoe law firm that represented Pennsylvania's big businesses and power brokers, clients with last names like Annenberg and Otis. The firm's alumni included judges, a mayor, a governor, state lawmakers, and a United States senator. Harmelin was a man who valued his reputation as a tough but honest and ethical negotiator, someone accustomed to success, million-dollar deals, and discretion.

Torsella looked nervous. Harmelin did not.

"How can we help you?" the lawyer politely asked.

I unfolded the seizure warrant and handed it to Harmelin. He looked surprised and put up his hands, making it clear they wanted no part of a crime, and said, "Whatever you need." He asked me if we planned to search Pratt's home and offices, or the offices of his experts and lawyers. "I've got the addresses, if you need them," he offered.

I shook my head. "Too risky."

They stared at me, silent.

I said, "If we execute a search warrant and fail to find the document, the sellers might get spooked and we might not see it again for a hundred years. They've already threatened to take it overseas, you know."

Harmelin and Torsella hadn't heard that. I related the saga of Richardson's cryptic 1995 attempt to sell the Bill of Rights to North Carolina and their mysterious visit to the experts at George Washington in 2000. I showed them Richardson's offer letter, the one with vague threats that the document might be lost if the nervous sellers felt threatened.

Harmelin and Torsella were angry now. They felt duped and worried aloud that the whiff of scandal might somehow taint their great project. It was the perfect time for my pitch: "We want you to help us get it back. We want you to go through with the deal, have them bring the Bill of Rights here to your office, and we'll seize it." I tried to make it sound simple.

Torsella coughed. "You want us to go undercover?"

"Yes. It's the only way to keep it safe and in the country. The only way."

Harmelin stood and led Torsella into the hallway. They huddled privately.

When they returned, they said yes. Before we could get into the details, Harmelin did what any good lawyer does—he called a meeting of more lawyers to discuss contingencies, and they spent an hour coming up with things that might go wrong: What if the document is damaged in a scuffle? Who's liable? What if someone sues the firm for participating in a fraud? What if someone calls the state bar and accuses Harmelin of lying to a fellow lawyer? What if things get out of control or leaked to the press? What if Richardson demands a blanket indemnification clause? Does our firm insurance cover that? What if North Carolina sues the firm? What if . . .

"Guys!" I finally interrupted. "You're just coming up with ways it won't work." I turned to Harmelin and his $200 necktie. "It doesn't matter what you say to Richardson. It's all bullshit anyway. Just say whatever it takes to get him to bring the Bill of Rights to this room. Remember: You won't have to keep any promises you make."

This was a hard concept for a lawyer like Harmelin to digest, and he asked me if I wouldn't prefer to conduct the negotiations myself. I told him it was too late in the game to inject a new player. It might spook Richardson. "I'll play the role of the buyer," I said. "I'll be Bob Clay, patriotic dot-com mogul, eager to donate the Bill of Rights to the new Constitution Center."

Reluctantly, Harmelin got on the phone with Richardson, and spent the balance of the day pretending to negotiate. At first, there was a lot of throat-clearing legal-speak and I could see it pained him to give in so easily. But by late afternoon, Harmelin began to warm to the role. By the end of the final conversation that Friday, Richardson was asking about the benefactor, the person buying the Bill of Rights for the Constitution Center.

Harmelin winked at me as I listened in on an extension in his skyscraper office. "His name is Bob Clay. Dot-com guy. You can meet when you come up here Tuesday for the closing."

When he hung up, Harmelin was ebullient, comfortable enough to tease me.

"Agent Wittman?" he said as I headed out the door with Heine.

"Do me a favor? If you're gonna be an Internet hotshot on Tuesday, find yourself a nicer pair of shoes."

I WASN'T IN the conference room when the closing began.

I wanted Richardson to see familiar faces, get comfortable. So the only people in the room were the three men Richardson had met once before—Harmelin, a rare-documents consultant, and another Dilworth attorney. Inside his jacket, Harmelin carried a cashier's check for $4 million.

I waited in another room with Torsella. My backup, five FBI agents, including Heine, stood ready nearby.

We didn't wire the room for audio or video. I thought it would be too much of a hassle to get permission—recording a sting inside a law firm would have created more worry for the Dilworth lawyers and required layers of approval within the FBI. Besides, Richardson didn't seem like the violent type. If there was real trouble, we'd hear the shouts through the door.

Agents on surveillance reported that Richardson arrived alone and empty-handed. A few minutes later, the agents reported that a courier was on his way to the conference room with a large folio.

I waited a few more minutes and Harmelin fetched me to join him in the conference room. Laid flat on the conference table, beside stacks of fake closing documents, was the Bill of Rights. I made a show of studying it. It was three feet high, written on faded vellum, its texture varying from corner to corner, making some amendments easier to read than others. Considering the parchment's journey, it was in remarkable condition. Right there, on the bottom, I could make out John Adams's neat signature in two-inch-high letters.

I turned to Richardson and pumped his hand. I slapped Harmelin on the back. "Gentlemen," I said, "this is a wonderful day. This will be a great contribution to the National Constitution Center. I'm so pleased to be a part of this." I turned to Harmelin, giving him a reason to leave. "Steve, we need to get Torsella in here. He needs to see this."

The plan was to leave me alone with the document expert and Richardson. With the Bill of Rights essentially secured, it was time to try to make a criminal case. I wanted a few minutes with Richardson, to try to draw him into a discussion about the stolen parchment to see what he knew about its mysterious 125-year journey from Raleigh to Philadelphia. With his mind on a $4 million payday, this would present my best opportunity. I planned to start by asking him how careful I really needed to be, whether there were any marks on the document that would prove it was North Carolina's stolen copy.

I never got the chance.

As Harmelin left the room to get Torsella, he bumped the door to the office where my colleagues waited. They took it as a signal to move in, positioning themselves between the Bill of Rights and everyone else. Thompson, our squad supervisor, handed Richardson the seizure warrant.

"Am I under arrest?" he said.

"Oh, no," I said, trying to reassure him. I walked him quietly toward a corner.

"What's this all about?" he said.

At that point, with my cover blown, I felt compelled to tell the truth. "We're conducting a criminal investigation into an allegation of interstate transportation of stolen property," I said. "The document is now evidence."

As I feared, Richardson now refused to talk.

"Can I leave?" he said.

"Yes," I said. I didn't have a reason to detain him. We had no evidence that he knew the Bill of Rights was stolen property. "But first I've got to give you a receipt for the document."

"You've got to be kidding."

"Nope," I said. I took out a standard Department of Justice receipt for seized property, a form I'd filled out dozens of times in my career. As I wrote the words—"Description of item: Copy of United States Bill of Rights"—the history of the moment caught up with me. I thought back to my first day at the FBI Academy, when I took an oath to protect and defend the Constitution and the Bill of Rights. I'd always assumed I'd pledged to defend the ideals, not the actual documents.

Richardson was stammering at me, but I was lost in the moment and didn't hear what he said.

I just handed him his receipt.

He straightened his tie and walked out the door.

WE RECEIVED SUCH great publicity when we announced the Bill of Rights rescue, Headquarters didn't hesitate when we asked to use the FBI director's jet to fly the parchment home.

The flight to Raleigh was scheduled for April 1. That it was April Fool's Day was a coincidence, but it certainly made it easier to pull off our gag.

Before we left, I stopped by the touristy gift shop at the Independence Mall Visitor's Center and bought a souvenir copy of the Bill of Rights for $2. Then I went to a drugstore and bought a two-by-two-foot piece of poster board and some superglue. Heine and I mounted the fake Bill of Rights onto the board and slipped it inside the custom three-by-three-foot box holding the real Bill of Rights, which was held inside a special protective plastic sleeve.

When we touched down in Raleigh, four local FBI agents met us at the airport and drove us to their suburban office. The conference room was already jammed with agents, prosecutors, and marshals. We teased our audience by making a show of the official paperwork documenting the transfer of evidence. People started getting impatient.

"Oh, I'm sorry," I said. "Do you want to see it first?"

Of course they did. Heine started to open the box and I shifted strategically in front of him to shield our sleight of hand. He took out the fake Bill of Rights, started to hold it up—and fumbled it to the floor.

"Oops," I said as Heine bent over. "Geez."

I heard a slight gasp, and as I looked up, Heine gave it his best Three Stooges stumble, clumsily stepping on the damn thing, twisting the cardboard.

On cue, I screamed, "Oh my God!"

We heard more gasps and saw a supervisor's eyes bulge.

We waited a beat, then bust out laughing.

The Raleigh supervisor did not laugh with us.

Gingerly, we withdrew the real of Bill of Rights, laid it on the table, and signed it over to the U.S. marshal.

My parents, Robert A. Wittman and Yachiyo Akaishi Wittman, met when my father was stationed in Japan during the Korean War. When I was a toddler, we moved to Baltimore, where I sometimes felt the sting of racism against my Japanese mother and grew to idolize the FBI as protectors of civil rights.

In 1988, I finally realized my dream of becoming an FBI agent. At the Academy, I was a fish out of water, a thirty-three-year-old former newspaper publisher surrounded by macho ex-cops and former soldiers.

The theft of Rodin's *Mask of the Man with the Broken Nose*, the sculpture that helped inspire the Impressionist movement, launched my career in art crime.

The tragic death of my friend Special Agent Denis Bozella, and my five-year battle to clear my name, became a major turning point and was key in my decision to dedicate my career to battling art crime.

The theft of the world's second largest orb, which once belonged to the Dowager Empress Cixi, had baffled curators and investigators for years. My mentor in Philadelphia, Special Agent Robert Bazin, and I recovered the crystal ball in the most unlikely of places.

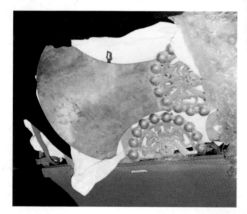

My first major undercover case, the rescue of an ancient Peruvian king's golden body armor looted from a royal tomb, signaled the start of something big. The recovery made international headlines, shocking FBI supervisors who figured no one cared about art crime.

Most art and antiquities thieves don't look much like Pierce Brosnan or Sean Connery. Rather, they look like George Csizmazia and Ernie Medford, the electrician and custodian who systematically stole more than $2 million worth of Revolutionary War and Civil War relics from a Philadelphia museum.

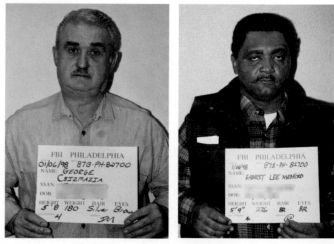

Because most museums can't afford to take routine inventories, they don't always know what's been stolen. In this case, the museum first thought they were missing only four swords and rifles. In Csizmazia's home, we found nearly two hundred stolen pieces.

Assistant U.S. Attorney Robert E. Goldman, who liked to call himself a frustrated history professor, was a kindred spirit. Despite the wishes of some narrow-minded supervisors at the Justice Department, he was willing to work with me on tough, esoteric cases—even when the unstated goal of an investigation wasn't an arrest, but the rescue of a stolen piece of art.

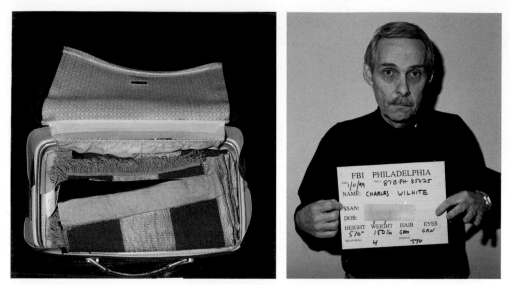

During an undercover sting at an airport motel, Charlie Wilhite, a callous Civil War collector and wheeler-dealer, brought me a near-sacred piece of African American military history. From a carry-on suitcase, he lifted the frail battle flag of the 12th Regiment Infantry, Corps D'Afrique—one of the first units of black soldiers to fight for the Union.

FBI Director Louis Freeh, Civil War reenactors, and fellow agents returned the battle flag to the U.S. Army's chief of military history during a ceremony at FBI headquarters. It was an emotional moment for me: I couldn't help but think about my parents—my dad and his military service, my mom and the racism she faced.

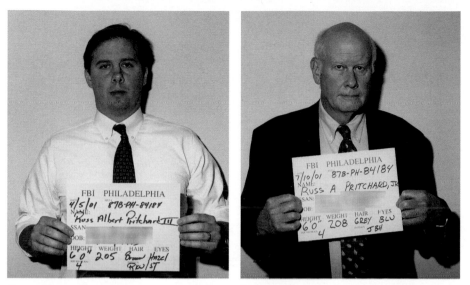

Russell Pritchard III, a preppy con man from Philadelphia's Main Line, swindled countless descendants of genuine war heroes. The investigation into his crimes became one of the longest of my career and singed the reputation of the beloved PBS program *Antiques Roadshow*. Sadly, Pritchard dragged his father, a respected former museum director, down with him.

In the patriotic months that followed the 9/11 attacks, Assistant U.S. Attorney David Hall (at far left) and I traveled to Rio de Janeiro to rescue three paintings by American icon Norman Rockwell, one of which, *Spirit of 76*, depicted Boy Scouts with the World Trade Center towers in the distance. Hall and Special Agent Gary Zaugg helped me negotiate the paintings' return from the shrewd Brazilian art dealer Jose Carneiro (at far right).

On my first international undercover case, I traveled to Madrid to try to solve Spain's greatest art crime—the theft of eighteen paintings worth more than $50 million, including the Goya painting *The Swing*. Hours before I met the chief perpetrator, I learned that he'd recently beaten a murder rap, and that the Spanish police wouldn't let me carry a gun when I met with him.

In 2003, I engineered an undercover sting to rescue one of the original copies of the Bill of Rights, handcrafted at the U.S. Capitol in 1789. Looted by Union troops from the North Carolina capitol building archives in 1865, the document had been lost for more than a century.

Facing a nervous Iraqi thug in a tiny Danish hotel room, I laid $245,000 in cash on the bed—payment for a Rembrandt worth $35 million and stolen at gunpoint during one of history's most brazen museum robberies. The bust was perhaps the FBI Art Crime Team's greatest achievement. It certainly garnered us the largest headlines.

In 2005, thanks to our high-profile successes, the FBI created a national, rapid-response Art Crime Team. I was named senior investigator and began to train young agents.

In 1990, two thieves dressed as policemen outwitted a pair of hapless guards at the Isabella Stewart Gardner Museum in Boston, stealing eleven paintings worth an estimated $500 million. By the time I received a credible tip in 2006 and went undercover in pursuit of the paintings, the Gardner theft represented not only the world's largest unsolved art crime but also the largest single robbery of *any kind* in the United States.

Theft Of Art From The Isabella Stewart Gardner Museum - Boston, Massachusetts
March 18, 1990

Rembrandt: The Storm on the Sea of Galilee

Vermeer: The Concert

Rembrandt: A Lady and Gentleman in Black

Manet: Chez Tortini

Flinck: Landscape with an Obelisk

Degas: La Sortie du Pelage

Degas: Program for an Artistic Soiree, Study 1

Degas: Program for an Artistic Soiree, Study 2

Degas: Cortege Aux Environs de Florence

Rembrandt: Self-Portrait

Degas: Three Mounted Jockeys

Napolean Eagle

Chinese Bronze Beaker or "Ku"

Any Information Contact:
SA Geoffrey J. Kelly
Federal Bureau of Investigation
Suite 600, One Center Plaza
Boston, Massachusetts 02108
(617) 742-5533

To ingratiate myself with a group of French mobsters offering
to sell the Gardner paintings, I set up a fake black-market deal
aboard a yacht near Miami. The man with me here is the
Marseille career criminal I knew as Sunny, who seemed
unnerved by all the attention undercover female FBI agents
gave him. Soon, his associates would threaten to kill me.

By 2008, the FBI was not the same agency I'd joined twenty years earlier. I took
my retirement and began an art-recovery and -security consulting business with
my wife, Donna, and our sons, Jeffrey and Kevin, and as always, drawing
inspiration from my mother, Yachiyo. My daughter, Kristin, a college student,
is already spending her summers working for museums.

CHAPTER 16

ART CRIME TEAM

Merion, Pennsylvania, 2005.

STANDING BEFORE A DOZEN FBI AGENTS AND SUPER-visors in the expansive main gallery at the center of the Barnes Foundation's museum, I pointed to a towering modern painting of a man and woman carrying flowers.

"This is *The Peasants*," I said. "It's a Picasso, very modern, but it has definite influences from Michelangelo. See the feet and the toes? The sinewy arms? The muscular legs? It's heroic."

Fourteen years after my yearlong class at the Barnes, I was returning to help with a daylong training session designed for agents from the FBI's newly formed Art Crime Team.

"Each gallery you'll see today is a classroom," I told my FBI colleagues. "The four walls in each gallery are your blackboards. They are the lesson plans. Each teaches us something about light, line, color, shape, and space. By the way, in this room alone, you're probably looking at a billion dollars' worth of art."

My pupils looked overwhelmed. Few agents knew much about art, and the dollar figures could be unsettling. "Don't be intimidated by what you see," I said. "We're not here to learn how to spot a forgery or know the value of this painting or that painting.

You'll learn that when or if you need to. We're here today to learn the basics. We're here to train your eye. To learn to see."

The group crowded into the second gallery. I swept my arm toward a cluster of paintings and said, "What's amazing here in this one gallery is that you look at this wall, and here's a Cézanne, there's a Cézanne, and another and another—Cézanne after Cézanne. They've got seventy of them in this museum, folks."

I stepped in front of a Renoir portrait. "Look at the color. Look at the palette, the shape of the people, and how it's done. See that? Now, look at the Cézanne. See how he paints the folds, the creases in the tablecloth? That's one of the hardest things to do. Compare the palettes: Renoir is rose, bright blue, cream, flesh tones. Cézanne is dark green, purple, violet, muted tones."

The group walked into the next gallery. "Now, in this room, can you tell which one is the Cézanne and which is the Renoir?"

The emboldened students began throwing out answers, and I could not have been prouder. I was no longer the sole FBI agent who cared about art crime.

THE FBI'S COMMITMENT to art crime was entering a new era. The creation of the Art Crime Team marked a great leap forward for the Bureau—and a natural progression from our successes following the high-profile Rockwell, Koplowitz, *Antiques Roadshow*, and Bill of Rights cases.

The FBI had assigned eight agents scattered across the country to the Art Crime Team, and I was named senior investigator. The agents would not work art crime full-time as I did, but they would take cases as they developed in their regions, and would be prepared to deploy rapidly. The FBI's new commitment did not compare to the Italian art crime effort—the Carabinieri force numbered three hundred. But it was a start.

Gone, or so it seemed, were the days when the FBI would get by with one or two agents who expressed an interest in art crime—

when an agent like Bob Bazin would handle cases, then informally pass the mantle to someone like me. Historically speaking, I knew of only two other FBI art crime experts beside Bazin and both had worked in New York. In the sixties and seventies, it was Donald Mason, probably best known for his recovery of a stolen Kandinsky, and in the seventies and eighties, Thomas McShane, who once recovered a stolen van Gogh in the carport of a New York gas station.

To bolster the new Art Crime Team, the Department of Justice provided a team of prosecutors—one of whom was Bob Goldman. They were granted special authority to prosecute art crime cases anywhere in the country. With great fanfare and a series of public events, the FBI unveiled an Art Crime Team website, a logo, and even created special souvenir coins. The press exposure and the accolades kept piling up. Just before the Art Crime Team was officially launched, I was awarded the Smithsonian Institution's highest honor for the protection of cultural property, the Robert Burke Memorial Award. Two years later, Goldman won the same honor. While we welcomed media coverage, I was careful to keep my identity secret so I could continue to work undercover. I never let photographers take my picture and I always remained in the back of the room, out of view, during press conferences. Whenever I appeared on television, I did so with my face blacked out.

In the months after the Art Crime Team's formation, we kept busy with smaller cases, using each to raise our profile. In Pennsylvania, I recovered eight Babylonian stone signature seals purchased by a U.S. marine as souvenirs at a flea market near Baghdad, the first such FBI case of recovered Iraqi artifacts in the United States. In a St. Louis hotel-room sting, I arrested a fake Arab sheik who tried to sell me a forged Rembrandt for $1 million. In a federal courtroom in Philadelphia, Goldman and I squared off against two antiques dealers who defrauded a wealthy collector during the sale of historic Colt revolvers.

Perhaps most important to our cause, we gained two earnest

and well-placed advocates at Headquarters in Washington. The first was Bonnie Magness-Gardiner, a veteran State Department cultural property analyst with a Ph.D. in Near Eastern archaeology. She became the Art Crime Team's program manager. Magness-Gardiner was well-versed in the ways of Washington and international diplomacy and, as it happened, was the spouse of an accomplished artist. She ably spearheaded our public outreach and education efforts and played an advisory role during investigations.

The second boost came when Eric Ives, a forward-thinking supervisor with a strong background in a wide range of property crimes, was named chief of the Major Theft Unit, the section that supervised the Art Crime Team. Ives asked me to visit him in Washington his first week as unit chief. I met him in a windowless office on the third floor of the J. Edgar Hoover Building, and in minutes I knew we would become good partners, despite the differences in age and experience. He was a former U.S. Marine with close-cropped sandy hair and intense green eyes, eager for action. Before Ives joined the FBI, he had worked for the Target retail store chain, chasing thieves who targeted bulk shipments. As an FBI agent in Los Angeles, he went after the same kind of thief, and came up with a marketing gimmick that helped catch a few. To solve the crimes, he posted pictures of wanted thieves on highway billboards, figuring this was a great way to get the photos in front of the most likely witnesses, truckers. Ives and I soon found that we shared a passion for property theft and a knack for taking chances that paid off.

In Washington, Ives came up with another novel approach. He proposed to aggressively promote—in effect, market—the Art Crime Team, raising awareness inside and outside the FBI. "The Bureau has thirteen thousand agents and we have fewer than a dozen working part-time on art crime," he said to me. "We need to exploit two things we have working to our advantage—one, the notion that the FBI was founded in 1908 to stop the interstate transport of stolen property, and two, this romantic allure of art crime, the Hollywood view, as projected by *The Thomas Crown Affair* and *National Trea-*

sure." He knew that the Hollywood version was a caricature, but believed we could leverage the misconception to our advantage. In our first marketing venture, Ives, Magness-Gardiner, and I drew up a Top Ten Art Crimes list. Written in the style of the FBI's Ten Most Wanted, our list generated a nice, moderate wave of publicity. I liked Ives's style; for a supervisor, he didn't think like a bureaucrat. All the better, my new boss was a fellow salesman.

Ives and I spoke nearly every other day, and he traveled as my handler on my undercover cases, watching my back, a rare role for such a senior supervisor. Traditionally, unit chiefs at Headquarters stuck to administrative and supervisory duties and rarely ventured into the field. But Ives took a special interest in art crime. My direct supervisor in Philadelphia, Michael Carbonell, was wise and secure enough to let me work independently and with Ives. It wasn't always easy for Carbo—his bosses in Philadelphia, who paid my salary, were always pestering him to ask where I was and what I was doing, and how the hell art crime was relevant to the local division's mission. A legendary fugitive hunter and no-bullshit supervisor, Carbo shared my work credo: Just get the job done and the office politics will take care of itself.

By the fall of 2005, with support from Carbo, Ives and I were ready to cut our ambitions loose.

And we aimed high.

CHAPTER 17

THE OLD MASTER

Copenhagen, 2005.

"IS IT ALL THERE?"

The Iraqi counting stacks of $100 bills on the narrow Danish hotel bed didn't answer or even look up. So I asked again. "All there?"

Baha Kadhum grunted. He didn't lift his eyes. He just kept flipping through the inch-high piles of cash I'd brought him, $245,000 neatly arrayed on a rumpled white bed sheet. In exchange, Kadhum had promised to bring me a stolen Rembrandt worth $35 million. Presumably, one of his colleagues held it downstairs or just outside the hotel. It was always possible the thug would offer a forgery—or worse, rob me. I kept my eyes on his hands.

Kadhum looked younger than his twenty-seven years, certainly younger than I had expected. Olive-skinned, with an aquiline nose and a mound of tousled black hair, he wore tight jeans, a pink polo shirt, black buckled leather shoes, and a gold chain around his neck. I doubted he was armed, but I took him for an amateur—desperate, and worse, unpredictable.

Kadhum believed that I was an American mobster, or at least some sort of art expert working for the mob. As a vouch, the father of one of his good friends had introduced us. The father, Kadhum believed, could be trusted because he'd hidden a stolen Renoir painting for their gang near Los Angeles for several years. But Kadhum remained wary, and for this reason I could not take the precautions I had taken in Madrid, insisting that I meet the bad guy with three "bodyguards." On the Copenhagen job, I was working alone and unarmed.

The missing masterpiece was tiny, a four-by-eight-inch Rembrandt self-portrait painted in 1630 at age twenty-four. One of the few the artist crafted on gilded copper, the painting glowed as if backlit. Still, *Self-Portrait* remains a sober piece. Young Rembrandt wears a dark cloak, a brown beret, and a half-smile as inviting and mysterious as the *Mona Lisa*'s. Once a centerpiece of the collection at the Swedish National Museum in Stockholm, *Self-Portrait* had vanished five years earlier, during one of the largest and most spectacular art heists in history.

THE WELL-EXECUTED THEFT began three days before Christmas, 2000.

About a half hour before the 5 p.m. closing time, a gang of six, possibly eight, Middle Eastern men spread out across Stockholm. It was already dark, the winter Scandinavian sun having set by mid-afternoon; sub-freezing temperatures kept most roads and sidewalks slick with packed snow and ice. The museum lies at the end of a short peninsula accessible only by three central Stockholm streets, and the thieves used this to their advantage, creating a set of barriers to cut it off from the rest of the city. On the first of the three streets, a gang member set a parked Ford on fire, creating a scene that drew the police, the fire department, and dozens of curious residents. On the second street, a gang member set a Mazda afire, drawing more fire trucks. To block the third road, the thieves laid spiked tire strips. Along the river at the museum's edge, two gang members quietly docked an orange fifteen-foot getaway boat.

A few minutes before closing, three men wearing hoodies—one carrying a machine gun, the others pistols—burst through the

gallery's double glass-door entrance. They ordered guards and patrons to the floor.

"Stay calm," the man with the machine gun said in Swedish.
"Stay quiet and you won't be hurt."

As one gunman held a handful of tourists, guards, and docents at
bay, the others vaulted up the museum's grand marble staircase to the
second floor. The thieves turned right and pushed through a set of
double doors, past marble sculptures and oil-on-canvas paintings. One
headed straight for the Dutch Room and Rembrandt's postcard-sized
Self-Portrait. The other hit the French room and selected two Renoirs
from 1878—*Conversation with a Gardener* and *Young Parisian*.

Each thief pulled clippers from his pocket, snipped wires holding the frames to the walls, and stuffed the paintings into large
black duffel bags. The three paintings were among the smallest in
the museum—and that made them among the easiest to carry away.
Together, they were worth an estimated $40 million. The men scur-
ried back down to the lobby, rejoined their colleague, and ran out
the front door. The entire robbery took just two and a half minutes.
The three men, each carrying a stolen treasure across the icy street,
turned left and ran for the waterfront, where they met their moored
boat and roared away. The police, stuck in traffic caused by the di-
version, didn't arrive until 5:35 p.m., a good half an hour after the
thieves left the dock.

THE THEFT OF *Self-Portrait* and the Renoirs bruised not only the
international art world, but also Swedish pride. The National Museum, a city landmark and model of Florentine and Venetian architecture that opened in 1866, held four centuries' worth of European
treasures, many of them collected by the enlightened King Gustav III.

The Swedish police began their investigation with one big clue:
During the robbery, another boater saw the three thieves dart down
the dock and jump into their getaway boat. Their hurry, particularly
in such icy conditions, caught the boater's curiosity. Quietly, the

witness followed the getaway boat as it sped across the Norrström River and snaked into a canal about a mile away. He found the orange boat abandoned by a small dock, still rocking in its own wake.

The witness called police, and a picture of the boat was published in the next day's newspapers. Within twenty-four hours, a man came forward to say he'd sold the orange boat for cash a few days earlier. The buyer had used a fake name but made the mistake of giving the seller his real cell phone number. Police traced the cell phone's logs and this led them to a crew of small-time suburban crooks.

Using phone wiretaps and surveillance, Swedish police were able to identify most members of the gang. In a quick sweep, they arrested a native Swede, a Russian, a Bulgarian, and three Iraqi brothers. In a search, police found Polaroid pictures of the missing works— blackmail-style photographs of the paintings next to recent newspapers. They did not find the actual paintings. Although a Swedish court convicted one man and sentenced him to several years in prison, the paintings remained at large.

A year later, underworld sources in Sweden tipped police that someone seemed to be trying to sell one of the Renoirs on the black market. The police set up a sting in a Swedish coffee shop and recovered *Conversation with a Gardener*. From my base in Philadelphia, I was pleased to read of the arrest. But for the next four years, no one in law enforcement heard a word about the other Renoir or the Rembrandt.

Then, in March 2005, I got a call from the FBI art crime investigator in Los Angeles, Chris Calarco.

"I'm not sure what we have yet, or if this is anything, but I wanted to give you a heads-up," he said. "A couple of guys on a wire out here heard something."

"Yeah?"

"They think the subject might be trying to sell a Renoir."

"What do we know about him?"

"Bulgarian. Here illegally since at least the 1990s. Moved here from Sweden, I think."

Sweden. "I'll be damned," I muttered to myself, and then I asked Calarco, "Is the painting he's trying to sell *Young Parisian?*"

Calarco said he would check and I filled him in on the 2000 Stockholm heist. He called back a week later. Yes, he said. It was *Young Parisian*. The target not only mentioned the painting by name, but he also seemed to speak regularly with a son still living in Stockholm. The target's name was Igor Kostov, and he was suspected of dealing drugs and fencing stolen goods. He was sixty-six years old, an illegal East European immigrant living near Hollywood, worked at a pawnshop, and almost always wore a Members Only windbreaker that covered his sagging stomach. Kostov was a former boxer, an occupation confirmed by his flat nose and forehead scars.

On the wire, Kostov spoke in rapid-fire, staccato sentences laced with his thick Bulgarian accent, and the agents found his incessant bragging amusing. I asked Calarco to thank the agents for their patience on the wire, for being smart enough to recognize the clues that suddenly transformed their case from a run-of-the-mill drug investigation into an international art rescue.

This can't be overstated. Most people don't realize that working a wire is grunt work. Wiretaps can provide phenomenal tips and evidence, but the reality is that recording them is a tedious task, far less glamorous than portrayed in the movies or hour-long episodes of *The Wire* or *The Sopranos*. Wiretaps require hours, weeks, and often months of patience, waiting for calls, staring at a computer screen, typing notes, trying to string together snippets of conversations, interpreting code words, waiting for the bad guys to slip up and say something stupid. In the United States, unlike most other countries, the job is incredibly time-consuming because agents can't simply record every call, then retrieve them all at the end of the day. To protect civil liberties, agents must listen to all calls *live* and record only those portions of a call that are relevant to the case. Thankfully, the case agents, Gary Bennett and Sean Sterle, had been paying attention when Kostov began talking about the Renoir.

Bennett and Sterle reported that Kostov was offering to sell the painting for $300,000 and a sale appeared imminent. The FBI faced a swift decision: Keep the drug investigation going or save the painting. It was not a difficult decision.

The agents rushed to stake out his house. A few hours later, Kostov came out carrying a square package about the size of the Renoir and put it in his trunk. As he walked to the car door, the agents moved. They cut Kostov off and ordered him to the ground. They asked to see the package in the trunk. Sure, he said. The excited agents popped the trunk and pulled the package out. Inside, they found dry cleaning. Kostov laughed.

Unamused, the agents took Kostov back to the FBI office for questioning. They sat him down in a windowless room and latched one of his handcuffs to a ring bolted to the top of the Formica interrogation table. They grilled him about the drugs, the stolen goods, and the painting.

The Bulgarian professed innocence and played tough guy. Sterle and Bennett persisted: They calmly explained that they had hours of wiretaps. They told Kostov he faced ten years in prison. He'd get out when he was seventy-seven, if he lived that long. Once they had him sweating, the agents used a standard police interrogation tactic—they gave him an "out," a way to stay out of prison. They promised that if he helped the FBI find the painting, they would urge the judge to go easy on him. The first step is yours, the agents told Kostov. Tell us where the painting is.

Kostov melted slowly, like an ice sculpture in the L.A. heat. Ultimately, he admitted that his son had smuggled the Renoir to him from Sweden to sell on the American black market. Kostov sent the agents to a pawnshop, where they found *Young Parisian* hidden against a dusty wall, wrapped in towels and grocery shopping bags. The Renoir had a slight superficial scratch but otherwise looked OK.

We were thrilled but kept the recovery secret. We planned to use Kostov as our vouch to try to rescue the remaining missing painting, the Rembrandt.

We asked Kostov to call his son and say that he'd found a buyer willing to purchase the Renoir *and* the Rembrandt. Kostov agreed, promising to betray his son to save his own skin.

Throughout the summer, I received updates on Kostov's negotiations. I winced as I read the transcripts of calls with his son, the middleman in the talks with the thieves.

"These guys are crazy," the son warned from Stockholm.

The father in Los Angeles seemed unimpressed, heartless even. "What are they going to do, kill you?" he said sarcastically. "Will they shoot you?"

The son sounded resigned. "I don't know. I don't give a shit anymore."

Kostov did a nice job haggling the sellers down from $1.2 million to $600,000. Although we'd be getting the cash back, we had to negotiate as if real money was at stake. We agreed to pay $245,000 in cash up front and provide the balance once the paintings were sold. Kostov told them he would fly to Stockholm with an American art broker and the cash in September.

Everything seemed lined up—until we contacted the Swedish authorities. International police operations are never easy. Every country has its own laws and procedures, of course, and they have to be respected. Whenever you work overseas, you have to remind yourself that you're a guest of a foreign country. You can negotiate diplomatically but you can't dictate terms. You've got to play by the host nation's rules.

Though extremely grateful to hear about the Renoir and eager to rescue the Rembrandt, the Swedes lamented that they simply could not grant permission for Kostov to enter the country. He was still a wanted man there, albeit for minor, decades-old crimes. Under Swedish law, the warrants could not be suspended for any reason, even temporarily.

We'd have to find another way.

* * *

THE DIPLOMATS' SEARCH for a solution gave me time to brush up on the Old Master.

There is a romantic notion that Rembrandt rose from tough roots to greatness. It makes for a nice story, but I doubt it's true. I say I *doubt* it's true because most of what's been written about Rembrandt is educated speculation. He didn't keep a diary or copies of his letters and he gave no interviews. The artist compared most often to Mozart and Shakespeare had no contemporary biographer. In the twentieth century, historians wrote dozens of thick books about Rembrandt, many with differing accounts. Scholars can't even agree on how many siblings he had. In recent years, some of Rembrandt's later paintings have become suspect. Did the master really paint them? Or did his students? Was he playing games with us? I like all this uncertainty. It just adds to the Rembrandt mystique. In the months that I chased his *Self-Portrait,* I enjoyed getting to know the man.

Rembrandt Harmenszoon van Rijn was just twenty-four years old when he painted *Self-Portrait* (1630). The painting isn't significant because it's a self-portrait—Rembrandt painted or sketched more than sixty self-portraits in his lifetime. It's significant because he painted it during a seminal period in his life, within a year of his father's death and of his decision to leave the comfort of his hometown for Amsterdam. Within four years, Rembrandt would be married and famous.

He lived in what was arguably Holland's greatest century, in a prosperous and peaceful democratic country between major wars. He was born in the Dutch town of Leiden, just south of Amsterdam and about a day's walk from the North Sea coast. His father was an earnest fourth-generation miller who owned several plots of land, making him semi-prosperous. His mother was pious and bore nine children (or ten, depending on which scholar you believe). Five (or three) of them died at an early age. Rembrandt was among the youngest siblings and he spent more time in the classroom than working for his father. He attended the Latin School in Leiden from ages seven to fourteen, and then enrolled at the University of Leiden.

Rembrandt didn't last long in college. He knew it couldn't prepare him for life as a painter. After one year, he quit to begin a three-year apprenticeship with a mediocre architectural painter, notable mostly because the artist taught him to sketch using stuffed animals. He took a second apprenticeship with the artist Pieter Lastman, who would become his more important mentor. Lastman worked with Rembrandt for about a year and is credited with teaching him how to paint with emotion.

The Dutch master began his professional career at age nineteen or twenty, sharing a Leiden studio with Jan Lievens, a slightly older, more accomplished painter and a former child prodigy. Lievens and Rembrandt shared models, mimicked one another's style, and began a lifelong friendship. Later, Rembrandt would be wrongly credited as the painter of some of Lievens's best pieces.

By 1630, the year *Self-Portrait* was painted, Rembrandt and Lievens began attracting notice as rising stars. That year, the poet Constantijn Huygens, secretary to the Prince of Orange, ruler of Holland, visited their studio. Afterward, Huygens wrote effusively of Rembrandt's talent: "All this I compare with all the beauty that has been produced throughout the ages. This is what I would have those naive beings know, who claim (and I have rebuked them for it before) that nothing created or expressed in words today has not been expressed or created in the past. I maintain that it did not occur to Protogenes, Apelles, or Parrhasius, nor could it occur to them, were they to return to earth, that a youth, a Dutchman, a beardless miller, could put so much into one human figure and depict it all."

The stolen Rembrandt might be the most significant self-portrait from the master's final years in Leiden. In 1630, he was experimenting with what would become a signature technique—chiaroscuro, painting in light and shadow, varying shades of darkness to project shape on three-dimensional figures. The colors and shades are subtle.

During this experimental period, Rembrandt painted and sketched himself in a dizzying array of emotions and appearances. Between

1629 and 1631, he captured his face in a dozen classic moments of surprise, anger, laughter, scorn. In one self-portrait, Rembrandt is middle-class, inquisitive, confident in a wide-brimmed hat. In the next, he appears as a beggar, forlorn, confused, even crazed. In nearly every painting, hair and lips take center stage—the hair, a wild, frizzy tangle or smoothly matted under a beret; the mouth, closed and pensive or cocked half-open with a whiff of mischief.

Why did Rembrandt paint so many self-portraits?

Some historians believe it was a form of autobiography. The scholar Kenneth Clark subscribes to this romantic view. "To follow his exploration of his own face is an experience like reading the works of the great Russian novelists." More recently, other historians have come to a more practical conclusion. They believe the Dutch artist's intentions were economic: He crafted so many self-portraits because he was a businessman and shrewd self-promoter. Self-portraits—in particular, expressive head and shoulder images known as "tronies"—were in vogue in seventeenth-century Europe, prized by wealthy aristocrats. For Rembrandt, the early self-portraits served the dual purpose of paying the bills and promoting the artist's brand.

I'm not sure which theory I like better. I don't doubt that Rembrandt became a keen salesman later in life, but I'm skeptical he was thinking about this at age twenty-four, when he painted *Self-Portrait*. I think the painting is simply an honest representation of an important snapshot in art history. The atmosphere is sober, the hair neat, the mouth closed, the lips fused. Rembrandt looks pensive, mature, like a guy ready to set off from home to make his fortune in the big city.

ULTIMATELY, THE DANES came to our rescue.

Police in neighboring Denmark agreed to host our Rembrandt undercover sting in Copenhagen, which is easily accessible by train from Stockholm. In our Iraqi targets' eyes, the change of venue only burnished Kostov's criminal bona fides. When he explained—truthfully—that he was a wanted man in Sweden and couldn't get a visa, they reacted with empathy.

In mid-September, I flew to Copenhagen and met with Kostov, the three Los Angeles agents, our American embassy liaisons, and the local police. We were also joined by Eric Ives, the Major Crimes Unit Chief in Washington.

The next morning I flew to Stockholm. Chief Inspector Magnus Olafsson of the Swedish National Police picked me up at the airport. On the ride to his office, he warned me about the two Iraqi suspects, brothers named Baha Kadhum and Dieya Kadhum. They were smart and ruthless, obviously violent. The Swedes were still wiretapping their cell phones and reported that the brothers were arguing over whether to trust me.

"They are very cautious," Olafsson said. "I don't think they'll be fooled by you."

At his desk, the chief inspector handed me color photographs of the front and back of the Rembrandt. I spent more time studying the back than the front. I'd already studied blow-ups of the front. It looked just like the postcard, and, since the painting was so small, it wouldn't take much to make a decent forgery. The backs of paintings often offer better clues. The rear of the mahogany frame was scarred with gouge marks; most of it was covered by three museum stickers, including a set of hanging instructions in Swedish. The Rembrandt was latched to the frame by six clips screwed into the wood. Two of the clips stood at odd angles.

I returned to Copenhagen the following day and we began our play. We gave Kostov a brand-new, untraceable, prepaid cell phone to call his son. The moments before that first in-country call still made me nervous. You've already spent all those resources, flown everyone overseas, made promises to foreign police officials, and put the FBI's reputation on the line, all the while assuming the bad guys are still on board. The first two calls went unanswered. Shades of Madrid.

What if we called and the Iraqis blew us off? What if Kostov was just stringing us along, hoping for a free flight to see his son before he entered prison? What if the targets didn't even have the painting?

Thankfully, Kostov reached him on the third call, and the sellers were still eager. The son, Alexander "Sasha" Lindgren, agreed to take a five-hour train ride to Copenhagen the following day to meet his father, me, and my money.

In the morning, undercover Swedish surveillance officers trailed Lindgren from his suburban home to the train station and then to the border, where Danish officers picked up the trail. We met in the lobby of the Scandic Hotel Copenhagen, a modern business hotel about a half a kilometer from the city's famed Tivoli Gardens.

The son brought with him a surprise, his three-year-old daughter, Anna. He rolled her into the foyer in an umbrella stroller, and Kostov knelt down to meet his granddaughter. Lindgren figured that bringing his happy little blond-haired daughter provided perfect cover.

I was pleased to see Anna, too—it meant her father and granddad were less likely to try to rob me when they saw the money.

After giving them a few moments, I interrupted the family reunion, taking command. "Sasha, you and your daughter will come upstairs with me. I will let you in my room; I will leave and get the money. You can count and make sure everything is all right." Boris translated and the four of us squeezed into the elevator.

I did not have my usual suite. This room was tiny and a third of it was consumed by a twin bed. I left the three of them alone inside for a few minutes and strolled up one flight to the command center, where I could see them on a grainy black closed-circuit picture. I took the satchel of cash and scooped up a few pieces of candy for Anna.

I returned to the room, handing the bag to Lindgren and the candy to Anna. He counted the cash in less than a minute, then handed it back to me. "What do we do now?" he said.

Simple, I said. You go back to Stockholm and bring the Rembrandt. And, I added, I'll only deal with one person. "Room's too small."

Moments after Lindgren wheeled his daughter from the room, a SWAT team hustled me out and took me to a safe house. It was smart, a routine precaution against a setup. There was always the worry that after seeing the money, Lindgren might simply return with a gun and take the money.

Late that night, the Swedish police called to report that Lindgren had returned to the Kadhums' apartment across the border in Stockholm. The lights stayed on late, they reported.

The next morning, the Swedes called to say that Lindgren and the Kadhum brothers, Baha and Dieya, were on the move. Dieya, the youngest, carried a shopping bag with a large square object inside.

Over and over, I reminded everyone to stay cool, so as not to spook the targets. I knew this was especially tough for the Swedish police. Their agents were following men they believed to be carrying a stolen Swedish national treasure, and they were supposed to watch these guys just slip out of the country with it.

When the train crossed the border into Denmark, which meant they would arrive at the hotel within the hour, I began last-minute preparations. I made my quick call to Donna in Pennsylvania, my silent reminder not to get too caught up in the mission. The Rembrandt might be priceless, but it wasn't worth my life.

I cleared my head and went through a mental checklist of how things were supposed to go down: Kostov meets a Kadhum brother in the lobby, brings him and the painting to my room. We meet, I leave to get the cash, return, and let him count it. Kadhum shows me the painting, brings it back without Kostov. I authenticate it, Danish SWAT officers burst in.

I thought about that last detail, the SWAT team. I went to check in with the commander next door and repeated the go-code—"We have a done deal." Almost as an afterthought, I decided to test the duplicate electronic key card the commander planned to use to enter my room. I stuck the key in my door and it didn't work. I tried again and again. Unbelievable. Exasperated, I ran down to the lobby to get a new set of keys, sweating by the time I returned. This was always the way. Despite all the support staff and backup, the undercover operative knows he is truly on his own. I left the new key with the SWAT commander. He was munching on a sandwich.

AT 6:17 P.M., an FBI colleague called me from the Danish command center to report the Kadhum brothers' arrival in the lobby. Baha Kadhum, empty-handed, was headed up with Kostov, he said. Dieya Kadhum was staying in the lobby, holding the package.

Damn, I thought. We were just getting started and already the plan was changing.

I heard a soft rap at my door.

I told the FBI agent, "Look, buddy, talk to you later." I hung up the phone and moved to the door.

I let Kostov and Baha Kadhum inside.

Kadhum was all business. "You have money?"

"There's no money here," I said. "Not yet. It's in another room. I have to go get it."

Kadhum cocked his head, confused. I played the patient but experienced mobster. "If I lose the money," I said, pointing a finger at my head, pulling an imaginary trigger, "boom—they shoot me dead." Kadhum smiled. I smiled back.

I raised my hands, palms up. The Iraqi understood. I was a fellow criminal and needed to pat him down, to make sure he wasn't armed or an undercover cop wearing a hidden microphone.

I went through the motions, patting Kadhum's ribs, even lifting his shirt slightly, pretending to check for a wire, but I stopped short of a full search, hoping to gain a bit more of his trust. "I don't worry about you," I lied.

He smiled, and I said, "Just sit back and I'll get the money." The

moment I entered the hallway, I exhaled. At the end of the stairway, I moved up a flight of stairs to a safe room where FBI agents
Calarco and Ives waited. Ives handed me the black bag with a
quarter of a million dollars, cash.

On the grainy surveillance video, we could see Kadhum sitting
on the bed, fidgeting with his cell phone, checking text messages.
Kostov tried to chat him up in Arabic, but Kadhum seemed annoyed, distracted. He focused on his phone and gave the older man
curt answers.

I returned and plopped the black leather valise on the bed. Kadhum quickly dug his hands in. I looked over at the TV, and pointed
at the variety show on the screen. "I like this," I said, and laughed.
Kadhum, eyes on the money, ignored me.

That's when I knew we had him. Kadhum had *the look*, the one
most criminals get when they believe they're going to get away with
it, when they think their plan is going to work. Kadhum wouldn't
back out now. He was too close. He was holding $245,000 cash in
his hands.

Kadhum put one stack on the bed and pulled out another one.
He flipped through the bills to make sure each one was real. He
placed that stack on the bed and grabbed the next one.

I said, "Is it all there?"

He grunted and kept counting. Kostov stood silently by the
door.

When Kadhum finished, I said, "You bring a bag?"

"No, I didn't."

I laughed, and offered him mine. I unzipped a side pocket and
took out my tiny art tools and put them on the table. It was all part
of the show.

Kadhum took his eyes off the money. "Can I see?"

I took out the tools, one by one. "This is a black light. . . . This
I use to measure. . . . This is a microscope. See the light on it? This
is the flashlight I use in case I have to look at something dark."

Kadhum quickly lost interest and turned silent. His mobile phone chirped; he checked a text message and frowned. He studied my face. Something seemed wrong.

He was deep in thought and at this point I didn't want him to think. I just wanted him to finish the deal. What was he up to? Why the delay? Did he really have the painting? Or was this a shakedown, a robbery? I tried to move things along. "You want to go down and get the painting?"

"OK."

Another text message arrived and he looked annoyed, confused.

I tried to retake control. I said, "I'll put the money back, and then what happens is we'll go down, we'll go get the painting and bring it back up and if it's good, I'll get the money and you can have the bag."

Kadhum had his own plan. He wanted to show me the painting downstairs, and then return to the room for the money. I didn't like that. I wanted everything to happen in the hotel room, where it would be videotaped, where no one else could get hurt, where I could control the environment, where armed Danish police could storm the room at a moment's notice.

I said, "I'll wait here for you, OK?"

"It's up to you," Kadhum said.

At 6:29 p.m., he left with Kostov.

I counted silently to thirty, then grabbed the bag with the money and bolted into the hallway. I burst into the stairwell, raced up one flight, and handed the bag to Calarco.

I went back to the hotel room and waited. After a few minutes, I checked in with Bennett, the FBI agent stationed in the Danish police command center. He was keeping in touch with the police watching the man in the lobby who was holding the bag with the painting. We were expecting him to hand Kadhum the bag.

He had bad news. "Subjects just ran from the hotel. . . . Headed down the street toward the train station. . . . Stand by. . . ."

Shit. I started pacing, anxious. Where were they headed? Did they know it was a sting? If so, how? Was it something I said? Something

Kostov said? I slumped on the bed. Would the Danes move in now? Would they try to grab the package the Kadhum brother ferried from Stockholm?

Just then, my borrowed Danish cell phone lit up. It was Bennett. "Hold tight. Subjects went to a second hotel and came out with another package. They're on their way back."

A second hotel, a second package. Smart, I thought. The first was a decoy, designed to test the Swedish police during the train ride. They'd sent the painting ahead with a fourth man.

At 6:49 p.m., I heard two knocks at the door.

It was Kadhum—and Kostov. I was furious to see Kostov, but tried not to show it. My unpredictable cooperator was violating my explicit instructions to get lost when the painting arrived. He knew I did not want an extra body in that tight space during the handoff, the most critical time, but he'd come anyway.

I was uncharacteristically blunt. "We don't need you here. You're welcome to stand in the hallway." He lingered anyway.

Kadhum handed me the shopping bag and offered to be frisked again.

I knew he'd been under surveillance the entire time he'd been gone. "I don't have to worry about that," I said. I did eye the bag with suspicion. If this were a robbery, it might be booby-trapped.

I looked at the package. "You wanna take it out for me?"

"No," he said. "I don't want to touch it."

I knelt on the bed and pulled a package from the bag. It was about the size of the stolen Rembrandt, and wrapped tightly in black velvet cloth with string. I struggled to get it open. I laughed as if this was no big deal, but it wasn't funny. I pressed my knees on the bed to give myself more leverage, but the damn thing wouldn't come undone. "I don't know how to untie it."

Kostov wandered over, trying to be helpful. He stood between the hidden camera and me, blocking the agents' view.

"Sit down," I whispered to Kostov. "You make me nervous."

"I don't make you nervous," Kostov said loudly. "Don't worry."

Kadhum got curious. "You know each other long time?"

Kostov, again helpful: "We know each other from Los Angeles."

I cut him off. "Nah, I don't know him too well. I'm an art dealer."

Kostov nodded. "He's an art dealer in Los Angeles." The guy could not keep his trap shut. He was going to blow it. He was breaking the cardinal rule—needlessly spouting lies we couldn't back up. I didn't know L.A. well enough to cover us. It was as dumb as my mistake of telling the backflap smugglers I was a lawyer.

I masked my growing irritation with a laugh. "And New York and Philadelphia. Everywhere." I tried to change the subject to the matter at hand, the string. "It's not coming off."

Kostov leaned closer, crowding me. I dug my nails into the knots, bit with my teeth and then, finally, the string came undone. I peeled away the velvet cloth and lifted the frame. I checked the back. All six back clips were still in place, two slightly skewed, just like in the museum photographs.

I looked up. "The frame is correct. You never took it out of the frame, huh?"

Kadhum was incredulous. "We wouldn't dare. It's a Rembrandt."

I kept a straight face. "Are you an art lover?"

"No, I just want the money."

I stood up and grabbed my tools, ready to inspect the painting. "I need to go in a dark room. I can't see it in the light."

Kostov mumbled something. I couldn't understand him, but I played along anyway. "Could be," I said. "But the varnish is a little thick."

Kostov, still the fool: "Yes, the varnish, it's very fresh. You can see for yourself."

Gently, I lifted the painting and carried it toward the bathroom. I motioned to Kadhum to follow me. I pulled a tiny ultraviolet scope from my pocket, and flipped the lights off in the bathroom. I squinted as I raked the ultraviolet light across the painting, about an inch from the surface. An untouched, original work carries the same uniform dull glow throughout the surface. If the painting has been retouched, then the paint fluoresces unevenly. The test is simple, but it can catch the most frequent frauds—usually sloppy attempts by sellers who try to fake a signature or a date. So far, so good. If this was not the real thing, it was a great fake.

With Kadhum over my shoulder, I put the scope by the sink and took out a thirty-power magnifier and a ten-power jeweler's loupe. Every painting has a fingerprint: the crackling that forms over the years as the varnish dries, creating a random and distinct pattern. From enlargements of museum photographs, I had studied the right-hand corner of *Self-Portrait,* just above Rembrandt's ear, and memorized the pattern. It matched, but I didn't let on. I pretended to keep studying the painting, waiting for the Iraqi to grow bored and walk away. When the sting went down, I wanted to be alone in the bathroom. In a firefight, it would be the safest place. Bathroom doors lock. Most have tubs made of steel or some other hard composite capable of slowing bullets.

A few seconds later, Kadhum's cell phone buzzed and he drifted into the bedroom to check a text message.

I gave the signal to the SWAT team. "OK," I said loudly. "This is good. We've got a done deal."

I heard footsteps in the hallway and leaned out of the bathroom to check the door.

The key-card clicked, the handle turned, and then—the door jammed.

Shit.

Kadhum whirled and our eyes locked.

We started to race for the door and heard the key-card click again. This time, it banged open violently. Six large Danes with bulletproof vests dashed past me, gang-tackling Kadhum and Kostov onto the bed.

I raced out, the Rembrandt pressed to my chest, down the hall, to the stairwell, where I found Calarco and Ives.

* * *

THE NEXT DAY we met the U.S. ambassador and Copenhagen police chief for a round of atta-boys. We posed for trophy photographs with the cash and the Rembrandt. I stood in the background, doing my best to keep my face out of the pictures.

That afternoon, I took a stroll into Tivoli Gardens with one of the FBI agents from California. We found a table in a café and lit Cuban cigars. He ordered a round of beers and I took one, my first in fifteen years.

THE REMBRANDT CASE garnered headlines worldwide, raising the Art Crime Team's profile to new heights, inside and outside the FBI. Within weeks, our tiny squad would have trouble keeping up with all the attention.

On the flight home, I thought about all I'd accomplished in a little less than a decade. I'd gone undercover a dozen times, solved cases on three continents, and recovered art and antiquities worth more than $200 million. At this point in my career, I felt prepared to overcome almost any obstacle any case might present, foreign or domestic.

Indeed, just nine months later, I embarked on the most challenging case of my career: I would go undercover to try to solve the most spectacular art crime in American history, the $500 million theft from the Isabella Stewart Gardner Museum.

It is a story that begins with an auction in Paris in 1892.

OPERATION
MASTERPIECE

CHAPTER 18

MRS. GARDNER

Paris, 1892.

O N THE AFTERNOON OF DECEMBER 4, 1892, THE AUC-
tion at the famed Hôtel Drouot reached item No. 31.

The Dutch painting was offered without fanfare. No one could
know that it was destined to become the centerpiece of the twentieth century's largest and most mysterious art heist.

As the bidding began, Isabella Stewart Gardner of Boston held a
lace handkerchief to her face. This was the signal to her broker to
keep bidding. No. 31 was an oil on canvas, a work by Johannes
Vermeer, the seventeenth-century Dutchman whose genius was not
yet universally recognized. He called the painting *The Concert*. The
work portrayed a young lady in an ivory skirt with black and gold
bodice playing the harpsichord. A second woman in an olive, fur-
trimmed housecoat stood by the edge of the instrument, studying a
note card as she sang. At the center of the painting, in more muted
hues of brown and green, a gentleman with long black hair, his back
to the painter, sat sideways in a bright terra-cotta-backed chair.

Although works by Vermeer were not nearly as popular or as
valuable then as they are today, Gardner faced tough competition
as she vied for No. 31. The other bidders making a play for *The*

Concert were agents representing the Louvre and the National Gallery in London.

From her seat in the auction room, Gardner could not see her straw bidder. She simply trusted that he could see her.

The bids climbed steadily past twenty-five thousand francs and Gardner kept her handkerchief in place. The bidding slowed, rising in smaller and smaller increments, until Gardner's man won it with a final bid of twenty-nine thousand. Afterward, she learned that the Louvre and the National Gallery had dropped out because each wrongly presumed that Gardner's bidding agent also worked for a large museum—in that day, it was considered bad manners for one museum to drive up the price against another. The museums were dismayed to hear that the winner, this cheeky woman with the healthy checkbook, was an American, and that she planned to take *The Concert* home to Boston.

I DON'T KNOW if Isabella Stewart Gardner ever met Albert C. Barnes—she died in 1924, the year before he opened his museum outside Philadelphia.

But Dr. Barnes and Mrs. Gardner strike me as kindred souls: Each assembled an astounding private art collection. Each built a museum to showcase these works to the public, displaying them in an eclectic, educational style. Each lived on the grounds of the museum, and each left a strict will that stipulated that the galleries remain precisely as arranged, not one frame moved, not ever.

Gardner was not a self-made millionaire like Barnes; few women of the nineteenth century were. She inherited the fortune her father had made in the Irish linen and mining industries. Yet Gardner spent the final thirty years of her life in the same manner as Barnes. She traveled extensively to Europe, snatching up important Renaissance and Impressionist works, pieces by Titian, Rembrandt, Vermeer, Michelangelo, Raphael, Botticelli, Manet, and Degas. Her ample resources and skilled negotiators enabled her to compete against the world's great museums.

Gardner and her husband, Jack, traipsed the globe on grand adventures, and she documented them in a diary with broad cursive strokes. An entry from November 17, 1883, is typical. She wrote of a trip by oxcart to Angkor Wat: "A small Cambodian, naked to the waist, fans me as I write. Within the walls of Angkor Thom have already been discovered one hundred and twenty ruins. . . ." Gardner returned repeatedly to her favorite city, Venice, island of art, music, and architecture. When she decided to build a public museum for her collection in Boston, she found a plot of marshland along the Fenway and designed a building in the style of a fifteenth-century Venetian palazzo, filling it with as many authentic European pieces as possible. She imported columns, arches, ironwork, fireplaces, staircases, frescoes, glass, chairs, cassoni, wood carvings, balconies, fountains. Like Barnes, Gardner disliked the cold, clinical museums of the day, in which paintings hung side by side with affixed labels explaining the significance of each work. She arranged her museum the way Barnes would twenty-five years later in Pennsylvania, decorating it with more subtle forms of art—furniture, tapestries, and antiques. She designed a great, glass-roofed, flower-filled Mediterranean courtyard in the center of the four-story museum, allowing the warm light of the sun to fall into the most important galleries. Gardner built an organic museum, one to be appreciated as a living thing. As the museum's official history notes, "Love of art, not knowledge about the history of art, was her aim."

The Dutch Room, home to the Vermeer and four Rembrandts— and later the scene of a great crime—was arranged in typical Gardner style.

She flanked the entryway with a pair of husband-and-wife portraits by Hans Holbein the Younger and hung a large bronze knocker of Neptune on the door. On the left, between a Van Dyck painting and the door, Gardner placed her first important purchase for the museum, a dark Rembrandt self-portrait from 1629, a painting similar to the one I rescued in Copenhagen. Underneath *Self-Portrait,* she placed a carved oak cabinet framed by two Italian chairs. To the side of the cabinet, she nailed a postage-stamp-sized framed Rembrandt etching, *Portrait of the Artist as a Young Man.*

Virtually everything Gardner displayed in the Dutch Room was an imported work of art, most of it from the seventeenth century. The red marble fireplace was Venetian; the refectory table, Tuscan; the tapestries, Belgian. The Italian ceiling was decorated with scenes from mythology—Mars and Venus, the Judgment of Paris, Leda, Hercules. The floor was covered with rust-colored tiles specially commissioned from Mercer's Moravian Pottery & Tile Works in Doylestown, Pennsylvania.

On the south wall, against patterned olive wallpaper above sets of salmon, aqua, and rouge chairs, Gardner hung seven paintings. There were works by the Flemish artists Rubens and Mabuse, but the wall was dominated by two of Rembrandt's better paintings, *A Lady and Gentleman in Black* and *The Storm on the Sea of Galilee,* his only seascape. Around these paintings, Gardner arranged Barnes-style accoutrements, including a twelfth-century Chinese bronze beaker.

The most unusual arrangement in the room stood along the wall by the exterior windows. There stood an easel with two paintings positioned back to back. In front of each painting, Gardner set a glass case filled with antiques and a chair. The first faced the rear wall: *Landscape with an Obelisk,* an oil painting on oak panel that was long thought to be a Rembrandt but later discovered to be the work of Govaert Flinck. The second painting faced the entrance to the Dutch Room, and the position of the chair beneath it seemed to mimic the bold square splotch of terra cotta on the chair at the center of the painting.

The Concert was the most valuable piece in the room.

CHAPTER 19

COLD CASE

Boston, 1990.

THE LARGEST PROPERTY CRIME IN U.S. HISTORY began very early on a Sunday morning in March 1990.

St. Patrick's Day fell on a Saturday that year and revelers across Boston were still stumbling from bars into a light drizzle and growing fog. Inside the Gardner museum, two young security guards worked the graveyard shift. One made rounds through the third-floor galleries. The other sat behind a console of cameras on the first floor.

At 1:24 a.m., two men dressed in Boston police uniforms approached the museum's service entrance along Palace Road, the narrow one-way street forty yards from the main doors on The Fenway. One of the men pressed the intercom button.

The guard at the desk, a college kid with dopey curly black hair that fell below his shoulders, answered. "Yeah?"

"Police. We have a report of a disturbance in the courtyard."

The guard was under strict instructions: Never open the door for anyone, ever, no exception. He studied the images of the men on the security camera. They wore badges on their sharp-edged police hats. He saw large radios on their hips. He buzzed them in.

The men in police uniforms pulled open the heavy wooden exterior door, moved through a second unlocked door, and turned left to face the guard at his station. The two men were white, each roughly thirty years old—one tall, perhaps six foot one, the other a few inches shorter and wider. The shorter man wore square, gold-framed glasses that fit snugly on his round face. The taller guy was broad-shouldered but lanky from the waist down. Each wore a false mustache.

The tall one did the talking. He said, "Anyone else working?"

"Yeah," said the guard behind the desk. "He's upstairs."

"Get him down here."

The guard picked up his radio and did as he was told. When the tall policeman motioned for him to step out from behind his console—away from the button for the silent alarm—the guard did that, too. Before the second guard arrived, the tall policeman said to the first guard, "You look familiar. I think we've got a default warrant on you. Show me some ID."

The guard dutifully dug out his driver's license and Berklee College of Music identification. The policeman took a quick glance and without a word spun the young guard around against the wall and handcuffed him. When the confused guard realized the cops hadn't frisked him, it hit him: *These guys aren't cops.* But it was too late. When the second guard, also a part-timer and aspiring musician, arrived, the policeman slapped cuffs on him before he could speak.

"You're not under arrest," the thief told them. "This is a robbery. Don't give us any problems and you won't get hurt."

"Don't worry," the second guard sputtered. "They don't pay me enough."

The thieves led their captives down the stairs into the basement, a damp warren of aging, low-hanging pipes and ducts. They took one guard to the end of a passageway and cuffed him to a pipe by a janitor's sink. They wrapped duct tape around the young man's eyes and ears, and from the base of his chin to the top of his forehead. They led the other guard to the other end of the basement, to a darker, harder-to-find corner. They wrapped his head in tape in the same manner and latched him to a pipe.

Most museum robberies are over in a matter of minutes, simple smash-and-grab jobs. But the Gardner thieves were able to take their time. Confident that they had prevented the guards from tripping the silent alarm, and likely carrying radio scanners that picked up police frequencies, the Gardner thieves spent an astounding eighty-one minutes inside the museum. They did not even begin to try to remove paintings until 1:48 a.m., twenty-four minutes after they entered the museum. They would then spend a full forty-five minutes in the galleries, ripping masterpieces from the walls, and another twelve minutes shuttling works of art out the service door. We know these minute-by-minute details because motion detectors installed throughout the Gardner tracked the thieves' movements. Although the robbers grabbed a printout of this record from the security chief's office before they fled, a computer hard drive preserved a backup copy.

At 1:48 a.m., the thieves headed up the main staircase. They turned right at the second-floor landing, moving along a hallway overlooking the courtyard, and directly into the Dutch Room, through the door marked with the Neptune knocker. The paintings were secured by little more than simple hooks, and the thieves quickly removed the four Rembrandts and rudely set them on the tile floor, scattering shattered and splintered glass from one of the frames. At the easel, they grabbed the Flinck, perhaps believing it to be a Rembrandt, and, shoving the glass case aside, got to work on the Vermeer. Very neatly, probably using box cutters, one of the thieves began slicing the works from their frames.

The other thief headed back past the stairway through the Early Italian Room, turned right, moved through the Raphael Room, past a priceless Botticelli and a pair of Raphaels, arriving in the Short Gallery at 1:51 a.m. This thief easily broke into a cabinet filled with framed sketches, a collection secured only by a century-old lock. In one of the center panels, the man removed five Degas sketches, works in pencil, watercolor, and charcoal. The sketches were relatively minor pieces compared with the far more valuable artwork within

arm's reach of the Degas—a Matisse, a Whistler, and a Michelangelo. Perhaps the thief was a Degas fan; perhaps he was following
orders; perhaps he was confused in the darkness and his hurry.

At 2:28 a.m., both thieves were back in the Dutch Room. They
abandoned the Rembrandt self-portrait on wood, presumably because it was too heavy or could not be properly cut from its frame,
and carried the five Dutch paintings and five Degas sketches downstairs. They removed the videotape from the recorder, ripped out
the printout of the recordings by the motion detector, and made for
the door. They opened the service entrance door twice, at 2:41 a.m.
and 2:45 a.m.

The thieves stole three other works of art from the Gardner that
misty morning, creating clues that have long intrigued investigators.
They took two relatively valueless items—a Chinese vase from the
Dutch Room and a gilded Corsican eagle finial from the top of a
Napoleonic banner in the Short Gallery. Why take such minor pieces?
Were these souvenirs? Or red herrings designed to trick investigators?

The third clue is most befuddling. The thieves took a three-foot-
tall Manet, *Chez Tortoni,* from the Blue Room. This was the only
work stolen from the first floor, and most curiously, the motion detectors did not pick up any movement in this gallery during the robbery. Absent a malfunction, this meant the Manet was moved *before*
the thieves confronted the guards, raising the specter that the Gardner heist was an inside job. Additionally: Whoever took the Manet
left its empty frame on the chair by the desk of the security chief, a
gesture many interpreted as a final insult.

The mystery of the Manet is like most Gardner clues—intriguing
but ultimately useful only to the countless armchair detectives in the
bars and salons of Boston and the art community.

THE THEFT SHOCKED Boston and the art world, but it shouldn't
have.

As the value of artwork, from Impressionists to Old Masters, rose steadily at auction houses from the early sixties to the late eighties, so too did the pace of art crime, especially in New England. The thieves began slowly, targeting the region's many colleges. Schools made prime targets because, as the thieves soon discovered, they held valuable but poorly guarded art and artifacts donated decades ago by long-dead alumni—Hudson Valley School paintings, ancient coins, rifles from the Revolutionary War. If a painting vanished from the walls of the English Department reception room, embarrassed college officials assumed it to be a prank or the work of the town delinquents, not the work of a growing cadre of Boston burglars who found it easier to steal art from a college or a mansion than to rob a bank. Emboldened by success, these thieves expanded their horizons and targeted museums. The most successful New England art thief was Myles Connor, who would become one of a number of Gardner suspects. Beginning in 1966, Connor burglarized the Forbes House Museum, the Woolworth Estate, the Mead Art Museum at Amherst College, the rotunda of the Massachusetts State House, and the Museum of Fine Arts, Boston. By the late 1980s, museums had begun to recognize the threat, but moved slowly to address it. When a new director was named to lead the Gardner in 1989, she ordered a review of her museum's security measures. It was not completed before the 1990 crime.

Hundreds of FBI agents and police officers investigated the Gardner theft, and as the years passed, the mystique and mystery of the heist only grew. Investigators navigated a growing thicket of speculation, one fueled by a cast of characters featuring con men, private detectives, investigative journalists, and wiseguys—all chasing a reward that would climb to $5 million.

No lead went unchecked. Detectives and agents searched a trawler in the harbor, a city warehouse, a Maine farmhouse. When a pair of tourists visiting a Japanese artist's home spotted what they believed to be *The Storm on the Sea of Galilee,* an FBI agent and a Gardner curator dashed to Tokyo. They found a fine copy, but no Rembrandt.

Every now and then a con man approached the media and the media bit. One got face time on *60 Minutes,* the other on *Primetime Live.* The con artist who appeared on ABC claimed to be working with Connor, and he repeatedly teased the U.S. attorney's office in Boston, claiming he could return one of the paintings within an hour, if paid $10,000 and granted immunity.

One newspaper reporter didn't just investigate the story. In 1997, he became part of it. Under the blazing headline "We've Seen It!," the *Boston Herald* reported that one of its star journalists, Tom Mashberg, was led blindfolded to a Boston warehouse in the dark of night, and shown a curled, badly damaged canvas that resembled *The Storm on the Sea of Galilee.* Mashberg's source later sent him photographs of the Rembrandt and paint chips supposedly of seventeenth-century vintage. Although an initial analysis suggested the chips were authentic, further tests by the government showed they were not.

Shady mob links to the Gardner heist surfaced repeatedly, and most drew breathless press coverage across Boston. Four times in the space of a decade, the papers reported, a wiseguy with alleged ties to the Gardner case died under suspicious circumstances. When two more reputed mob associates were arrested for conspiring to rob an armored car, they alleged that FBI agents had set them up as part of a scheme to win the paintings' return. As all of this mob-Gardner speculation swirled, alleged Boston mob boss Whitey Bulger—a man the media identified as a prime suspect in the Gardner case—fled the United States on the eve of his arrest for unrelated murders.

Almost every new twist and detail from the Gardner investigation made the papers and the eleven o'clock news—from the dead, indicted, and fugitive mobsters to the false sightings in Japan. The *Herald* reporter recounted his story for a national audience in *Vanity*

Fair and inked an option for a movie deal. Harold Smith, a respected private art detective, was featured in a well-received documentary film about the heist.

Even the normally tight-lipped FBI joined the fray, feeding the hype. For a story marking the anniversary of the crime in the mid-1990s, the lead FBI agent in Boston gave an on-the-record interview—highly unusual for a street agent working an active case. He told the *New York Times,* "I can't imagine a whodunit as nightmarish as this, considering the pool of potential suspects. It's mind-boggling."

Mind-boggling, perhaps. Frustrating, for sure.

And then, in 2006, sixteen years after the crime, after all the false leads and con games, the FBI received a credible lead.

That tip landed on my desk.

CHAPTER 20

A FRENCH
CONNECTION

Paris, June 1, 2006.

A LITTLE OVER A CENTURY AFTER GARDNER WON *THE Concert* at auction in Paris, I traveled there to give a lecture. And to follow up on the hot tip.

Each year, the men and women who supervise the world's undercover law-enforcement operatives convene in a major capital. The conference goes by a secret name as bland as Universal Exports.

The agenda includes lectures on crime trends, updates on important international legal developments and treaties, and presentations on successful operations—war stories told by undercover agents on famous cases. In the spring of 2006, the group invited me to give a lecture on the Rembrandt sting in Copenhagen. I flew to Paris with an old Philadelphia colleague, Daniel DeSimone, the FBI's unit chief for Undercover and Sensitive Operations. We looked forward to meeting and socializing with our counterparts, making the kind of personal connections that can be invaluable during international investigations. The undercover group planned a Seine dinner cruise and a behind-the-scenes tour of the Paris Opera, the venue immortalized by Renoir.

During one of the luncheons, I introduced myself to DeSimone's counterpart in Paris, the chief of the French undercover unit called

SIAT. The SIAT chief was busy hosting the conference, shaking lots of hands, making small talk, but when we met, he arched an eyebrow.

He put down his glass of red wine. "You've of course heard what we heard about these paintings?"

We spoke in vague, veiled terms. There were a lot of people around. But I knew he was referring to the tip that the French had just passed to the FBI: Two Frenchmen living in Miami appeared to be trying to broker the sale of two stolen masterpieces. One was a Rembrandt, the other a Vermeer. The world was missing only one Vermeer—the one from Boston.

"You should meet the officer who received the tip."

"I'd like that."

"Good. He works for another department, but I will find you his mobile number."

I MET THE SIAT contact at the tourist entrance to the Louvre, outside the large glass pyramid.

We spied each other easily in the thick crowd of tourists in T-shirts and shorts—we were the only ones wearing suits. He was a grizzled Police Nationale officer who worked the busy undercover art crime beat in Paris. He was heavyset with a leathered face and narrow blue eyes, and introduced himself as Andre. We shook hands and laughed at ourselves: two hotshot undercover art sleuths meeting in coat and tie at France's best-known museum! Andre and I strolled away from the mob in the warm sun, tossing back and forth the names of cops and museum chiefs we both knew.

Three minutes later, we were turning right on the cobblestones, following the sidewalk through one of the great arches and out of the palace complex. We crossed Rue de Rivoli and its cheap souvenir shops, moving north up Rue de Richelieu. I was eager to dive in, start peppering him with questions about the Gardner tip. But this was his town, his tip. I let him lead.

After two blocks, the crowds thinned. We kept walking, and Andre said, "You know in France, we have two different national police departments, the Police Nationale and the Gendarmerie Nationale?"

I did, but treaded carefully, having heard about the rivalries. "Kind of a complicated arrangement, huh?"

"*Oui*. There are important differences and it is important for you to understand." Andre laid it out for me: The Gendarmerie, created during medieval times, is an arm of the Defense Ministry.* Their officers carry themselves with military bearing and discipline, and are deployed mostly in rural regions and the ports, but by tradition the gendarmes also keep a strong presence in Paris. The Police Nationale, created in the 1940s, is an arm of the French Interior Ministry. The force focuses mostly on urban crime. Andre worked for the Police Nationale.

"Sometimes the Police Nationale and Gendarmerie investigate the same case, compete, and this gives us headaches," he said.

There was one other important nuance I needed to know, Andre said. "You must understand SIAT."

SIAT was a division of the Police Nationale created in 2004, the same year the French repealed a decades-long ban on the use of evidence obtained by undercover officers. During the ban, France had used undercover officers sparingly, but in an informal, no-paperwork-involved manner, often with a wink and nod from the local magistrate. Back then, each unit in the Gendarmerie and Police Nationale had used their own people to go undercover. When the law changed and the SIAT was created, many undercover officers had transferred to the new unit. But some veterans, like Andre, had stayed where they were. They found the rule-heavy SIAT culture and configuration too bureaucratic and turf-conscious to be effective. Andre was warning me that SIAT would insist on running the show if this case involved any undercover operations inside France.

* This changed in August 2009, long after this case ended.

"Who runs the art crime team?" I asked.

"Complicated also: It is under the jurisdiction of the Police Nationale, but for political reasons the chief is always a Gendarme."

"How's the chief?"

"This one we have now is very good, very smart," Andre said. "He would rather return an important statue to a church or a painting to a museum than put a man in jail. The problem was that Sarkozy, before he became President of France, was the Minister of the Interior and he didn't agree. He was very much about law and order. For the Police Nationale, Sarkozy cared only about results—arrests, arrests, arrests. Sarkozy cared only about the statistics. He wanted to show he is fighting the criminals."

"Sounds like the FBI. We're not wired to recover stolen property, art. We're wired to count convictions in court because that's how you're measured. We've got guys so cynical they call cases and convictions a 'stat.' We have arguments over which FBI office gets credit for the 'stat.' " I smiled at Andre. "You have your Police Nationale–Gendarmerie-SIAT issues, we have our own problems."

"Yes, I have heard this, though I thought all this changed after 9/11."

"That's what everyone thinks, but it's probably only true in terrorism cases," I said. "When it comes to everything else, not much has changed." The FBI remains a largely decentralized law enforcement agency, divided into fifty-six field offices spread across the country. Each of these fifty-six field offices operates as its own fiefdom. Once a field office begins an investigation, it rarely cedes its turf. The FBI's investigatory protocol is sacrosanct: Absent extraordinary circumstances, investigations are run and supervised by the agents in the field office in the city where the crime was committed—not by anyone at headquarters. "The case we're talking about now is being run out of Boston because the paintings were stolen from Boston."

"The FBI agents in Boston are experts in art crime?"

"No. Bank robbery. SWAT, that kind of thing."

Andre cocked his head, confused.

"That's the FBI, my friend," I said. I didn't want to go into too much detail because Andre still seemed to be sizing me up, deciding how much to tell me about the Florida tip. So I did not explain that despite my expertise, Eric Ives's enthusiasm from headquarters, and the Art Crime Team's worldwide successes, the Gardner case would almost certainly remain under the control of the Boston office. I would work for them. In theory, Headquarters could overrule a field supervisor or wrest a case away from a field office. But in reality, that rarely happened. It would be viewed as an insult to the field office supervisor and create a blot on his record, a slight he and his friends would never forget. The FBI is a giant bureaucracy—middle-management supervisors are rotated to new jobs every three to five years, between the field offices and Washington. This dynamic makes supervisors at Headquarters reluctant to make waves. The supervisor you cross today may become your boss tomorrow.

"But don't worry about it," I said. "I've been doing this a long time and never had a problem with that sort of thing. I just do my cases."

We kept walking, crossing another busy boulevard.

The Frenchman said, "You know, Bob, you must be subtle in art crime. It is important to use discreet methods, sometimes methods that are not illegal but not by the book. Our chief understands that in some situations you have to be subtle."

I nodded.

The French cop stopped on the sidewalk and looked me in the eye. "These are dangerous people, the guys who have your paintings. Corsicans. I'm going to put you in touch with someone in Florida." Andre said his French contact in Florida did not know he was a cop, and that he had discreetly used the man's information in the past. "All very quietly, you understand?"

"Of course."

"I will give him your number in the U.S. What name will you use when he calls?"

"Bob Clay, art broker from Philadelphia."

"Good."

I said, "Let me ask you—just so I'm clear, the paintings for sale are . . . ?

"*Oui*, a Vermeer and a Rembrandt."

"A Vermeer, huh?"

"*Oui*," he said, and walked off.

ANDRE RANG MY cell phone a short while later.

"Now," he said. "I've told this guy you deal in fine art, big, multimillion-dollar deals. You're based in Philadelphia and we've done business, made a lot of money."

It was the vouch.

"Excellent," I said, "I appreciate it. So, he'll call me?"

"*Oui*," he said. "This guy, his name is Laurenz Cogniat."

"You know him well?"

"Laurenz? He is a fugitive. An accountant for many years in Paris. Worked with organized crime. Money laundering. Very smart, very rich. Moved to Florida. Big house, big car, Rolls-Royce. Knows many people still, here in France, Spain, Corsica."

"Can I trust him?"

The Frenchman laughed. "He is a criminal."

"If he says he can get the Vermeer—"

"Let me tell you something about Laurenz," the cop said. "I do not think he will lie to you about this. Laurenz is not a con man. He is an opportunist. He views himself as a businessman, a man who makes deals in the space between the black and the white. You understand?"

"Sure."

"But this man Laurenz can be trouble if you try to control him too much," Andre said. "Be patient. He will take you in many directions, but I think he will lead you to what you want."

CHAPTER 21

LAURENZ AND SUNNY

Miami. June 19, 2006.

L AURENZ DID NOT DISAPPOINT.

Two weeks after we began speaking by phone, I flew to Miami to meet him. He took me for a ride in his Rolls, an FBI surveillance team in slow pursuit.

Laurenz wore a salmon Burberry dress shirt with a cursive *LC* monogram on his breast, blue jeans, brown sandals; and a gold Rolex Cosmograph Daytona. He was forty-one years old, trim, with short-cropped curly brown hair.

"Nice car. New?" I asked because I knew the answer—I'd checked his motor vehicle records—and was curious if he'd tell the truth.

Laurenz answered honestly. "A year old. I get a new one every eighteen months. I don't like to drive a car with more than twenty thousand miles on it. Not good for the image."

I admired the cherrywood console, running a finger across the frosted silver lettering, PHANTOM. I said what he wanted to hear. "Very nice."

Laurenz nodded. "If it's good enough for the Queen . . ."

I laughed, and realized I couldn't tell if he was joking.

"Her Majesty drives one just like this," Laurenz added. He spoke English fluently, but with such a thick accent that it sometimes took an extra moment for what he said to register. "If you've never driven this car, you will never understand how smooth it is. You hear nothing outside. You speed up to seventy and you feel nothing. You go to one-ten and you feel like you are driving seventy. Everything is top of the line. The sunroof, the steering, the brakes. There are two DVD players in backseat. For many years, this was an old car for old people. But the new ones are magnificent. I have a guy who comes every month to do the leather. And a boy who washes the car every two weeks."

He rapped the window with his knuckles. "Bulletproof glass. Custom armor-plated exterior. Four hundred and fifty thousand dollars."

"Impressive."

He sniffed. "That's the point."

Laurenz steered the Rolls onto the Dolphin Expressway, headed west toward the airport. An irritating pop song played on the radio—all synthesizer and falsetto. Laurenz cranked it up. "Good sound, huh?"

I studied Laurenz and wished I'd been carrying a recorder. What my handling agents and supervisors would make of such banter! Two weeks into the Gardner case and the FBI agents involved were already falling into two camps—those who believed Laurenz might be able to deliver the stolen Boston paintings and those who were skeptical. I fell squarely in the middle, not yet ready to pass judgment, still working him. With undercover cases, especially art crime, you never know until you vet it out. Was Laurenz a fool? A con artist? The real deal? We wouldn't know until I sized him up.

Clearly, Laurenz liked to talk about himself and I didn't mind listening. It was an easy way to ingratiate myself with him, and so far, I hadn't caught him in a lie. His claim that he was worth $140 million was impossible to verify because his holdings were scattered across Florida, Colorado, and Europe in a variety of names and corporations, and Laurenz seemed to spell his first and last names a variety of ways, probably on purpose. But our most basic checks of public records showed that he was worth millions, if not tens of millions, of dollars, at least on paper. What really mattered was that the French police confirmed Laurenz's connections to the Western European underworld, particularly gangs that dealt in stolen art.

Laurenz and I didn't directly discuss my background on the phone. With the vouch from his friend in Paris—the undercover cop—it wasn't necessary to talk about such things on an open line. After a few calls, Laurenz had asked me to fly down to meet him. He said he had a friend arriving from France, someone I should meet.

At Miami International Airport, Laurenz pulled the Rolls into the short-term parking and we walked toward the international arrivals terminal. We had forty-five minutes to kill and Laurenz bought two bottles of Fiji water.

I took a sip. "Looks like you've done all right for yourself. How long have you been in Florida?"

"Ten years. But I've lived all over the world. I speak seven languages."

"Seven? How did you learn seven?"

"When I was younger, I was working for Club Med around the world. French Polynesia, Brazil, Sandpiper, Japan, Sicily."

"What'd you do for Club Med?"

"Didn't matter. I was twenty. Whatever they asked. Pool, beach, bartender, waiter. I was only thinking about eating, drinking and, you know, girls. When you are this age, you get three, four girls a week minimum, every week for three years."

I laughed.

"Then I returned to France and I studied accounting, finance, and I started working for this guy. A wiseguy in Paris. I was twenty-five. I did things for him, and then I found out that he used my name as the president of his corporation. The business had many debts and I got into trouble because I was the president. This situation I could not handle—the only way out was to go into the life. Since I am accountant, this is what I do for them. I was very good, washing money, setting up foreign corporations in Luxembourg. You have one million euros and ten minutes later it is in another name, another country, another currency. You understand?"

"Yeah, sure." He was a mob accountant.

"I was very good. I had a nice office near the Champs-Élysées. It's good for a while. French and Italian wiseguys, some in Spain. We dealt in gold, cash, diamonds, paintings, whatever you like. Then I saw some bad shit. The Russians and Syrians, sloppy. So, things happened and I know too much. I must leave France. If not, I am dead or in jail."

I knew Laurenz had been arrested once in Germany and once in France on suspected currency violations, but freed after a few months. I also knew he was a wanted man in France for financial shenanigans. I didn't bring any of this up. The way he was talking, I expected him to get around to it soon enough. I said, "So you came here?"

"Right, Florida, 1996. I come here with just $350,000 and I get lucky with real estate. First month here, I meet an asshole, a Swiss guy who is losing his condo in foreclosure. I go to the courthouse for the sale. Don't get his condo but I get another. I pay $70,000 for a $400,000 penthouse in Aventura! You see, Bob, I understand the financial system, and it's easy if you do. I also know the right banker, the one who will take a few dollars in his pocket when he gets the loan."

I laughed at that. "The right banker."

We checked the board and saw the flight had landed. A team of undercover agents was waiting inside the customs area to see if Laurenz's friend had arrived with anyone else.

I said, "So what's the plan when we meet your guy?"

"We take Sunny to lunch. We talk business. Sunny is a wiseguy. Not a big guy, but he knows people in the south of France, and I think these people will have the paintings you want. He is trying to move here. Sunny wants to be a player. He will try to impress you and say he can sell anything."

"I'm only interested in paintings," I said. "No drugs, guns, nothing like that."

"Yes, yes, I agree," Laurenz said. He leaned in and gently grabbed my forearm. "Listen my friend," he said, "we are the sharks, you and me, and we have a small fish here who can lead us to the big fish. But these big fish, the guys with the paintings in France, are very bad guys. We must be serious. You must have the money. I will get the price down and then you and I will take our cut. We are partners?"

"You get me what I want," I said, "and you will be happy."

Sunny came through the doors a few minutes later, a short, plump man of fifty, his brown mullet matted from the long flight. He was rolling two large blue suitcases. We shook hands and headed outside, toward the Rolls.

As soon as we hit the fresh Florida air, Sunny lit a Marlboro.

WE BEAT RUSH hour and reached La Goulue, an upscale bistro north of Miami Beach, in about forty minutes.

The three of us sat around a white-linen tablecloth. Sunny ordered the seared calamari with basil pesto. Laurenz got the jumbo scallops. I tried the steamed yellowtail snapper. If nothing else, Laurenz knew where to get a good meal.

As we dined, Laurenz continued to dominate, talking, talking, talking. He dropped some names, presumed wiseguys in Paris. He talked about his new Jet Ski, and a sucker's deal he was working on a condo near Fort Lauderdale. He also vouched for me with Sunny, making up a story, saying we'd met years earlier at an art gallery on South Beach. Sunny listened quietly, shoveling calamari.

Finally, Laurenz turned to me. "Sunny can get you many things."

Sunny pursed his lips.

Laurenz said, "Bob is looking for paintings."

"Yes," Sunny said. "I've heard this." He looked at his plate and continued eating. For now, I let it drop. Laurenz picked up the check, conspicuously laying his black American Express card on the table.

On the way back to the hotel, we stopped off at a cellular phone store and Laurenz bought Sunny a mobile phone. I memorized the number. We'd need it if we decided to tap it.

THE FOLLOWING MORNING, the three of us met for bagels. As always, an FBI surveillance team hovered nearby.

When we sat down, Sunny asked to see our cell phones. "Please take out your batteries," he said.

Laurenz laughed. "Why?"

Sunny said, "The police, the FBI, they can track you through your cell phone, even when it is off."

"Oh, bullshit," Laurenz said.

"No, it is true," Sunny said. "I saw it on *24*."

"The TV show?"

"Just take them out."

We did.

"All right," Sunny said, "I can get three or four paintings. A Rembrandt, a Vermeer, and a Monet."

"Monet or Manet?" I asked.

Sunny looked confused.

"Monet or Manet?" I said again.

"Yes," he said, and I realized he didn't know there was a difference. In a way, his ignorance led credence to his offer. He was just passing on names he'd been given. If he'd been playing me, he would have done enough homework to know the difference.

"These paintings are good," Sunny said. His English was poor, but I could understand most of what he said. It was certainly better than my French. "The paintings were stolen many years ago."

"From where?"

"I don't know," he said. "A museum in the U.S., I think. We have them and so for ten million they are yours. You can do that? Ten million?"

"Yeah, of course—if your paintings are real, if you've got a

Vermeer and a Rembrandt. Look, Sunny, my buyer's gonna want proof. Do you have pictures you can send me? Proof of life?"

"I will see what I can do."

THE CASE INCHED through the summer.

At FBI offices in Washington, Miami, Boston, Philadelphia, and Paris, agents and supervisors expressed cautious optimism, exchanging e-mails and hosting conference calls. The French police fed us more information on Sunny and Laurenz, confirming their links to underworld art brokers. Authorities on both sides of the Atlantic arranged for wiretaps. I kept in touch with Laurenz by phone. He said Sunny was moving forward on the deal, slowly. I urged Laurenz to push him.

By early fall, we were moving toward an undercover buy in France. Eric Ives, the Major Theft Unit chief at Headquarters, began to arrange for a group of FBI agents to travel to Paris in mid-October for our first formal meeting with the French.

One morning after Labor Day, Eric called to chat.

"What do you think?" he said.

"What do I think about what, Eric?"

"Sunny, Laurenz, Boston."

"I think it's on," I said. "That's what I think."

IN THE FIRST week in October 2006, on the eve of our first big FBI–French police meeting in Paris, I flew down to Miami to see Laurenz and Sunny.

We met in the late afternoon at Laurenz's favorite haunt, a Thai-Japanese joint just off the 79th Street Causeway. Laurenz and Sunny were already there, phones on the table, batteries out.

I sat down and removed my phone battery. "*Ça va?* Good to see you, Sunny."

"*Ça va,* Bob."

I slapped Laurenz on the back and gave him a big wink. "Nice work, buddy. We're going to celebrate tonight, right?"

Laurenz beamed. "Absolutely. Already doing it." He pointed to the bowl of green tea ice cream, topped with whipped cream, Laurenz's idea of a celebration. He held up a glass of water in toast. "To the next deal!"

I said, "Amen, *mon ami*."

Sunny cocked his head, confused—reacting just as we had hoped. The "deal" we were celebrating was a complete fabrication, one that Laurenz and I concocted the night before. It was part of our play, designed to impress Sunny.

Laurenz leaned close to Sunny and whispered rapidly in French. He explained that he and I had just completed an $8 million deal for a stolen Raphael. We'd each cleared $500,000, he said. Laurenz was a pretty good liar. Sunny nodded, duly impressed.

The fake deal was all part of an expanding wilderness of mirrors: I was playing Laurenz, and Laurenz thought that he and I were playing Sunny. I'm sure Laurenz had his own angles thought out. And Sunny? Who knew what really went through his mind?

Laurenz and I continued to banter about the fake Raphael deal until Sunny finally broke in, taking the bait. "All right," Sunny said. "The paintings in Europe—we are ready. It can only be the three of us. We must work together to not get caught."

"Of course," I said.

"Yes, yes," Laurenz said impatiently.

"Just the three of us," Sunny repeated. "We'll go to the south of France and . . ." He launched into a convoluted scenario for the exchange, one that included a series of rotating hotel rooms—the money in one room, the paintings in another, a human life as collateral in a third. With Sunny's accent, I couldn't understand every word, but it didn't matter. We could clarify everything later. I just wanted to get things moving.

Sunny was quite clear on one point. "When you see the paintings, you will know that they are real. But once you see them, you must buy them. So let me say again that you must be serious about having the money. You see the paintings, you must buy them."

"I want to buy them," I said. "Vermeer and Rembrandt?"

"Yes, yes, we have," Sunny said. "The important point is not the money or the painting, but that we are all happy, all safe. Nobody wants trouble. Very important, from here on out, nobody gets involved in this except us."

Sunny grabbed a napkin and took out a pen.

"Now," he said, and he drew a triangle and scribbled a letter in each corner—*S, L,* and *B.* "This is Sunny, this is Laurenz, this is Bob. We are in this together. We cannot let anyone else in the triangle. This is all it can be, ever. This way, if anything goes wrong, we'll know it's one of us who betrayed."

CHAPTER 22

ALLIES AND
ENEMIES

Paris. October 2006.

THE TROUBLE BEGAN A WEEK LATER, JUST MINUTES
into our first formal Gardner case meeting with the French police.

An FBI supervisor from Boston—I will call him Fred—began
with an impolitic demand. "Since we'll be going along on the sur-
veillances, we're going to need to be armed."

Fred spoke louder than necessary, clumsily enunciating every
syllable. Just to be sure the French understood, he cocked his thumb
and index finger in the shape of a gun. "So we need to take care of
that, right off the bat."

Fred liked to be in charge and because of the FBI's sacrosanct
protocols he was considered the lead supervisor on the Gardner
case—back in 1990, the heist had been assigned to the Boston FBI's
bank robbery/violent crime squad, and Fred now led that unit. He'd
been an FBI agent for seventeen years, but his expertise was SWAT
and chasing bank robbers, not investigating art crime or running international undercover investigations. This was his first trip to a
foreign country. It didn't seem to occur to him that we were guests
on someone else's turf.

"We're here to get our paintings back," Fred said severely, as if puffing up his resolve would help get the job done. "The people who have our paintings will be armed. So will we."

It was such an outrageous thing to say that everyone else in the room—the six French police officials, six other FBI agents, and an American prosecutor—simply ignored it. Fred had been watching too many movies. As I knew from my experiences in Brazil, Denmark, Spain, and other nations, most countries don't allow foreign police officers to carry weapons.

One of the FBI agents stationed at the embassy politely cut Fred off, directing the conversation back to the matter at hand, our joint American-French sting operation.

This first major meeting raised the stakes on both sides. The French police had gotten into the spirit and hosted the meeting at the new Musée du Quai Branly, which showcased artifacts crafted by the indigenous peoples of Asia, Australia, the Americas, Africa, and the Polynesian region. It was one of the most interesting and confounding museums I'd ever visited—designed with a jungle theme, a thicket of trees and grass on the outside, dark passageways and dimly lit displays on the inside. It was easy to lose one's bearings.

The Gendarmerie lieutenant colonel chairing the meeting was Pierre Tabel, the chief of the national art crime squad. Andre, the undercover French police officer who'd provided me the initial tip, had spoken highly of Pierre, describing him as a rising star in the Gendarmerie, savvy with keen political instincts, a future general. The art crime job Pierre held was a sensitive one because the unit often became involved in international cases and investigations in which the victim was a celebrity, wealthy, or politically connected. Pierre understood that these cases sometimes called for discretion, or off-the-book methods in which the supervising magistrates agreed to look the other way.

Pierre and I had been talking shop over the phone since September, and I liked him. We'd built a tight working relationship, one I felt would be crucial to our success. I could immediately tell he was a good supervisor—someone who encouraged his people to get things done, without micromanaging or throwing up bureaucratic barriers. He understood that art crime cases could not be handled like other undercover cases, and we agreed that the goal here was to rescue the Boston paintings, not necessarily to arrest anyone in France. Besides, he explained to me, the maximum penalty in France for property theft of any kind was a mere three years in prison.

When I had arrived at Charles de Gaulle Airport from Philadelphia the previous day, Pierre had picked me up, a gesture both courteous and shrewd. He intercepted me before I could speak with anyone else, including my FBI colleagues at the U.S embassy, and on the ride into the city we talked over the case. Based on my undercover work in the United States and Pierre's phone tap and surveillance successes in France, we had agreed that Sunny and Laurenz would probably arrange for the sale of the Gardner paintings somewhere in France.

Pierre had cautioned that he would not be able to control every facet of operations in France. In a case with the potential for such huge headlines, he said, many supervisors from many agencies will want to play a role, claim credit, stand at the podium at the press conference, get their picture taken. "Everyone will want a piece of the cake," Pierre liked to say. Pierre warned me that the SIAT undercover chief would probably now demand a major role. Because the undercover laws in France were so new, the SIAT chief often acted cautiously, and this sometimes placed him at odds with Pierre's more adventurous art crime team. I warned Pierre about the FBI's pecking order and protocols, and we agreed that turf wars and intra-agency rivalries on both sides of the Atlantic were going to complicate things.

Sure enough, at the French-American meeting that afternoon, the SIAT chief followed Fred's speech with one of his own: He unilaterally announced that he planned to insert a French undercover officer into the deal. I explained that Sunny would probably resist adding a fourth person to the deal. I even sketched out the triangle on a piece of paper and spelled out what Sunny had said: "It can only be the three of us." The French SIAT chief replied that this was impossible. "There is a warrant for Laurenz in France," he said, "and so he cannot come to France." The SIAT chief added that he doubted I would be allowed to work undercover in France. The new French undercover law, he explained, was tricky.

"Sure, I understand," I said, careful not to become engaged in an argument in front of such a large group. If what the SIAT chief said was true, it would mean that two thirds of our triangle— Laurenz and me—were barred from doing a deal in France. That sounded ominous.

The most encouraging news from the briefing came from the two supervisors running Pierre's wiretap and surveillance groups. One said she was "ninety-nine percent sure" that the gang Sunny was speaking with held the Gardner paintings.

Pierre added, "On the phone calls, they talk in code to a person in Spain. But it's easy to understand. They speak of getting apartments for someone named Bob. One they say is located on Vermeer Street. The other they say is on Rembrandt Street."

"Do you know who Sunny is talking to?" someone asked.

"Yes," the French surveillance supervisor said. "They are Corsicans, a group known to us."* The French territory in the Mediterranean was infested with organized crime, and the national police officers were as unwelcome on Corsica as FBI agents are in Puerto Rico.

After the meeting broke up, Fred sauntered up to Pierre. I overheard the Boston supervisor again mention something about a gun and Pierre say, "I'm sorry, but . . ." I walked over to Pierre, pulling him aside to apologize.

"No problem," Pierre said, and he lowered his voice. "I have my problems also. What my SIAT chief said about you not being able

---

* To protect the safety of certain individuals, references to this group are intentionally vague.

to work in France? Not true. But he is a boss and I cannot make him look bad in front of the Americans."

I shook my head. Too many chefs. Too many FBI offices. Too many French law enforcement agencies. Too many competing interests. It didn't bode well for such a complex undercover operation, one that would require speed, flexibility, creativity, and risk.

Pierre seemed to sense what I was thinking and said, "Like I say, in this case, we're going to have a lot of managers; everyone wants a piece of the cake."

WHEN WE RETURNED to the United States, the case agent in Boston, Geoff Kelly, put together the necessary paperwork for a major undercover investigation, a seven-page form called an FD-997. He set the value of the Gardner art at $500 million, summarized the FBI's extensive efforts to recover it since 1990, and laid out the undercover plan for a sting in France.

Geoff also gave the case a name, Operation Masterpiece.

A FEW WEEKS after the Paris meeting, Laurenz called to tell me we'd be buying the paintings in Spain instead of France.

For me, the change of venue was fortuitous. I'd made plenty of friends in the Spanish police during the Madrid case—their cooperation would be virtually assured. The medal the Spanish government gave me hung in my den. The richest woman in Spain owed me a favor.

"Fine, no problem," I told Laurenz. "I love Spain."

"Sunny wants to know if you want the 'big one' or the 'little one' first." I didn't know if he meant the diminutive Vermeer, which was worth much more, or the gigantic Rembrandt, which was worth less.

"I want them both, so it doesn't matter," I said. "What are we talking about? Madrid? Barcelona? Couple of weeks?"

Laurenz said, "I let you know."

I called Eric Ives in Washington and gave him the good news. We put together a plan to travel to Madrid in ten days' time. On the eve of the trip, Eric arranged a conference call between all the FBI offices involved—Washington, Paris, Boston, Miami, Madrid, and Philadelphia. The call did not go well.

Fred began by announcing that the trip to Madrid was canceled, catching everyone except the FBI agents in Paris by surprise. This particularly embarrassed our agent in Madrid, because he'd already spent a lot of time with the Spanish police securing SWAT, surveillance, intelligence, and undercover support. The Boston supervisor cited unnamed "security issues" in Spain, suggesting that the police there were not trustworthy.

What's more, Fred made it clear he was furious that I'd been making arrangements without clearing every detail with him. "There are communication issues here," he said. "We've got to be careful not to leave people out of the loop." Fred chastised me for directly contacting the FBI agent in Madrid. I reminded Fred that Eric had already obtained Headquarters' approval for me to make the appropriate contacts in Spain—and that I knew our man in Madrid from the Koplowitz case. Fred didn't care. "Not your job, Wittman. I'm in charge."

I backed off for now. I didn't care if these guys barked at me. Whatever it took to move forward.

But I knew we'd never recover the Gardner paintings if we operated by committee.

After the conference call, I needed some air. I began wandering around the office, and landed at the desk of my friend Special Agent Jerri Williams, a twenty-four-year veteran and the FBI's spokesperson in Philadelphia. She'd replaced Linda Vizi, who'd retired.

"You don't look too good," Jerri said.

I told Jerri about the conference call.

She frowned. "It sounds like the kind of turf-war crap we get whenever we deal with other agencies, not inside the Bureau." She was right. The major federal law-enforcement agencies—especially the FBI, DEA, IRS, ATF, and Immigration Customs Enforcement—almost always wrestled for control of joint investigations; the public would be surprised to learn how often different law enforcement agencies hid things from one other, or tried to squeeze each other out. Jerri said, "Not getting much help from headquarters?"

"I'm trying, but . . ."

"Yeah, well, you know Boston isn't going to give up a case like this."

My concern only grew in the weeks that followed, as I found myself spending a great deal of time juggling calls between Eric in Washington, Fred and Geoff Kelly in Boston, and the agents stationed at U.S. embassies in Europe. Since I needed to verify what Sunny and Laurenz were telling me, I kept in close contact with Pierre, whose art crime investigators were wiretapping their phones. We agreed to check in every Thursday morning. On one of those calls, he warned me that his French bosses weren't happy that the case might be shifting to Spain. They would fiercely resist the move.

I didn't bother to ask Pierre why the French would object. It was obvious. If the bust went down in Spain, the big press conference would be held in Madrid and all the accolades would go to the Spanish police, not the French.

PIERRE'S BOSSES NEEDN'T have worried.

Shortly after Sunny returned to Miami in late November 2006, Laurenz called to let me know that the plan had changed once again: Sunny was now offering all eleven Gardner paintings in France, not Spain.

"How much would you be willing to pay?" Laurenz asked.

"Thirty million," I said. It was the standard black market price, five to ten percent of open market value.

"Cash?"

"If I buy them inside the U.S., yes," I said. "Otherwise, wire transfer."

Laurenz asked if I could put together some financial statements to prove we were serious, that we had access to thirty million.

"Shouldn't be a problem," I replied.

"Magnifique," Laurenz said. "If you can get the money and can get me into France, I think we can have the paintings in six days."

This was, of course, extraordinary news. The money wouldn't be a problem. Thirty million was just a number—a big number, yes, but ultimately just a number—money temporarily moved from one account to another. We weren't talking about flash money, cash on the street. The $30 million would never leave the bank.

I let Pierre know. "I think we're coming to France." I ran through the latest details.

"Good, good," Pierre said. "Do you think we'll be able to use our undercover man?"

"Don't know yet," I said, dodging the question. "Any luck on waiving Laurenz's warrant? Looks like we're gonna need him in France."

"Working on it, my friend, working on it."

WHEN I FLEW into Charles de Gaulle for our second big American-French meeting in late November 2006, Pierre picked me up again. We were late and Pierre used his blue lights and siren to part the morning traffic.

On the ride downtown, Pierre let me know that counter forces were at work. "You missed the nice dinner we had last night— Geoff and Fred, and your boys from the embassy."

What the hell? I was groggy from the overnight flight and figured I'd misunderstood. "Dinner?"

Pierre grinned. "Just games, my friend," he said. "Office politics. They came a day early to see us without you. I think they are scared of you."

Pierre caught my frown. "Don't worry, we took them to a cheap place," he joked. "Tonight, we will eat much better."

Pierre dropped me at my hotel, but the room wasn't ready. I showered in the fitness center, and when I came out I saw a welcome sight, Pierre chatting with Eric Ives from Washington. Eric, the art crime unit chief, was fuming because he had just learned that he, too, had been excluded from Fred's secret American-French dinner.

The briefing convened in a stark conference room inside a modern Defense Ministry building. Pierre began with an overview and quickly turned to his surveillance chief. She reported that Sunny had been spotted meeting with known Corsican mobsters on a street corner in Marseilles and that in wiretapped conversations he spoke of "frames for Bob."

We wrestled next with the thorny issue of how to get Laurenz inside France. The top French police official in the room insisted that the decade-old warrant against Laurenz for his financial crimes could not be lifted. The French warrant, he added, was valid in virtually every country in the European Union, so Laurenz couldn't travel to Spain, either. But, the senior French official wondered aloud, what if we allowed Laurenz to enter France under a fake name with a fake U.S. passport? The Americans looked at each other. It was a possibility.

Afterward, I pulled Pierre aside. "Why did your bosses all of a sudden come up with a way to let Laurenz inside France?"

He replied with a small smile, "Because they worried that you were going to take the case to Spain. They want the arrests to be in Paris."

Things finally seemed to be coming together. When I got back to my hotel, I called Laurenz and told him to be ready to fly to Paris on a few days' notice. I wanted to move quickly, I said. My buyer was eager to get going. He had cashed investments to rustle up the $30 million and it was now sitting in the bank, not earning much interest, and while we dickered, he was losing money. Laurenz said sure, he was ready and eager to do the deal—so long as it didn't interfere with his big ski vacation in Colorado.

"So maybe we do this in January, after the holidays?"

Stunned, I didn't know how to react. So I simply said, "Where you headed, Vail?"

"Crested Butte. Just sold a complex there—kept a condo for myself."

As I sat on the bed and digested the Laurenz conversation, rubbing my temples in bewilderment, an FBI agent from the embassy called. He said the bureaucrats were balking at the plan to furnish Laurenz with a fake U.S. passport. But the agent had come up with a new idea: What if we did the deal in Monaco? We could fly Laurenz from New York nonstop to Geneva, then charter a helicopter to fly him over French airspace to tiny Monaco, the independent principality on the Riviera. Since neither Switzerland nor Monaco belonged to the European Union, the French warrant wouldn't apply.

Hmm, I thought. Not a bad idea, not bad at all.

WHILE WE WAITED for everyone in Paris, Boston, Washington, Marseilles, and Miami to resolve the administrative and political issues in the Gardner case, Eric and I planned a quick side trip—an undercover mission to rescue treasures stolen from Africa.

Our plane to Warsaw left early the next morning.

CHAPTER 23

A COWARD HAS
NO SCAR

Warsaw, December 2006.

IN ZIMBABWE, THEY HAVE A PROVERB, "A COWARD HAS no scar."

When I received a tip that five national treasures stolen from a major Zimbabwe museum might be in Poland, Eric didn't hesitate when I proposed an undercover mission to rescue them. He didn't care that there was no American connection, or that we were in the midst of the Gardner case. Eric understood that it was the right thing to do, and that it would earn the FBI goodwill in two countries. Besides, the flight from Paris to Warsaw is just two hours and twenty minutes.

The Polish case was a model international investigation—completed in just three weeks, from initial tip to hotel sting, involving governments on three continents but minimal manpower and precious little paperwork. The longest meeting in the case was the hour-long briefing we held with the Polish SWAT team in Warsaw. They were the nicest group of bald-headed, bull-necked knuckle-draggers I've ever met. They even laughed at my jokes.

"The name of this case," I said, "is Operation KBAS."

"What's KBAS?" someone asked.

"Keep Bob's Ass Safe."

One of the first things we all agreed on was a media blackout. Because of the Gardner case, I wanted to keep a low profile in Europe, and the Polish police hoped to prosecute the case without using an undercover FBI agent as a witness at trial. As I understood it, the Polish police planned to keep every trace of FBI involvement quiet. Publicly, at least, Eric and I were never there, and neither was my FBI colleague from Philadelphia, John Kitzinger.

Our target was a Polish man named Marian Dabuski. On the Internet, he'd advertised for sale three Zimbabwean headrests, or *mutsagos,* and two Makonde helmet masks. When an honest dealer in Denver saw the offer, he tipped me. The headrests were sculpted concave pedestals, about a foot long and six inches high, and used as a sort of hard pillow during religious ceremonies: A worshiper would lie on his back, his neck supported by a headrest, close his eyes, and enter a Zen-like state in which he'd try to communicate with the dead. The headrests dated to the twelfth century, were crafted by the nomads of Zimbabwe, Sudan, Uganda, Kenya, and Tanzania, and looked a lot like the priceless artifacts I'd viewed at the Musée du Quai Branly in Paris. One of the headrests Dabuski advertised online matched one stolen the previous year at the National Gallery of Zimbabwe in Harare. In that theft, a middle-aged white man who looked remarkably like Dabuski had walked into the museum during the day, ripped four headrests and two helmet masks from a museum wall, and run out the front door. A guard chased him into the street and cornered him, but as the two began to tussle, people in the Harare crowd mistook the black guard for the criminal and began to beat him. The white thief slipped away with his loot.

I contacted Dabuski by e-mail—I said I was an American IBM executive based in Budapest, looking to expand my collection of African artifacts. He agreed to meet me in the lobby bar of the Marriott Hotel, across the street from Warsaw's Palace of Culture and Science. He and his wife showed up an hour late, but bearing three skull-sized boxes.

We went up to my room, which was wired for pictures and

sound. The Polish SWAT team was in the room on the left, and the commanders, including Eric and John, watched via video from the room on the right. As the Dabuskis unwrapped the masks, I pretended to closely study the craftsmanship, but I was really looking for the museum's serial numbers, etched just beneath the underside of each mask's chin. One had no tell-tale marks, but on another I noticed an odd smudge. It looked like brown shoe polish and it seemed to be concealing something. When I made out part of a number, perhaps a "3," bleeding through the polish, I knew these were the stolen masks. I agreed to their offer, $35,000 for the two masks and three headrests, and I gave the go-code.

Given my near disaster with the failing hotel key cards in Denmark, I tried a different approach in Warsaw. A member of the SWAT team simply knocked on the door, and I acted annoyed. "Who the hell could that be?" I grumbled. When I opened the door, the Poles yanked me out, rushed in and arrested the Dabuskis, throwing them on the floor and slapping black hoods over their heads. The police, following through on their plan to erase my role in the case, then put on a big show that in all the confusion I had somehow escaped.

Two surprises followed.

At checkout, the Marriott bill for the three rooms I'd booked on my Robert Clay credit card came in $800 higher than expected. It seemed that my friends from the Polish SWAT team had helped themselves to the minibars in the rooms, cleaning out all the liquor after I made my escape. Half amused, half annoyed, I paid the bill, knowing I'd face days of extra paperwork coming up with a way to justify the expense.

The second surprise came a few weeks later, after I returned to Philadelphia and the Gardner case.

I got a call from the FBI agent stationed at the U.S. embassy in Warsaw. He said that a Polish prosecutor, a man clearly in the dark about what really went down, had called with a request.

That conversation had gone something like this:

FBI agent in Warsaw: "How can I help you?"

Warsaw prosecutor: "Well, we've arrested a Polish man named Dabuski at the Marriott in Warsaw for trying to sell African artifacts to an American."

"Is that right?"

"Yes, but the American got away and we'd like your help tracking him down."

"Sure, I can try. What's his name?"

"Robert Clay."

The FBI agent didn't miss a beat. "OK," he told the prosecutor, "I'll get right on it."

CHAPTER 24

SUSPICIOUS MINDS

Philadelphia, January 2007.

FRED, THE BOSTON SUPERVISOR, REACHED ME ON MY cell phone late on a Sunday afternoon. I was home watching the NFL playoffs with my boys.

It was two months after our Paris meeting. While things remained promising, we were still waiting for the bureaucrats to clear Laurenz's fake passport, approve the Monaco scenario, or come up with some other plan.

I knew that Fred had been complaining about me to Eric Ives in Washington. He was angry that I'd been speaking directly with Pierre in Paris and that I'd warned every FBI official involved that if we didn't move swiftly, we'd lose our opportunity to buy the paintings. Fred believed I was usurping his role.

On the call, I grew uneasy as I detected a trace of satisfaction in Fred's voice. Then he said, "We're hearing that Sunny thinks you're a cop. So this changes everything, Wittman. We're gonna have to ease you out of this—insert one of my guys or the French UC."

Fred was quick to presume his tip was accurate. "How do you know Sunny thinks I'm a cop?" I asked.

"From the French," he said. Presumably from their wiretaps.

"Whoa, hold on a sec, Fred," I said. "This doesn't make sense. I spoke with Laurenz last night and he and Sunny are still in. I'm not surprised to hear Sunny worrying that I might be a cop. Hell, he might be talking about it on the phone to see if we react—just to test me and see if his phone was tapped. He's paranoid about everything. Remember the triangle he drew?" Criminals are always probing each other to figure out if this guy or that guy might be a snitch or an undercover agent. It's normal. I'd heard such talk during most of my long-term undercover cases. I'd heard it in Santa Fe, Madrid, and Copenhagen. Yet in the end, each time the criminal had succumbed to greed and followed through with the deal.

Fred made it clear he hadn't called to debate. He'd called to give me marching orders: I was on my way out.

"From now on," he said, "the French are going to deal directly with Laurenz. They'll use their guy in Paris"—Andre, the undercover cop—"to deal directly with Laurenz."

"Wait, I can't talk to Laurenz?"

"Right now, no."

"Fred, how's that supposed to work? He's gonna call me. What do I tell him?"

"We're working that out, gonna have some meetings."

I called Eric Ives in Washington. I told him about Fred's call and my new marching orders.

"That's ridiculous, Bob," he said. "Let me see what I can do."

I knew it wouldn't be easy for Eric. To overturn anything Fred had done, he'd need support from his bosses in Washington, who'd have to be willing to confront Fred's bosses in Boston. Unfortunately, supervisors in Washington are typically reluctant to confront supervisors in the field. They don't like to make waves, especially when it pits a veteran supervisor like Fred against a younger man like Eric. The FBI is very much an old-boys network.

Street agents have a saying that explains this mentality: *Mind over matter. The bosses don't mind and the agents don't matter.*

* * *

OF COURSE, LAURENZ called me the next morning.

I told him I might have to fade out from the deal for a while. A family medical emergency, I said. I kept it vague. I told him I might introduce him to a colleague.

Laurenz exploded. "Bob, what the fuck are you talking about? The deal, it is with the three of us. You, me, Sunny. You can't drop out. You have $30 million parked in the bank. I'm yelling at Sunny, telling him it is costing you $150,000 a month in interest and we have got to get moving, that you want to buy the Boston paintings. So what the fuck am *I* supposed to do now?"

"It's family, Laurenz," I said. "I've got a family problem. I don't know what to say."

Laurenz cursed again, screamed something at me in French, and hung up.

THE NEXT EVENING, shortly before midnight, Laurenz called me back. He was ebullient, and acted as if our previous conversation had never taken place.

He boasted that he'd just closed a $20 million real estate deal in Colorado, and now planned to buy the Gardner paintings in France on his own, and then sell them to me afterward. He spoke more rapidly and forcefully than usual. I wasn't even supposed to be taking his calls, but it sounded like we were on the verge of a breakthrough. I just listened. Laurenz said he planned to travel to Paris and that the French undercover cop Andre, the man who'd introduced us, would be arranging the sale.

The day after Laurenz's caffeinated call, Fred phoned. Before I could tell him about Laurenz's call, Fred began chatting about the latest plan. He said the French undercover cop Andre had told Laurenz that he would use his underworld contacts to sneak him into France, and that Laurenz and Sunny would buy the Gardner paintings in France on their own, then sell them to me.

"Yeah, I know," I said. "Laurenz told me about it last night."

Big mistake. Fred went nuts. He started shouting. "You spoke with Laurenz! You're not supposed to talk to him!"

"Fred," I said. "*He* called *me.*"

When Fred calmed down, he started talking about a series of more meetings, maybe in Miami or Paris or Boston or Washington. But by now, I wasn't really listening. I was seething. We were weeks away from solving the biggest property crime in American history, going up against Corsican mobsters to recover a set of long-lost masterpieces. Fred seemed more worried about protocols, meetings, and protecting his turf.

Soon, Fred was busy deploying that timeworn bureaucratic weapon, the memo. Inside the FBI, such memos are called "Electronic Communications," or ECs, because they are sent e-mail-style through the Bureau computers to each addressee. About a week after our heated call, Fred penned an outrageously slanted EC, one that not only presented a lopsided version of the way Operation Masterpiece had unfolded but raised questions about my integrity. The most damning section included a claim by a French participant that I planned to delay the Gardner sting until after my retirement in 2008, so that I could claim the $5 million museum reward for myself. It was a preposterous allegation. FBI agents aren't eligible for rewards for cases they've worked, even after they retire. Everyone knows that.

Steaming, I printed out a copy and walked it over to my direct supervisor in Philadelphia, Mike Carbonell. Mike and I were the same age, though he'd been with the FBI a decade longer. Mike held the same job in Philadelphia as Fred did in Boston—supervisor of the bank robbery/violent crime squad.

When I walked into Mike's office gripping Fred's slanderous EC, it marked the first time in a decade I'd come to a supervisor for help. I was used to fixing my own problems.

"You need to read this," I announced.

He closed the folder on his desk and took the document. To say that Mike uses foul language is like saying Rembrandt painted a few self-portraits. By the time he got to page two, the expletives were flying—"Holy shit . . . He put all this bullshit in a goddamn EC? . . . What the fuck?"

I asked him what he thought I should do.

But Mike wasn't done venting. "In twenty-eight years, never seen anything like this. . . ."

I told Mike that I'd made a call to France and had learned that the remarks Fred cited had been made in jest.

"Well, then it's obvious what's happening," he said. "You're on the cusp of solving a huge case and these guys want to cut you out."

"What should I do?" I repeated.

"You're the one whose ass is on the line. You know going undercover is always voluntary. It's up to you. You still comfortable going undercover with Fred or the guys in France who are running the operation? You trust them with your life?"

"No." The quickness of my answer surprised me.

I asked Mike about getting the case transferred from Boston to a supervisor in Philadelphia, Miami, or Washington.

"Doubt it," he said. "You know the drill. Nobody in Washington wants to risk pissing anyone off."

Mike, who was nearing retirement, didn't care if he made enemies. He forwarded his anger up the chain of command. And, in a rare move, Headquarters ordered Fred's EC deleted from the FBI system.

Ultimately, senior officials in Washington convened a come-to-Jesus meeting at Headquarters to hash out the differences and try to salvage Operation Masterpiece. The result: I was now permitted to resume conversations with Laurenz. But I was ordered not to speak to Fred, and presumably he was ordered not to speak with me. Left open was the question of whether I could work undercover in France or Spain—and, even if we could get permission, whether I would work with Fred.

After the Washington meeting, we returned to the job at hand, trying to come up with ways to shore up my backstory, ways to convince the sellers that I was a high-end art broker, a player, not a cop. We came up with several ideas to solidify Sunny's and Laurenz's confidence in me. Under one scenario, the three of us would travel to Los Angeles, party, and bump into a Hollywood starlet who often helps the FBI. The celebrity would recognize me, stop to chat for thirty seconds, and leave the impression that she and I once did a deal together.

We didn't end up doing the L.A. gig. Instead, we came up with a better way to ingratiate myself with them: I'd involve Sunny and Laurenz in two painting "deals," one in Miami, one in France—and in each case, I'd bring Laurenz and Sunny along as my "partners." As I had with Josh Baer in Santa Fe, I'd lead them to believe that we were partners in crime. Both deals, of course, would be fake, American and French undercover operations. In the U.S. deal, I'd sell forged paintings to undercover FBI agents posing as Colombian drug dealers aboard an undercover FBI yacht in Miami. The French deal would be similar, except that I'd sell fake paintings to French undercover agents in Marseilles.

I laid out the plan in a long e-mail to everyone involved. At the end, I wrote, "I caution everyone involved that in order to make this work we need complete cooperation and advocacy. Ladies and gentlemen, we all have to be on the same page on this."

Once I got the green light, I started making preparations. I called Washington and arranged to borrow a sack full of diamonds and a half dozen Krugerrands from an FBI forfeiture evidence vault. I called Miami to lease the yacht and dug up a bunch of fake paintings for the first sale—six forgeries seized by the government long ago, imitations of works by Degas, Dalí, Klimt, O'Keeffe, Soutine, and Chagall. The Miami division agreed to supply a cadre of undercover FBI agents to help.

When everything was squared away, I called Sunny and Laurenz. The call to Sunny was easy. I told him I needed his help as muscle. He was so eager to make some cash, he said yes, no questions asked.

I approached Laurenz differently. He didn't need money and he didn't fancy himself a man of muscle, so I played to his weakness—he was so rich and so bored that he'd developed an odd passion for danger. He was an adrenaline freak. Laurenz loved to Jet Ski, skydive, snow ski, and make outrageously risky real estate deals. So when he balked at joining me on the yacht deal, I teased him about his manhood.

"I've known you for a year now, Laurenz," I said. "You certainly talk a good game, drive a Rolls and all, but the truth is I've never seen you in action. And we're talking about doing a $30 million deal together. Let's just say I'd like to see how you handle something like this before I commit to something like that."

"OK, OK, I do it with you, Bob," he said. "But I can't do it next week."

"Why not?"

"Going on vacation."

I bit my tongue. "Skiing again?"

"Hawaii."

LAURENZ WASN'T THE only one headed to Hawaii.

Just as we geared up for the Miami yacht operation, my best ally in Washington, Eric Ives, was transferred to Honolulu. The move was unrelated to the Gardner case, simply part of the routine FBI rotation of young supervisors around the country every three years. But it was a huge loss. During the Gardner investigation, Eric repeatedly stood up to turf-conscious supervisors. On his final day, he even sent an e-mail imploring them to give me the space I needed to do my job.

The FBI did not replace Eric. It left his position as chief of the Major Theft Unit open, creating a vacuum. Many months later, things turned worse. The FBI reorganized its operations and eliminated the Major Theft Unit, scattering its programs to other sections.

The Art Crime Team was reassigned to the Violent Crime Section, where it instantly became a low priority, eclipsed by the FBI's bread-and-butter duties, like catching kidnappers, gangsters, drug dealers, bank robbers, and fugitives.

Inside the bureaucracy, the Art Crime Team lost its juice.

WITH LAURENZ ON vacation, the Miami/Marseilles boat stings remained on hold. But my supposed colleagues in France stayed busy.

On a Thursday call with Pierre, I learned that the French SIAT undercover chief and a Paris-based FBI agent now planned to try to squeeze me out and run the operation entirely in France. The same SIAT chief who'd once told me it was impossible for Laurenz to enter France now planned to sneak him in and do the deal without me. I was dumbfounded. It was one thing for the Boston supervisor to try to tell a street agent like me what to do, but it was quite another for an American colleague in Paris to conspire against me with a foreign police officer.

I told Pierre about Fred, his crazy EC, his rants, and the Washington meeting. I told him about losing Eric as unit chief and how it would hurt the FBI Art Crime Team. Pierre and I talked about the Miami boat deal, and when I mentioned that it would be delayed for three weeks because Laurenz was going on vacation in Hawaii, Pierre burst out laughing.

"What's so damn funny?" I asked.

"My guys in Paris, your guys in Paris, Fred in Boston, Laurenz off sunning himself at the beach when you want to do a deal, losing your friend Eric from Washington," he said. "Everyone is giving you the banana to slip on."

THE NIGHT BEFORE the Miami yacht deal, I brought the six fake paintings to Laurenz's house. Sunny helped me carry them inside.

The three of us sat under palm trees by the pool and smoked cigars, steps from the dock and Laurenz's beloved Jet Skis.

I laid out the plan—the six paintings for $1.2 million. Laurenz tried to act cool, but I could tell he was excited. I doubted Laurenz ever got his hands dirty; he paid others to do it. Sunny sat quietly and smoked, sipping a bottle of Evian. When I finished, I asked Sunny if he had any questions.

"*Non*, I am OK," he said. "I have my insurance. Got my gun."

"No, no weapons," I said. "If they pat us down on the boat, it'll insult our hosts. I've never done a deal with a gun. Never needed it."

Sunny laughed. "And I've never done a deal without one!" Sunny turned to Laurenz. "Tell Bob what Patrick said." Patrick was one of their contacts on the French Riviera.

"He wants to sell us about ten paintings," Laurenz said. "There is a Monet and I think others. He will send pictures. He says they are worth forty million euros and he wants six million."

"What's that in dollars?" I said. "Ten million?"

"Mmm, maybe more like nine," Laurenz said. "You interested? With these guys, you don't screw around. Once you agree to buy the paintings, you must follow through."

"Or?" I said, acting dumb to try to provoke a reaction.

Sunny scoffed and stood, agitated, pacing, and speaking rapidly in French. Laurenz translated: "We must be entirely serious. We do not want to go to war with these people. They are stone-cold killers. They killed my best friend. He was driving in his car and the assassin pulled up at a light on a motorcycle and shot him. We are dealing with loosely organized gangs. Maybe two hundred guys in all, in France, Spain, Serbia, Corsica. Different gangs have different caches of paintings. Some of these guys have been in prison for years, and have been hiding the paintings, waiting out their sentences. Some paintings are badly damaged because they've been taken from their original frames. One of the big Rembrandts you seek is badly damaged. Our friend Patrick is going to try to get it repaired."

Alarmed, I interrupted Sunny's spiel. "No, no. Tell him not to do that. It might make it worse, decrease the value. Let me get the professionals to do that. I know some guys."

I told Sunny I'd think about buying the Monet, but I really wanted the Old Masters, especially the Vermeer and the Rembrandts.

Sunny was adamant. "First, you must take what they offer."

WE DID THE Miami yacht deal the following afternoon.

We drove the six paintings to the harbor in Laurenz's new platinum Rolls. Sunny and I carried them onto the undercover yacht, *The Pelican*. We cruised Miami Harbor into the late afternoon, watched the undercover bikini babes dance and eat strawberries, and I "sold" the fake paintings to the fake Colombian drug dealers for $1.2 million.

The Colombians paid me with a phony wire transfer and with the diamonds and Krugerrands from the FBI vault. When we left the boat, I tossed the small sack of ten diamonds to Sunny and gave Laurenz a few of the gold coins. "For your help today," I said.

Sunny held the sack aloft and said, "Dinner's on me."

We drove to La Goulue to celebrate. On the ride up Miami Beach, Sunny seemed more interested in talking about the drug dealers and the bikini girls than the painting deal. While on the boat, he said, he'd talked to one of the Colombians about a possible cocaine deal.

"I don't know about those guys," Sunny said. "I don't know them. Maybe they are cops."

"Yeah, be careful—I don't know them well either," I said, trying to play it cool without discouraging him from considering the drug deal. "You don't want to be messing around with drugs anyway, Sunny. You make more money with art. But hey, man, if you like drugs, that's up to you. Maybe you know drugs better. And those guys, I know their money is good. But that's all you. I don't want any part of it."

"Mmm," Sunny said. "I don't know."

I dropped it, unsure if he would take the bait. The cocaine angle, created by the Miami agents, was designed to develop several opportunities in the Gardner case. At a minimum, we hoped it would allow us to introduce Sunny to more undercover FBI agents, men he might grow to trust. We could wait to see how the Gardner case was playing out and, if appropriate, bust Sunny on a serious drug charge and try to flip him—threaten him with a very long prison sentence unless he agreed to help us recover the Boston paintings. Also, we believed that a drug scenario might create a safety valve for use in an emergency. If we needed to make a sudden arrest of one of the Gardner conspirators, here or in France, we could always deflect blame to one of Sunny's new drug buddies, plant the idea that one of them was a snitch.

By the time we arrived at the French restaurant, the three of us were talking about art again, not cocaine. We discussed the plan to helicopter into Monaco, and whether Patrick, Sunny's French connection, could meet us there. I suggested that this would be a lot easier if Patrick and his partners simply flew to Florida to meet with us. Then we could hash everything out. Laurenz liked this idea and Sunny said he would call Patrick.

Then, out of the blue, Sunny asked me if I liked Picasso. When I said sure, he asked me if I'd heard about the recent heist in Paris, the theft of two paintings valued at $66 million from the apartment of Picasso's granddaughter. I told him I had. Laurenz and Sunny smiled slyly.

Our meals arrived and Sunny said, "We eat. We talk business later." We spoke of family, Jet Skis, Laurenz's Hawaiian vacation, and the deal he got on his new platinum Rolls-Royce. We never returned to the Picassos.

Everything seemed copacetic. The bill came while Laurenz was on a phone call and Sunny used the opportunity to politely excuse himself and slip away, sticking Laurenz with the check.

* * *

IN MAY, BOSTON and Paris launched a new paperwork salvo.

It was a clever setup to push me out and began with an EC from Boston to Paris. On the surface, the questions seemed innocuous enough: Given the "Bob is a cop" suspicion, did the French police believe that my undercover identity had been compromised? Could I safely travel undercover to France to meet with the people offering to sell the Gardner paintings?

The answer from Paris: While there was no direct evidence that my cover was blown, the Paris office noted that "a significant degree of danger will exist" if I worked undercover in France.

I studied the two documents and shook my head. Of course an international undercover operation would pose "a significant degree" of danger! You didn't need to be an FBI agent to know that. But in the risk-averse culture of the FBI, I knew that a memo like that would set off alarm bells and flashing yellow lights. Everyone was now on notice that I might be hurt or killed in France, and no supervisor wanted that on his record, especially when we'd all been warned in writing.

No one was directly saying I couldn't remain on the case and work undercover in Paris, but the vibe was chilling. My supervisors in Philadelphia got on the line with Fred and his bosses, then with the FBI supervisors in Paris and Miami. Afterward, my Philadelphia bosses told me that the atmosphere had grown so toxic that Boston didn't even want me to play a consulting role. The internal strife was so intense that it now jeopardized the case and the safety of the agents involved, including me. My Philadelphia bosses advised me to withdraw from the Gardner investigation. Reluctantly, I agreed.

But how to tell Laurenz and Sunny without ruining the case?

I kept it short, sweet, and as close to the truth as possible. It was nice working with you guys, I explained, but my boss has lost confidence in me and wants someone else to step in. I told them I could no longer take their calls.

Hysterical, Laurenz left me voice mails and sent several unsettling e-mails, rants that revealed desperation and vulnerabilities he had never displayed in person.

"Good evening!" Laurenz wrote in one e-mail in broken English and peppered with capital letters and exclamation points. "I am very sad. I am really in a difficult situation tonight. Why doing all the risks, my life, my future, my time? For nothing! Why? I was thinking we could really get these paintings and now I know it is just an illusion? Why? Why? I REALLY NEED SOME EXPLANATIONS. Good night! Sweet dreams!"

I felt compelled to reply, but did so with an incredibly bureaucratic, cover-your-ass e-mail, one that conveyed the warmth of a corporate customer service representative. "I understand your concerns and questions and have relayed them . . ." I felt awful, but I didn't have a choice.

Laurenz responded in minutes. "It's ridiculous! I am spending/investing a lot of money and now you throw me a DOG BONE? Be nice? Talk to someone else? No! The only person I will talk to is BOB! ONLY BOB! I don't trust anyone else."

I let the FBI offices in Boston and Paris know about the e-mails and calls and they were not pleased. In short order, they sent a request to my boss in Philadelphia, demanding all recordings and investigative notes of my contacts with Laurenz. The memo read like a subpoena.

It marked the lowest moment in my FBI career since December 20, 1989, the night of the accident. I began growing irritable, sleepless. I tried to hide it from the kids, but Donna bore the brunt of my frustration. She understood I was one year from retirement, and encouraged me to fight for my reputation.

Few inside or outside the FBI knew of my despair. On the surface, everything seemed fine and my success as the FBI's top art-crime sleuth only grew. That summer, I recovered the original, hand-edited manuscript of Pearl Buck's Pulitzer Prize–winning novel *The Good Earth*. The press conference was well attended, but as I took my usual place, out of sight behind the television cameras, I couldn't help feeling hollow.

FOR A FEW weeks, I followed orders and didn't call anyone involved in the Gardner case. But I couldn't stop Laurenz or Pierre from contacting me.

One afternoon in mid-July, Laurenz sent me several e-mails I couldn't ignore.

Attached to each e-mail was a photograph of a Picasso painting beside a week-old copy of a Paris newspaper. I instantly recognized these "proof of life" pictures as the paintings stolen from Picasso's granddaughter's apartment—the ones Sunny and Laurenz had mentioned offhandedly at the restaurant a few months earlier. Laurenz wanted me to buy them.

I didn't respond, but I let my supervisors know. Soon, Pierre was calling from Paris.

"You know of the Picassos stolen in Paris?" he said. "I have now seen the e-mails."

"Right," I said, cautiously.

"There is more," Pierre said. I knew Pierre was tapping many phones, including Sunny's, and his team was doing its best to monitor any calls Laurenz made to France. "On the wiretaps, Sunny and Laurenz are talking to these bad guys who have the Picassos about selling the paintings to our undercover man, Andre. And on the phone, they say that Andre can be trusted because he works with a man named Bob in Miami. And I do not think there is another Bob in Miami who they are talking about."

"Probably not, no."

I shook my head as I untangled the logic of the situation. At the beginning of the Gardner investigation, Andre had vouched for me to Laurenz, leading him to believe that Andre and I had worked together as shady art dealers. But now that Laurenz and Sunny believed the three of us had actually committed a major crime together—the "sale" on *The Pelican*—the vouch had doubled back on itself. Sunny and Laurenz were now telling the thieves that Andre could be trusted because *Bob* could be trusted. Yes, Laurenz was annoyed with me because I'd pulled out of the Gardner deal, but he still believed I was trustworthy. After all, we'd done business together and no one had been arrested. What could be better evidence of my criminal credentials than that?

"So, this has created a problem because of the Boston case," Pierre said. "Your friends Fred and the others at FBI, they ask us to wait. To not take the paintings right now. You understand why?"

"Yeah, I do." The moment Andre and his fellow officers completed their sting in the Picasso case, making arrests, the thieves would know that someone involved was actually an informant or an undercover cop. Suspicion would likely turn to Andre and perhaps to his American partner, Bob, the man whose bona fides Sunny and Laurenz had used to convince the thieves to work with Andre in the first place. If that happened, it might ruin any chance of using Laurenz and Sunny to recover the Gardner paintings.

I also understood Pierre's dilemma. He couldn't let $66 million worth of Picassos slip away. If word got out that he had failed to recover the artwork as a favor to the FBI, it would create a scandal and probably scuttle his career.

So I offered Pierre a suggestion: When you make the bust, pretend to arrest your undercover police officer. That way the thieves won't know who betrayed them. At a minimum, it will buy us time.

Pierre liked the idea. "You are a good chess player," he said, and promised to make it happen.

Incredibly, Pierre's orders were not carried out during the Paris sting—the French SWAT team failed to arrest their undercover officer with the thieves. Worse, during an interrogation, another French policeman confirmed to one of the thieves that the buyer was in fact an undercover agent. It didn't take long for the thieves in Paris to make the link from Andre to Laurenz and to me.

Pierre called and apologized profusely for the screwup. It wasn't intentional, he said, and I believed him.

Unfortunately, the consequences were immediate and severe.

LAURENZ CALLED IN a panic a few days after the Picasso sting.

"They want to kill me! They want you! You and me! They want to assassinate us both!"

I told him to calm down and start from the beginning. Associates of the Picasso thieves were in Miami with Sunny, he said, demanding answers from Laurenz and money for the thieves' legal bills.

"I was at the Blockbuster," Laurenz sputtered. "You know I go every Tuesday for the new releases? They follow me there and they want to put me in the car and take me away. I told you these guys don't fuck around."

"How'd you get away?"

"I saw them from inside the Blockbuster and have my wife call 911 and when the police come I go out to talk to them."

"Smart. Where are you now?"

"A hotel. The Loews. They take my dogs here." Laurenz loved his two mutts, took them everywhere. He began bragging about the size and cost of his suite, and I let him prattle on. I needed time to think.

I wanted to know more about the goons threatening Laurenz. For one thing, they might lead me to the missing Gardner paintings. For another, they were threatening my life. But I had to find a way of stepping in that would be plausible to Laurenz and remain in character for Bob Clay. Here I held an advantage: Laurenz didn't know that I knew he had floated my name as Andre's partner to the Picasso thieves. As far as I ought to know, the French thieves had never heard of me.

So I said, "Laurenz, back up a second—you said they want to kill me, too. Why would they want to kill me? All I did was look at e-mails you sent me. I was never in this deal."

Laurenz fell into the trap, and blamed Sunny. "Sunny said to them that you are a partner with Andre, and that we can trust Andre because we trust *you*. So now they want to know where you live. They want assassinate you because you are responsible for their friend being in jail."

I exploded. "What the—? Why would Sunny say that? Never mind! Who do these guys think they are? I want to meet them! You set it up!"

Laurenz called back the next day. We'd meet the two Frenchmen at the bar at a luxury hotel in Hollywood, Florida. In three days.

THE OP PLAN for the hotel meet was a compromise, hashed out by committee. As one FBI employee later handwrote across the coversheet of his after-action report, it looked like "a total clusterfuck."

Given the circumstances, I was officially brought back on to the case, but Fred made it clear the move was only temporary. He insisted that I use the meeting to introduce his undercover agent from Boston into the mix. The agent who would replace me was named Sean, and he often played a Boston mobster. I was instructed to vouch for Sean, to explain that he was taking over for me on the Gardner deal. I doubted it would work. Sean was a nice guy, but he didn't know anything about international art deals. Besides, the Picasso case had already spooked the Frenchmen—this was the point of the meeting. It seemed like the worst possible time to get them to start dealing with a complete stranger.

"What if these guys refuse to deal with Sean?" I asked. "What if they insist on working with me? What do we say then?"

"We tell them to take their business elsewhere," Sean replied.

I laughed. "Seriously? What about leaning on them? Take control of the situation? Maybe make a veiled threat?"

"No threats, not me," Sean said. "This special agent is not going to be on tape threatening anybody."

Sean was more worried about covering his ass than protecting mine. I didn't waste effort arguing with him.

Before I left to meet Laurenz in the lobby, I stuffed a handgun in each pocket. It was the first time in my nineteen-year career I'd carried a weapon while working undercover. But this situation felt different, and I'd already been threatened. The people I planned to meet weren't looking to sell me a priceless piece of art; they wanted to know why they shouldn't kill me.

As I stashed the guns, Fred shot me a look. I said to Fred, "If these guys start to fuck with me, I'm going to kill them."

"Please," Fred said. "Don't shoot anybody."

"I don't want to shoot anybody—never have—but these guys have already told Laurenz that they want to kill me."

That got Sean's attention. "Are these guys that dangerous?"

"Yeah, they're that dangerous," I said. "Listen, Laurenz told me a story about one of these guys. He has a thing for knives. The guy cut himself the first time he met Laurenz to show how tough he was. Sliced his arm and sat there, letting it bleed, real menacing-like, blood dripping down. And he says to Laurenz, 'I don't have any problem with pain. This is what real life is all about.' So yeah, Sean. A guy like that? I take him seriously."

SEAN AND I met Laurenz in the lobby.

Before we entered the bar, Laurenz described the two would-be assassins waiting with Sunny for us. He called them Vanilla and Chocolate. Vanilla was the white one—long, stringy dark hair and a crooked nose. Chocolate was black, bald, and wore silver braces across his teeth. He was the one with the knife fetish and was built like a linebacker.

We met them at the bar and the six of us took seats around a corner table—Laurenz, Sean, and me on one side, Sunny, Vanilla, and Chocolate on the other.

Vanilla and Chocolate were large, but they were not stupid.

They treaded carefully, treating me with feigned respect. If I was who I claimed to be—a shady art broker with access to millionaire clients—the Frenchmen knew I could make them a great deal of money. It would be foolish to insult me before they got to know me. If, on the other hand, they concluded that I was a snitch or a cop, they could deal with me later.

Sensing their hesitation, I put them on the defensive. "Look," I said aggressively, my hands under the table, inches from the hidden guns, "it's obvious someone in France gave your guy up and now we're all in trouble because of this. Your problem is in France."

Chocolate said, "The FBI is involved in this. That's not in France."

I shot back, "Don't you think I know the FBI is involved? They came to my house, woke me up, scared my wife to hell, asking us questions about Picasso and this guy and that guy in Paris. This is not good for business, having FBI agents showing up at my home. I've got a reputation."

Chocolate wanted to know why my name had surfaced in Paris. How did the undercover French policeman know to use it to lure the Paris thieves?

I smiled and sat back in my chair. "A damn good question," I said. "I've been wondering the same thing. I wish I knew." I pointed to Sunny. "Maybe they're tapping his phone. You know Sunny and I are working on all kinds of things."

Chocolate asked about his arrested friends' legal expenses for the Picasso charges. Would Laurenz help pay them?

Laurenz loved playing tough guy, but he knew there was but one correct answer if he wanted to stay alive. "*Oui,*" he said sharply. He looked away.

Problem solved, I moved my hands away from my pockets and changed the subject, introducing Sean. He stuck out his hand in greeting, but Chocolate and Vanilla just stared back.

Sean spoke gruffly, like a tough guy in a '40s movie. "OK, here's the deal. From now on," he said, "you deal with me. You don't talk to Bob. I'm the one you contact for business. As far as you are concerned, I am the business. You go through me."

Sunny and his French friends looked confused, as if to say, what the hell is this? Laurenz translated for them. Chocolate spoke rapidly in French to Sunny, and then turned to Sean. "*Non,* we deal with Bob, Sunny, and Laurenz—only."

Sean shook his head. "You call me from now on or we're done."

Chocolate sputtered a small laugh. He said to Sean, "Who are you again?"

Fred's lame game plan was falling apart. I cut in. "Call Sean. It's good. Tell you what: Let's cool off for thirty days and then we get back in touch, OK?"

Chocolate didn't commit either way. He began talking with Sunny again in French. The waitress came by and Sean clumsily jumped to get the check. He shoved a credit card at her. What was his hurry?

Sunny and his friends stood and walked off, headed toward the beach. Laurenz, Sean, and I went the other way, toward the lobby and the valet stand. Laurenz remained uncharacteristically quiet until he and I were alone, back inside the Rolls. He started to open his mouth, but his cell phone rang. It was Sunny. They spoke in French and Laurenz began laughing.

Laurenz hung up, shook his head. "They say of your friend Sean, they say, 'Who is this fucking guy?' They say they wish to stuff him in the trunk of their car but they cannot because it is a rental and he is too big to fit.' Sunny says they think he's an idiot and they won't deal with him."

"What do *you* think?"

"He is a joke," Laurenz said. "And I think he might be a cop."

"What do you mean?"

"He is no wiseguy. This I know."

"Why do say that?"

"He is a pussycat. He say, 'Oh, you don't deal with me, I walk away.' Oh, I am so scared. A real wiseguy, he look you in the eye and say very quietly, very calmly, 'Fuck me? Fuck you. You tell me why I should not kill you today. Tell me now or you are dead before the day is over. Thank you. Good-bye.' This is what the real wiseguy say."

"Well—"

Laurenz floored the Rolls, rocketing away from the valet stand. "This guy Sean, he use green American Express card to pay the bill! A real wiseguy doesn't use a credit card. He uses cash. Always, always! And he never takes a receipt! Never! Never!"

I didn't know what to say. He was right.

Laurenz turned toward the causeway and downtown Miami.

After a few moments, he said, "I drop you at your hotel and then maybe I not see you again. Because if we had not done the deal on the boat, I would be thinking for sure you are a cop. But now"—Laurenz took his eyes off the road for a moment and squinted at me—"I don't know if you are a cop and I don't care. I am in fucking bad shape, OK? We are through."

Laurenz stepped on the accelerator and cranked the radio.

He was out.

WITH LAURENZ GONE, the Boston FBI office shut down Operation Masterpiece.

Wonderful, I thought. Bureaucracies and turf fighting on both sides of the Atlantic had destroyed the best chance in a decade to rescue the Gardner paintings. We'd also blown an opportunity to infiltrate a major art crime ring in France, a loose network of mobsters holding as many as seventy stolen masterpieces.

Our failure convinced me that the FBI was no longer the can-do force it was when I'd joined in 1988. The bureau was becoming a risk-averse bureaucracy like any other government agency, filled with mediocrity and people more concerned about their career than the mission.

The Art Crime Team, launched with such promise, seemed

headed for that fate too, roiled by constant turnover. We'd not only lost Eric Ives as unit chief, but our best prosecutor as well, Bob Goldman. Petty and insecure bosses in Philadelphia had given my best friend an ultimatum: Drop art crime and return to garden-variety drug and bank robbery cases or find another job. Goldman had called their bluff and quit, abruptly ending a twenty-four-year career in law enforcement. Perhaps worse, half of the original street agents assigned to the Art Crime Team had now moved on, looking to advance their careers. It was disheartening.

As I began my final twelve months as an FBI agent in the fall of 2007, I planned to finish up a few lingering cases, train an under-cover replacement, and start thinking about my retirement party. I'd travel with Donna, visit my sons in college, attend my daughter's high school recitals.

Then one afternoon that fall, my undercover cell phone buzzed.

It was Sunny.

CHAPTER 25

ENDGAME

Barcelona. January 2008.

FOUR MONTHS AFTER SUNNY'S PHONE CALL, I FOUND myself in a frayed Barcelona hotel room, negotiating with his boss, Patrick.

Six of us crammed around a flimsy table and two single beds. Patrick and I sat on opposite sides of the table by an open window. Sunny and an undercover Spanish police officer perched on the edge of one bed. My muscle, the two FBI agents from Miami, still posing as Colombian drug dealers, lounged on the other bed.

A hidden camera in the ceiling fan recorded everything. A Spanish SWAT team waited next door.

Patrick, a lithe and cocksure Frenchman of Armenian descent, perhaps six foot three, sat a foot from my face, chain-smoking Marlboro reds. He was sixty years old, with close-cropped gray hair and a day's white stubble on his chin. He kept his brown eyes locked on mine, patient and as focused as a sniper. His words came deliberately and in short sentences.

"We are older men, you and I," Patrick said in French. "Money is nice, but liberty is very important."

I'd hoped to bring along a French-speaking undercover FBI agent to translate, but the bureau hadn't been able to find anyone qualified. So the Spanish officer did the job. He moved from French to English and English to French with speed and gusto, but also with an unsettling lisp and effeminate voice that belied the tense negotiation. I could imagine the macho FBI agents watching on video in the next room, snickering at the incongruity.

I said, "I don't want to go to jail either."

"Yes, we know what is important."

"So," I said, hoping to get a confession on tape, "tell me about the robbery."

Patrick was only happy to.

I ALWAYS TELL rookies that you've got to run down every lead. You never know which one will pan out.

Sometimes long shots pay off.

When Laurenz had dropped out of the deal, the agents at the Boston FBI office had thrown up their hands and closed the file. But the Miami division had not given up on Sunny; its agents opened a new investigation, Operation Masterpiece II, and lured Sunny back with the promise of a large cocaine deal. Soon, Sunny was calling me again to talk art.

At first, we spoke of the Vermeer and Rembrandt. But he also began to offer a second set of paintings—four works, including a Monet and a Sisley—stolen the previous summer from a museum in Nice. The two sets of paintings were held by different sets of gangsters, Sunny said.

I made it clear that I wanted the Boston paintings, not the Nice paintings. Sunny said I had to buy the Nice paintings first. It was a way to build trust, he said.

With the window to the Gardner paintings cracked open again, I had agreed and Sunny had set up the meeting in Barcelona to negotiate a price for the Nice paintings. I found it curious that Sunny chose Spain as a meeting spot—we knew from the wiretaps that the Vermeer was likely held in Spain.

I also figured we couldn't lose. If Sunny was merely stringing me along about the Gardner paintings, we'd still recover the Nice paintings and help my friend Pierre solve a big art heist. On the other hand, if a deal for the Nice paintings led to a Gardner deal, we'd hit a grand slam.

Still, I approached the Spain meeting with extreme caution. I'd recently learned that a few weeks after our Florida hotel confrontation, Sunny had pulled an FBI informant aside and offered him $65,000 to have Laurenz killed.

IN THE BARCELONA hotel room, I let Patrick spool out the details of his big Nice museum heist. He was proud of his work.

Patrick explained that he had picked a Sunday in August, the slowest visitor day of the week during the slowest month of the year. He'd chosen the apricot-and-cream-colored Musée des Beaux-Arts because it is set off the beaten tourist track, perched on a hill in a residential neighborhood. I knew that the Musée des Beaux-Arts shared something in common with the Gardner and the Barnes—it was the inspiration and former residence of a single patron of the arts, a nineteenth-century Ukrainian princess. The museum still held important works, though its once grand vista of the city's Bay of Angels was now obscured by a forest of bland apartment buildings.

Patrick described his four accomplices as two close friends and two nobodies, gypsies. The five of them dressed in blue city maintenance jumpsuits and shielded their faces with either bandanas or motorcycle helmets. Security was a joke. No surveillance cameras. No alarms. The half dozen guards on duty were unarmed, pimply-faced kids. Pushovers, Patrick recalled. With their ill-fitting blazers and drooping khakis, the guards were perhaps the worst-dressed males in France.

Patrick said his crew was in and out in four minutes.

Wielding handguns, the thieves pushed open the glass door at the entrance and ordered the guards and a handful of visitors to the floor. The gypsy henchmen held everyone at bay in the foyer as the others sprinted toward their targets. One thief ran through a sky-lit ground floor garden to a rear gallery, removing two paintings by the Flemish artist Jan Brueghel the Elder, *Allegory of Water* and *Allegory of Earth*. Patrick and an accomplice vaulted up sixty-six marble steps to the second floor, then scampered another thirty-four paces, past a Chéret mural and a Rodin rendering of *The Kiss,* to a room lined with Impressionist paintings, each hanging by a single hook. Patrick and his buddy lifted Monet's *Cliffs Near Dieppe* and Sisley's *Lane of Poplars at Moret-sur-Loing* and raced back downstairs. The thieves escaped by motorbike and blue Peugeot van.

I'd already read the French police file and knew the story well. But as Patrick related his tale, I reacted with awe at his cleverness and derring-do.

As a favor to Pierre, I began by pushing hard for the Sisley and Monet. Pierre sought these above the others because they were property of the French national government, on loan from the Musée d'Orsay in Paris. The Brueghels were owned by the city of Nice and less valuable.

Patrick opened the negotiation by valuing the paintings at $40 million. I told him he was crazy, that the four paintings were worth no more than $5 million on the open market, which meant they were worth $500,000 tops on the black market. We negotiated for more than ninety minutes in the foul hotel room, with its dingy drapes and air stale with cigarette smoke. The air conditioner didn't work and I didn't dare flip on the ceiling fan because I worried it might gum up the hidden camera and microphone.

Patrick was a fierce negotiator and I found myself in an unusual position. In other cases—with the Rembrandt in Copenhagen, the Geronimo headdress in Philadelphia, the Koplowitz paintings in Madrid—I'd been able to offer any amount, knowing I'd never have to pay the money. But here, it was possible we might let the money for the Nice paintings walk—*if we were near certain it would lead to the Gardner paintings.*

As the afternoon waned, Patrick dropped his offer from $4 million to $3 million. Patrick was hungry to cash in. He'd planned this great heist, pulled it off, and all he had to show for it was four pretty pictures that could land him back in prison. He'd said he'd left the Nice paintings in France and had come only to talk. But what he if was lying? What if he had the paintings close by? Could he be tempted by a bag of cash? And what of the Gardner paintings?

I threw out a couple of options.

What if I gave Patrick $50,000 cash on the spot for the four Nice paintings with the balance due after I sold them? If I didn't sell them, I told Patrick, I'd return the paintings and he could keep the $50,000. He said no.

OK, I said, what if I gave him the $50,000 for just the Monet and Sisley? He could keep the other two while I tried to sell them. Again, Patrick said no.

I gave it one last try and swung for the fences. On the chance that Sunny had lied, and that Patrick somehow had access to the Gardner paintings, I made a proposal. I pointed to my friends from Miami on the bed and told Patrick that they had a boat moored on the coast here, ready to smuggle the paintings back to Florida. Now, I said, Sunny knows I've got $30 million sitting in the bank, cash ready to be wired the moment I receive the Vermeer, the Rembrandt, and the other Boston paintings. So while I'm here, I said, why don't we just do that deal too, and put all the paintings on the boat?

Sunny looked away from both of us, quiet. Patrick switched from French to English. He said, "You want Vermeer? I'll get you Vermeer."

"Can you get it?" I asked.

"No problem," he said confidently. "I get anything you want. I find you one. There are many Vermeer." He was offering to steal one for me.

"No, I don't want a new one—they're too hot," I said. "I want an old one, missing for many years."

Patrick nodded. "I sell you paintings from Nice. Then we talk more with Sunny."

"Right," I said. "OK." So Patrick had no access to the Gardner paintings. But Sunny, I still believed, was using the Nice sale to test me. If I could win his trust with this buy, we still had a chance.

Patrick and I negotiated for another hour and finally settled on a tentative price for the Nice paintings, a little less than $3 million.

Patrick took a long drag on his cigarette. He blew smoke from the corner of his mouth, toward the translator. In English, he said, "Bob, very important, we would like business but very quiet business. You understand what I say?"

"I understand."

"Very, very quiet."

"*Silencieux*," I said.

"*Voilà*," Patrick said and stubbed out his cigarette.

AFTER BARCELONA, I never saw Sunny or Patrick again.

We spoke by phone in code but once we settled on the price I told them to work out the logistics with the undercover FBI agents in Miami. I was a financier, I explained, not a smuggler.

Four months later, when Patrick and a French friend visited Sunny in South Florida, I told them I was too busy to see them. My colleagues in Miami treated Sunny, Patrick, and their friends to one last party aboard *The Pelican*, and they set the final handover of the Nice paintings for June in Marseilles. The French were still refusing to allow me or any other FBI agents to go undercover in Marseilles, and Sunny knew better than to meet with anyone but me. Luckily, Patrick was calling the shots now, and he was dumb and desperate enough to agree to deal with my buyer in Marseilles—who was, of course, a SIAT agent, a member of the French undercover police.

The final takedown was imminent.

ON THE MORNING of June 4, 2008, a blue Peugeot van pulled out of a garage in Carry-le-Rouet, a tiny coastal Riviera town west of Marseilles. A compact beige jalopy followed close behind, Patrick at the wheel.

Undercover French officers watching nearby radioed ahead, noting that the van was heading southeast, as expected. The vehicles wove through downtown Marseilles on side streets, doubling back to avoid detection in Wednesday morning rush-hour traffic. But they did not shake Pierre's surveillance men. How could they? The French police knew precisely where they were headed. The thieves were on their way to meet a SIAT agent, a man they believed to be working for me.

When the van and the jalopy reached the old harbor, they headed for the Corniche John Fitzgerald Kennedy, the picturesque road that hugs the rocky Riviera coast, rising fifty feet above the lapping waves of the glimmering Mediterranean Sea. The gangsters with the paintings came armed for battle. One of the men in the van brought an automatic weapon. In the small car that followed, Patrick carried a Colt .45 under his jacket. His passenger, a hulking man with shoulder-length blond hair, gripped a Czech-made hand grenade.

The vehicles snaked their way past the four-star Pullman Marseille Palm Beach, a mod-style hotel cut into the seaside beneath the roadway. Pierre and a small army of French police officers were coordinating the sting from the Pullman, two hundred meters from the takedown site, staffing a command center with a SWAT team and, in case it was necessary, a suitcase full of euros.

Beyond the Pullman, the thieves' cars rolled into a valley flanked by curved public beaches and a dog track, and anchored by a series of boardwalk by-the-sea pubs and shops, a spot the police chose be-cause it was easy to block all exits. It was still early—the morning sun still growing from the eastern hills, casting a warm orange glow across the wind-whipped beach—and so the thieves found plenty of free parking on the street.

Patrick and his friend with the grenade stepped out on the side-walk and stretched, fifty meters from the sea. The guys in the van stayed put.

The French undercover officer waiting to authenticate the paint-ings began walking down the sidewalk, toward Patrick. The cop was alone, but plenty of colleagues wandered nearby in disguise—sweeping a storefront, walking a dog, sitting at a bus stop.

The thieves and the cop met by the beach.

Over the radio, someone gave the order.

A force of twenty policemen converged, weapons drawn and with overwhelming force, tackling Patrick, the friend with the grenade and—well done!—the undercover cop, too, preserving his identity and possibly mine.

IT WAS 2 a.m. in Philadelphia, but Pierre called anyway to fill me in. The French police found all four paintings in the blue van. They were in good condition.

He asked me about Sunny and Laurenz.

Laurenz wouldn't be charged with a crime, I said, because he wasn't involved in the Nice deal.

Sunny would be arrested at dawn at his home near Fort Lau-derdale, I said. The press releases would start flowing in the after-noon.

AMERICAN GRAND JURY indictments can be written two ways.

There is a short form: A one- or two-page double-spaced vague statement of the law violated. The short form is preferred when the case is routine or when the government wants to deflect attention from an ongoing undercover aspect of the case.

Then there is the long-form indictment: A multipage, detailed document with a long narrative, a "speaking indictment" that summarizes the crime and every meeting between the accused and the undercover officers. Prosecutors almost always use the long-form indictment when they plan to convene a press conference. They do this because the rules require them to stick to the facts contained in the indictment. The more titillating facts they stuff into the indictment, the more they can repeat in front of the television cameras.

I didn't see the American paperwork in the Nice case until after the indictment was unsealed and the press release went out.

I was disappointed but not surprised. Although Sunny was charged with just one felony count, prosecutors detailed the case in a long-form indictment that included my role as an undercover agent. The prosecutors didn't mention the link to the Gardner investigation, or use my name, but the way they wrote it, they might as well have. If Sunny's associates truly held the Gardner paintings in Europe, they now knew to never trust me, or anyone else connected to Sunny. The public indictment, posted on the Internet, left no doubt that I was an undercover FBI agent.

Angry, I called Pierre to let him know of the screwup.

Pierre said, "Like I say, everybody wants a piece of the cake and wants to have their face in the picture." Everyone wanted credit.

We joked about supervisors for a few moments, and I reminded him that he was on his way to making general. We spoke about when we might see each other next, dancing around the big question.

Finally, I said, "Pierre, do you think we had a chance?"

"You mean for the Boston paintings?"

"Yeah."

"*Absolument,*" he said. "We have a good idea who has them. We know to whom Sunny was speaking. But now that we arrest Sunny and say Bob is FBI, the case is gone. We will not have this chance again for many years. Perhaps you will get to try again?"

"No, I'm done," I said. "I retire in three months."

"Who will take your place?"

I hesitated because the query hit a raw nerve. I was eager to help train and brief my replacement, but the FBI didn't seem to be grooming anyone.

I said, "I don't know, Pierre. I don't know. It's a good question."

AUTHOR'S NOTE

UNDERCOVER WORK IS BY NATURE OFTEN SENSITIVE and dangerous. For me, the risks were part of the job, and the thieves I arrested now know my true identity. They do not, however, know everything, and I think it's best left that way. Most of all, I don't want to jeopardize the fellow law-enforcement officers and others who risked their lives to help me. Many of the criminals we caught are not gentlemen thieves; they are thugs who I fear would not hesitate to retaliate against my friends. To protect my colleagues' identities and to protect certain FBI methods, I have omitted or slightly altered a handful of details. The essence of what happened remains unchanged.

Priceless is a memoir, not an autobiography or exposé. It's my version of what happened—no one else's. Much of this book is based on what I recall. My collaborator, John Shiffman, and I strived to reconstruct events as accurately as possible. We reviewed news accounts, government reports, art crime books, art history books, personal notes, video, photographs, and receipts—as well as official and unofficial documents and transcripts. We revisited crime scenes and museums in the United States and Europe. To re-create dialogue during several stings, we reviewed surveillance audio, video, and transcripts. We also leaned on friends and family to help re-create conversations and provide critical context. I thank them again for helping me craft a memoir that hews as closely as possible to the truth.

ACKNOWLEDGMENTS

October 5, 1979.

SINCE WE OPENED EVERY CHAPTER WITH A DATE, IT makes sense to begin the acknowledgments with the most important date in my life—the day I met my wife, Donna, the person without whom I would not be the man I am today. She has led when I followed, given me her strength when I was weak, and carried me when I couldn't walk, through trial and tribute. Without her, the stories in this book and the lines of my life could not have been written. Thank you, my love, for choosing and believing in me for all of these years. We have lived this tale together.

My three children—mature, quiet, and studious Kevin; boisterous, outgoing, and sure-of-himself Jeffrey; intelligent, beautiful, apple of my eye Kristin—have been a grand source of inspiration. They have taught me many things, not the least of which is the importance of staying focused to devotion to a cause, and to family. I am proud to say they are all better people than me. My parents, Robert and Yachiyo Wittman; my brother, William D. Wittman and his wife, Robin; and my uncle Jack Wittman and his wife, Doris, taught me to aim high and encouraged me to pursue my ambitions. Thanks also to Donna's family—her mother, Geraldine, and father, William T. Goodhand Sr.; her brother, William T. Goodhand Jr., and his wife, Susan—who stood by me during the bad times as well as the good.

This book would not have been possible without the help of many individuals. First and foremost is John Shiffman, my cowriter. He is brilliant and I think this will be the start of a long and successful book-writing career for him. It was my pleasure to help him fulfill a dream. His wife, Catherine Dunn Shiffman, worked diligently to ensure that we stayed on course and kept the book accessible. My agent, Larry Weissman, and his partner, Sascha Alper, who believed in me and the project from the beginning, were instrumental in seeing it through. Rick Horgan and Julian Pavia, my editors at Crown, are true gentlemen and made many insightful edits and excellent suggestions.

At the FBI, I owe a special debt of gratitude to Linda Vizi for her help and counsel throughout the years. I would also like to thank my former squad supervisors—John Louden, Tom Dowd, Mike Thompson, Henry James Sweeney, Mike Carbonell, and John Kitzinger. It was my pleasure to serve under them. The Special-Agents-in-Charge of the Philadelphia office during my tenure—Bob Reutter, Bob Conforti, Jeff Lampinski, Jack Eckenrode, Jody Weis, and Jan Fedarcyk—were enlightened enough to support art crime investigations, even when they weren't a headquarters priority.

I never worked alone—it was always a team effort. And while no list of street agents would be complete, I would be remiss not to mention a few who were and are dearest in my heart. First is Stephen J. Heaney, a talented and dedicated investigator and my surrogate little brother, who always had my back when organizing undercover sting takedowns in Philadelphia. Thanks also to Special Agents Doug Hess, Pam Stratton, Michael A. Thompson, Jay Heine, Mitch Banta, Judy Tyler, Konrad Motyka, Sean Sterle, Alejandro Peraza, Gary Bennett, Chris Calarco, Eric Ives, Bob Bazin, Joe Majarowitz, Frank Brostrom, Cathy Begley, Brian Midkiff, Amanda Moran, Lou Vizi, Jack Garcia, Tom Duffy, Jesse Coleman, Al Bodnar, J. J. Klaver, Martin Suarez, Henry Mercadal, Vince Pankoke, Mike German, Jason Richards, Tim Carpenter, Jim Wynne, Johanna Loonie, Greg Johnson, Joaquin "Jack" Garcia, Marc Barri, Leo Tadeo, Ron Kozial, and Ron Nolan. In the front office, Jerri Williams, R. J. Saturno, John Thomas, and Ron Hosko were always friends and often advocates. At FBI headquarters, Lynne Richardson and Bonnie Magness-Gardiner, who managed the art-theft program, deserve kudos for trying to keep the program alive by continuing to stir the pot with managers.

Special thanks to my other comrades in law enforcement: prosecutor Maureen Barden, who taught me the ropes and also how to be compassionate; the trio on the jewelry theft gang case—prosecutor Chris Hall and police officers Edward Quinn and Jack Quinn— who taught me how to *really* conduct a criminal investigation; Fish and Wildlife Special Agent Lucinda Schroeder, for her excellent undercover work in the Joshua Baer and Geronimo war bonnet cases; police Col. Pierre Tabel, the former chief of the French national art crime team; French police officer Damien Delaby; Karl Heinz-Kind and Fabrizio Rossi of Interpol; Gen. Giovanni Nistri, chief of the Italian art crime team; Col. Matthew Bogdanos of the U.S. Marines; and Vernon Rapley and Gary Oldman of Scotland Yard.

I also wish to thank the civilians who helped me during my career—men and women who care deeply about preserving art and antiquities for future generations: Herbert Lottier and Mark Tucker of the Philadelphia Museum of Art, Bob Combs and Wilbur Faulk of the Getty Museum, Ron Simoncini of the Museum of Modern Art, J. J. McLaughlin of the Smithsonian Institution, John Burelli of the Metropolitan Museum of Art, Dick Drent of the Van Gogh Museum, Dennis Ahern of the Tate Museums, Anthony Amore of the Isabella Stewart Gardner Museum, Milton Esterow of *ArtNews,* Renee Bomgardner at the Barnes Foundation, Kristen Froelich at the Atwater Kent Museum, Clark Erickson, C. Brian Rose, Pam Kosty, Therese Marmion, and Steve Epstein at the University of Pennsylvania, Charlene Bangs Bickford of the First Federal Congress Project, Stephen Harmelin of Dilworth Paxson LLP, Walter Alva of the Royal Tombs of Sipan Museum, Andy Newman of Newman Gallery, Carl David of David Gallery, art dealer George Turak, Bo Freeman of Freeman Fine Arts Auction House, Bill Bunch of William Bunch Auctions, Robert Crozier, William O'Connor and the ICEFAT community, Sharon Flesher of the International Foundation of Art Research, and Chris Marinello and Julian Radcliffe of the *Art Loss Register.*

To the world's three best lawyers, Mike Pinsky, Bob Goldman, and Dave Hall: Thank you, counselors. I wouldn't have accomplished anything without you.

Finally, to my friend Denis Bozella, whom I think about every day.

Robert K. Wittman
Philadelphia, Pennsylvania

* * *

JOHN SHIFFMAN WOULD also like to thank Bill Marimow, Vernon Loeb, Tom McNamara, and Avery Rome in Philadelphia; Tom Mashberg in Boston; Vincent Noce and Aline Magnien in Paris; Eleni Papageorgiou in Milan; Blythe Bowman Proulx in Richmond; and Caitlin Lukacs and Brooke Shearer in Washington. Thanks also to my terrific writing and traveling partners, Bob and Donna Wittman. To Peter Franceschina, *grazie mille.* Special thanks to Paul, Sevah, Belle, Will, Jake, Nick, and Sam. Cathy is, of course, priceless.

ABOUT THE AUTHORS

ROBERT K. WITTMAN spent twenty years as an FBI special agent. He helped create and was senior investigator for the bureau's Art Crime Team. He has represented the United States around the world conducting investigations and instructing international police and museums in investigation, recovery, and security techniques. He is president of the international art security firm Robert Wittman Inc. Contact him at www.robertwittmaninc.com

* * *

JOHN SHIFFMAN is an investigative reporter for *The Philadelphia Inquirer*. A lawyer and former associate director of the White House Fellows program, he has won a dozen journalism awards and was a 2009 finalist for the Pulitzer Prize. Contact him at www.john shiffman.com